World Englishes

The spread of English around the world has been and continues to be both rapid and unpredictable. *World Englishes* deals
with this inescapable result of colonisation and globalisation
from a social and linguistic perspective. The main focus of
the book is on the second-language varieties of English that
have developed in the former British colonies of East and West
Africa, the Caribbean, South and South-East Asia. The book provides a historical overview of the common circumstances that
gave rise to these varieties, and a detailed account of their
recurrent similarities in structure, patterns of usage, vocabulary and accents. Also discussed are debates about language in
education, the rise of English in China and Western Europe,
and other current developments in a world of global travel
and migration.

RAJEND MESTHRIE is Professor of Linguistics in the Department of English at the University of Cape Town. His recent
publications include *Language in South Africa* (2002) and *A Dictionary of Sociolinguistics* (2004, with Swann, Deumert and Lillis).

RAKESH M. BHATT is Associate Professor of Linguistics in the
Department of Linguistics at the University of Illinois. He is
the author of *Verb Movement and the Syntax of Kashmiri* (1999).

KEY TOPICS IN SOCIOLINGUISTICS

Series editor:
Rajend Mesthrie

This new series focuses on the main topics of study in sociolinguistics today. It consists of accessible yet challenging accounts of the most important issues to consider when examining the relationship between language and society. Some topics have been the subject of sociolinguistic study for many years, and are here re-examined in the light of new developments in the field; others are issues of growing importance that have not so far been given a sustained treatment. Written by leading experts, the books in the series are designed to be used on courses and in seminars, and include suggestions for further reading and a helpful glossary.

Already published in the series:
Politeness by Richard J. Watts
Language Policy by Bernard Spolsky
Discourse by Jan Blommaert
Analyzing Sociolinguistic Variation by Sali A. Tagliamonte
Language and Ethnicity by Carmen Fought
Style by Nikolas Coupland

Forthcoming titles:
Bilingual Talk by Peter Auer
Language and Identity by John Edwards

World Englishes

The Study of New Linguistic Varieties

RAJEND MESTHRIE AND RAKESH M. BHATT

CAMBRIDGE
UNIVERSITY PRESS

CAMBRIDGE UNIVERSITY PRESS
Cambridge, New York, Melbourne, Madrid, Cape Town, Singapore, São Paulo, Delhi

Cambridge University Press
The Edinburgh Building, Cambridge CB2 8RU, UK

Published in the United States of America by Cambridge University Press, New York

www.cambridge.org
Information on this title: www.cambridge.org/9780521797337

First published 2008

Printed in the United Kingdom at the University Press, Cambridge

A catalogue record for this publication is available from the British Library

Library of Congress Cataloguing in Publication data

Mesthrie, Rajend.
World Englishes: The study of new linguistic varieties / Rajend Mesthrie and Rakesh M. Bhatt.
    p.   cm – (Key topics in sociolinguistics)
Includes bibliographical references and index.
ISBN 978-0-521-79341-4 (hardback) – ISBN 978-0-521-79733-7 (pbk.)
1. English language – Great Britain – Colonies.   2. English language – Commonwealth
countries.   3. English language – Variation – Great Britain – Colonies.   4. English language –
Variation – Commonwealth countries.   5. Second language acquisition.   6. Sociolinguistics.
I. Bhatt, Rakesh Mohan.   II. Title.   III. Series.
PE2751.M47   2008
427.009171'241 – dc22   2008003210

ISBN 978-0-521-79341-4 hardback
ISBN 978-0-521-79733-7 paperback

Contents

Figures

Tables

Preface

The study of varieties of English that began as second languages under the experience of British colonialism is not new, going back to the nineteenth century. As in all matters pertaining to language contact the name Hugo Schuchardt comes to mind, with his 1891 study *Das Indo-Englische*, which examines the properties of varieties of English in India, in the light of the author's interest in Creole and other contact languages. Within the colonies, some scholars had also tried to inculcate the serious study of the local varieties of English, as opposed to satirical works or grammars, promising to weed out the unconventional in these varieties. The influence of Firoz Dustoor in the middle of the twentieth century at Allahabad and later Delhi is cited by Braj Kachru. It is safe to say that until the 1980s most work tended to discuss individual varieties of colonial English in isolation. The comparative study of what has more or less come to be called 'World Englishes' is due to the pioneering efforts of many scholars. ('New Englishes' is a near-synonym, which we occasionally employ.) Of these scholars Braj Kachru, once of Kashmir, then Edinburgh and finally Urbana-Champaign, probably deserves the most credit for establishing this subfield. It is due to his enthusiasm, vigorous insights and charisma that the area of study entered the mainstream of Sociolinguistics. Other scholars have played important pioneering roles. Manfred Görlach at Cologne has been equally vociferous in his role as researcher and publisher, and it is thanks largely to his efforts (and that of his successor, Edgar Schneider, at Regensburg) that German universities are important centres for World English studies today. His edited collection with another pioneer, Richard W. Bailey (1982), remains a primary resource. John T. Platt at Singapore wrote important articles and books in the late 1970s and 1980s which tried to integrate the study of New Englishes with the field of Pidgin and Creole studies, which had become established as the major branch of Contact Linguistics at the time. The tradition of World English studies as a result continues to thrive in Malaysia and (especially) Singapore. A fourth figure of influence is Tom McArthur who established the popular magazine-cum-journal *English Today* in Cambridge. In Africa early interest in the subject was sparked by the writings of John Spencer, K. A. Sey and Ayo Bamgbose.

The major impact of international migration and globalisation in the late twentieth and current centuries has made World Englishes an essential part of modern culture and sociology. Creative writing in English from the former colonial territories is an essential part of this prominence (e.g. those of Ben Okri, Vikram Seth and Arundhati Roy, to name a few). In this book we have endeavoured to give a sense of the main concerns of the field, drawing in large part upon the foundational writings of the linguists cited above. We have also included some discussions of the debates surrounding the ideology of the spread of English. However, as the main focus of our interest is on linguistic structure, space allocated to the themes of ideology, neocolonialism and even New English literature is not as large as they might deserve. That space belongs to another kind of book. We have brought some of our own interests within Linguistics into the book too: a section on what linguistics might make of the variable structures in stable second-language varieties is offered in a section on Optimality Theory (written by Rakesh Bhatt), and a major part of a chapter is devoted to parallels with Pidgin and Creole studies (written by Rajend Mesthrie). In addition, we have tried to bridge the paradigm gap between studies of Second Language Acquisition (which often focuses on individuals) and New Englishes. Inevitably our coverage has come from varieties we are most familiar with: Indian English (Bhatt) and Black and Indian South African Englishes (Mesthrie). But we have not neglected the major second language varieties of English to be found in West and East Africa, Singapore and Malaysia, and what have become first languages in Ireland and in places like the US reservations. Finally, in respect of areal coverage, we examine the current growth of English in China and Europe.

In terms of organisation, the first chapter covers the history of the spread of English. The second and third chapters give a broad overview of the recurrent morphological and syntactic features that differentiate New Englishes, at a prototypical level, from standard metropolitan varieties. These two chapters double up as an introduction to why New Englishes deserve linguistic attention, and as a reference grammar. A concluding section introduces a more integrated analysis from other branches of Linguistics, namely Variation Theory and Optimality Theory. The second half of this section on Optimality Theory is aimed at readers with some familiarity with modern approaches to

Syntax and Phonology. It can be skimmed over by readers without this background. Chapter 4 continues the structural overview, with respect to recurrent aspects of vocabulary and phonetics. Chapter 5 moves from structure to discourse, pragmatics and code-switching, with some applications from literary and colloquial sources. Chapter 6 offers an overview of how the diverse structures found in New Englishes can be viewed from frameworks offered by Second Language Acquisition Theory and Creolistics. In Chapter 7 we conclude by looking at more practical and applied aspects of the field of World Englishes, covering issues relating to education, communication in the era of global air travel, and the continuing post-modern linguistic interfaces between Centre and Periphery. Truly this is an important global subject that deserves rigorous sociolinguistic investigation. We hope we have made a small dent in this direction.

For the research administrators whose task it is to catalogue and evaluate research, it is necessary to stress that this work, like its predecessors in the series, is an original, research-based work that draws on existing studies and extends them via the intellectual leanings and academic stamp of the authors. We envisage a readership that covers researchers in the field, academics, their advanced undergraduate and beginning graduate students.

Acknowledgements

This text is a collective product of the myriad influences that have shaped our thinking on the subject of New Englishes, and which can be easily deduced from the preface and the text that follows. Rakesh Bhatt owes a professional debt to Professors Yamuna and Braj Kachru who have been most active in his training in this field. They have also been gracious and stimulating hosts to Rajend Mesthrie on his several trips to Urbana-Champaign. We also owe thanks to Professors Ramakant Agnihotri and Rajendra Singh who have provoked a re-thinking on some of the taken-for-granted concepts and consequences of this relatively new field within Contact Linguistics. Many thanks to other colleagues and friends in the field with whom one or both of us have had the opportunity to discuss parts of our work over the years: Gillian Sankoff, John Singler, Salikoko Mufwene, Suresh Canagarajah, Vaidehi Ramanathan, S. N. Sridhar, Monica Heller, K. P. Mohanan, Tara Mohanan, Miriam Meyerhoff, Meena Sridhar, Rajeshwari Pand-haripande, Hans Hock, James Yoon, Abbas Benmamoun, Karlos Arregi, Silvina Montrul, Eyamba Bokamba, Nkonko Kamwangamalu, Jean D'Souza, Anne Pakir, Tammy Valentine, Tej Bhatia, Vijay Bhatia, Kimberley Brown, Peter Lowenberg, Margie Berns, Agnes Bolonyai, Rick Hallett, Shahrzad Mahootian, Matt Ciscel, Roger Lass, Joan Swann, Ana Deumert, Kay McCormick, Bertus van Rooy, John Baugh, Edgar Schneider, Manfred Görlach, Bernd Kortmann, Christian Mair, Tom McArthur, Chris Jeffery, Jan Blommaert and others.

Our past and present students at Urbana-Champaign and Cape Town deserve a special mention for their interest in the subject and contribution to our thinking and presentation. Large parts of the manuscript were tried on students in Cape Town in the spring of 2005 and on an uncomplaining group of Masters students at the University of Regensburg in the cold northern winter of 2005: Rajend Mesthrie remembers them fondly and thanks Edgar Schneider, the facilitator-cum-host.

Many thanks to our research assistants, Jill Ward and Jennifer Cramer in Urbana-Champaign, and Rowan Mentis and Germain Kouame in Cape Town, for immense editorial research and bibliographical assistance.

Some sections from our previous writings occur here in a revised form, for which we express our gratitude to the original publishers. The section on Optimality Theory draws on Rakesh Bhatt's article 'Optimal Expressions in Indian English', *English Language and Linguistics* 4 (2000): 69–95. The following articles/chapters were originally authored by Rajend Mesthrie: parts of Chapter 1 appeared as 'World Englishes and the Multilingual History of English', *World Englishes* 25/3–4 (2006): 381–90; parts of the section on pidgin and Creole linguistics in Chapter 6 do double duty with sections in Singler and Kouwenberg (eds.), *A Handbook of Pidgin and Creole Linguistics* (2007); and the section on phonology in Chapter 4 is adapted from Schneider *et al.*, *A Handbook of Varieties of English*, vol. I (2004). We are grateful to Manfred Görlach, Braj Kachru and (especially) Tom McArthur for permission to reproduce the circles diagrams in Chapter 1.

Colleagues who commented on parts of the manuscript include Edgar Schneider, Claire Cowie and Devyani Sharma. We express our gratitude to the staff at Cambridge University Press for their patience in waiting for a manuscript that was on their forthcoming list for many a year, and to Andrew Winnard for his involvement in the series.

And finally, to our families. Rakesh gives heartfelt thanks to his wife Barbara, son Ashish and daughter Priyasha, for standing by during the writing process. Rajend thanks his wife Uma and daughter Sapna likewise. It is to them that we dedicate this book.

Abbreviations

AAE	African American English
Af	African
Am	American
ATC	Air Traffic Control
AUX	auxiliary
Bl	Black
Cam	Cameroons
CFl	Cape Flats
colloq	colloquial
Comp	Complement
CP	Complement Phrase
E	East
EAL	English as an Additional Language
EFL	English as a Foreign Language
EIL	English as an International Language
ELC	English Language Complex
Eng	English
ENL	English as a Native Language
ESL	English as a Second Language
Ghan	Ghanaian
HKng	Hong Kong
Ind	Indian
Ir	Irish
L1	first language
L2	second language
Mal	Malaysian
N	North
Nig	Nigerian
NP	Noun Phrase
OT	Optimality Theory
Pak	Pakistani
PD	Pro Drop

Phl	Phillipines
pl.	plural
pro	pronoun
S	South
sg.	singular
Sgp	Singaporean
SLA	Second Language Acquisition
Spec	Specifier
SrLnk	Sri Lankan
Std	Standard
TL	target language
V	verb
W	West
WE	World Englishes
Φ	zero
*	ungrammatical

1 History: the spread of English

1.1 INTRODUCTION: THE ENGLISH LANGUAGE COMPLEX

This book is concerned with an important topic in modern Sociolinguistics: the globalisation of English and the linguistic consequences of this process. The rise of English can be studied from a number of perspectives:

- as a topic in Historical Linguistics, highlighting the history of one language within the Germanic family and its continual fission into regional and social dialects;
- as a macro-sociolinguistic topic 'language spread' detailing the ways in which English and other languages associated with colonisation have changed the linguistic ecology of the world;
- as a topic in the field of Language Contact, examining the structural similarities and differences amongst the new varieties of English that are stabilising or have stabilised;
- as a topic in political and ideological studies – 'linguistic imperialism' – that focuses on how relations of dominance are entrenched by, and in, language and how such dominance often comes to be viewed as part of the natural order;
- as a topic in Applied Linguistics concerned with the role of English in modernisation, government and – above all – education; and
- as a topic in cultural and literary studies concerned with the impact of English upon different cultures and literatures, and the constructions of new identities via bilingualism.

Since the 1980s many of these topics have risen to prominence in books and journals. Important early studies drawing attention to this new field were Bailey and Robinson (1973); Bailey and Görlach (1982); Kachru (1982 and 1986); Pride (1982); and Platt, Weber and Ho (1984). These works were concerned with describing the status and functions

1

of English around the world and their linguistic characteristics. The ideology behind the spread of English is documented in Richard Bailey's (1991) *Images of English*, Robert Phillipson's *Linguistic Imperialism* (1992) and in Alastair Pennycook's *The Cultural Politics of English as an International Language* (1994). Two popular books that describe in highly readable terms the growth of English and its many manifestations are David Crystal's (1997) *English as a Global Language* and Tom McArthur's (1998) *The English Languages*. Mention of collections of articles should not exclude the comprehensive volumes edited by Cheshire (1991), Burns and Coffin (2001) and the Manfred Görlach sequence *Englishes* (1991), *More Englishes* (1995), *Even More Englishes* (1998) and *Still More Englishes* (2002). Accessible introductory books with a sociolinguistic orientation include Jenkins (2003) and Melchers and Shaw (2003). Three large handbooks devoted to English throughout the world have large sections devoted to varieties treated in this book: Hickey (2004a), Kortmann *et al.* (2004) and Schneider *et al.* (2004). A handbook devoted entirely to World Englishes in forty-two chapters appeared just as this book went to press (Kachru, Kachru and Nelson 2006). And the growth of interest in English around the world as an academic area of study from the 1980s onwards can be seen in the establishment of three journals that form the mainstay of the field: *English World Wide* (founded in 1979), *World Englishes* (founded in 1985) and the more 'popular' *English Today* (founded in 1984). If the field is well served by books and articles, why the appearance of one more? Our motivation for the present work is that we feel the time is now ripe for a synthesis of the increasing body of research in the area; to identify gaps in the field; and – most importantly – to emphasise perspectives from other branches of Linguistics. Platt, Weber and Ho's (1984) book was the only one, to our knowledge, to attempt a unification of the field by describing the recurrent features of different varieties. This work was slightly premature in that it did not have a range of in-depth empirical studies to draw on and consequently reads as somewhat skimming the surface. In fairness to the authors it could equally be said that they were ahead of their time and that they had put their fingers on a number of significant issues. Our inspiration comes from the works cited above, as well as from the fields of Language Contact (including Creolistics), Language Acquisition, and Phonological and Syntactic Theory. As the chapter titles of this book show, our interest is in the history of the spread of English, the ideology that promulgated that spread, the structure of the manifold Englishes of the world, the contexts in which these varieties emerged, their status, and the educational and social issues that surround them. Our main focus (in Chapters 2 to 4) will fall on the linguistic forms characteristic of new varieties of English and on ways of describing and understanding them.

1.2 THE FIELD OF 'WORLD ENGLISHES'

The terms most often used to describe the varieties we are interested in are 'New Englishes' or 'World Englishes'. It has become customary to use the plural form 'Englishes' to stress the diversity to be found in the language today, and to stress that English no longer has one single base of authority, prestige and normativity. There are at least four books bearing the main title *New Englishes*: Pride (1982); Platt, Weber and Ho (1984); Foley (1988) on Singaporean English and Bamgbose, Banjo and Thomas (1997) on West African English. The pluricentrism is also captured in the eye-catching book title *The English Languages* (MacArthur 1998). Yet, as we shall see, neither 'New Englishes' nor 'World Englishes' is an entirely satisfactory term. Kachru (1983a) pointed out that the 'New English' of India was actually older than English in Australia, which is not generally considered 'New' – since it is to a large extent a continuation of the norms of nineteenth-century first-language (henceforth *L1*) working-class British English. The second term 'World English' runs the risk of being over-general, since British English is not generally studied within this paradigm. Yet one might quibble that it is a 'World English' too (from a commonsense notion of the word 'world', anyway). The term is often cited as parallel to the term 'World Music', which covers 'non-Western' musical forms. In all of these terms there is a problem of perspective that is difficult to overcome. It is therefore necessary to find a cover term for *all* varieties of English: the one we will settle for is 'English Language Complex' (henceforth *ELC*), suggested by McArthur (2003a:56). The ELC may be said to comprise all subtypes distinguishable according to some combination of their history, status, form and functions. The following list of subtypes, which takes a largely historical point of departure, will be fleshed out in the rest of this chapter:

(a) *Metropolitan standards*: The term *metropolitan* (literally 'mother city/city-state') is an old one, going back to ancient Greece, denoting the relation between a state and its colonies. For the ELC the term would have once been applicable only to standard English of England. However, it is uncontroversial today, long after US independence and its subsequent espousal of distinctly American English norms, to acknowledge the existence of at least two metropolitan standard varieties, whose formal models are those provided by the radio and television networks based largely in London and US cities like Washington, Los Angeles and (for CNN) Atlanta.

(b) *Colonial standards*: The colonial history of English has made it an important language in Australia, New Zealand, Canada, South Africa and Northern and Southern Rhodesia (now Zambia and Zimbabwe). A fairly large number of English speakers formed an influential group of speakers in the early history of these 'Dominion' territories. The varieties spoken there are referred to in historical dialectology as 'extraterritorial' Englishes. It is possible to speak of 'colonial standards' since informal and (to a lesser extent) formal varieties have arisen in these territories that may be considered 'standard'. These standards were, until recently, not fully accepted within the territories, since the metropolitan standards exerted a counter-influence. Today the colonial standards are much more prominent as British influence recedes.

(c) *Regional dialects*: These are the varieties that may be distinguished on the basis of regional variation within metropolis and colony. A rule of thumb is that the older the settlement of English speakers, the firmer the regional differentiation within the language. Thus English dialects of the UK and USA are clearly definable in regional terms; this is less true of Australia, New Zealand, Canada, South Africa and Zimbabwe.

(d) *Social dialects*: Identifiable varieties within a region along the lines of class and ethnicity may occur. In London there is the difference between Cockney of the working classes, Received pronunciation (RP) of the upper-middle class and the intermediate 'Estuary English' (Rosewarne 1994). In Australia linguists identify Broad, General and Cultivated varieties (Mitchell and Delbridge 1965); the first is the most localized, while showing numerous traces of its origins in British working-class dialects; the third is historically oriented towards RP, while the second mediates between these two poles. Amongst ethnolects (or ethnic dialects) Black English (also known as African American English) is identifiable as a distinct linguistic variety in the USA (though it has some regional variation too).

Groups (a) to (d) are frequently labelled off as a special group, 'mother tongue' or L1 English or English as a Native Language (ENL), or in B. B. Kachru's (1988) terminology, which we discuss later on, *Inner Circle* varieties. Of equal interest in modern sociolinguistics are the other members of the ELC outlined below:

(e) *Pidgin Englishes*: Pidgins are defined prototypically as rudimentary languages that have no native speakers, though they may subsequently gain in complexity. They arise from trade and other – largely colonial – forms of contact. English-based pidgins like West African pidgin English may be considered to belong to the English family, since they are 'lexified' by English – i.e. English is the source of much of their vocabulary.

(f) *Creole Englishes*: Creoles are fully developed speech forms, which show so much restructuring as to bear little resemblance grammatically to their lexifiers. These languages are 'mixed' in the sense that typically their grammars and lexicons come from different sources – see Singler and Kouwenberg (in press) for recent debates over terminology in this field. Although a variety like Jamaican Creole is structurally an independent language, it has overlapping membership with the ELC in terms of its vocabulary and the possibilities of being influenced by English, which is the 'authorised' language of the education system.

(g) *English as a Second Language (ESL)*: Typically these are varieties that arose in countries where English was introduced in the colonial era in either face-to-face communication or (more usually) via the education system of a country in which there is, or had once been, a sizeable number of speakers of English. In ESL countries like Kenya, Sri Lanka and Nigeria, English plays a key role in education, government and education.

(h) *English as a Foreign Language (EFL)*: This category typically refers to the English used in countries in which its influence has been external, rather than via a body of 'settlers'. For EFL speakers English plays a role for mainly *inter*-national rather than *intra*-national purposes. Whereas ESL countries produce literature in English (and other languages), EFL countries typically do not use English in creative writing. The trend towards globalisation in economics, communication and culture has made EFL prominent in places like China, Europe, Brazil, etc.

(i) *Immigrant Englishes*: In the context of migration to an English-dominant country, varieties of English which originate as EFLs may retain some distinctiveness or may merge with the regional English of their territory, depending on a host of social and economic factors. Thus whilst English in Mexico is of the EFL variety, Chicano English of the USA shows greater affinity with general US English. However, Chicano English is still a distinct variety amongst many speakers which we classify as an 'immigrant English'. Our main reason for differentiating 'immigrant English' from ESL is in the degree of influence of metropolitan English over the former, since it is readily available in the local environment (we discuss this issue further below).

(j) *Language-shift Englishes*: These are varieties that develop when English replaces the erstwhile primary language(s) of a community. There is, nevertheless, frequently a sense of continuity with the ancestral language(s) and culture(s) in the shifting community. The difference between 'language-shift English' and 'social dialect' is one of degree; the former can, in time, shade into a social dialect. Essentially, a language-shift English has at some crucial stage of its development involved adult and child L1 and second-language (L2) speakers who formed one speech community. A social dialect in contrast is typically conceived of as having only L1 speakers. Thus Hiberno English is probably best classified as a social dialect in most areas of Ireland today; not so long ago it would have counted as a language-shift variety, with L1 and L2 speakers of the dialect closely interacting with each other.

(k) *Jargon Englishes*: Whereas a pidgin is a well-defined (if rudimentary) variety, with norms that are tacitly agreed upon by its speakers, a jargon is characterised by great individual variation and instability (hence also described as a pre-pidgin).[1] E.g. contact between South Sea Islanders and Europeans in the nineteenth century led to the formation of unstable jargons in many parts of the Pacific. One of these developed into a stable, expanded pidgin, Tok Pisin, which is now one of the official languages of Papua New Guinea.

(l) *Hybrid Englishes*: Also called 'bilingual mixed languages', these are versions of English which occur in code-mixing in many urban centres where a local language comes into contact with English. Although sometimes given derogatory names, like Hinglish for the hybrid Hindi-English of north Indian cities, these hybrids may have prestige amongst urban youth and the young at heart in informal styles.

A sketch typology like the one we propose brings as much controversy as clarity. Many issues raised in the characterisation of the ELC are worthy of closer scrutiny and debate. For example:

---

[1] The alternative sense of 'jargon' as the excessive use of technical terms does not apply here.

(i) is it really the case that jargons, pidgins, English Creoles and hybrids belong here?

(ii) do some of the categories not overlap considerably (e.g. language-shift Englishes with social dialects; immigrant with hybrid Englishes)?

(iii) does the category 'language-shift English' have any phenomeno-logical status?

A consideration of points such as these will sharpen our characterisation of the ELC, and possibly open up new dimensions in the history of English.

In the first place our characterisation suffers from focusing on 'products' rather than 'processes'. Sociolinguists generally try to avoid the bias of conceiving of language in terms of already codified forms (as in grammars and dictionaries) or written norms (as in literature or print media). They argue that language is constantly being made and remade by speakers in terms of their situation, need, interlocutor, audience, knowledge of other 'languages', general strategies of communication, etc. The classic account is perhaps that of focusing and diffusion – Le Page and Tabouret-Keller (1985); it is implicit in Bakhtin's (1981) idea of dialogism; it also finds favour in the work of some creolists (e.g. Baker 2000; Mufwene 2001). An analogy might help to make this more concrete. Although we think of fluent adult speech as the prototype of English, the developing capacity of a three-year-old child is also 'English'. Yet, it is not possible to draw a strict line as to when exactly 'child language' turns into 'English proper'. The same principle applies to the transitions shown by adults in moving from a minimal ability in English (as sometimes eventually manifested in jargons, pidgins or early fossilised interlanguages) to increasing development towards an accepted community norm of 'English'. That is, jargons and early inter-languages are perhaps no less, and no more, varieties of English than a very young child's developing variety of L1 English. This issue goes to the heart of conceptions of English and of the 'native speaker of English', which are still debated in sociolinguistics and which we take up again in section 1.6.

Secondly, we advocate a 'prototype' definition of the term 'English', with some varieties considered clear-cut examples (e.g. middle-class English in Edinburgh, the L2 English of teachers in Nigeria, rural people's English in the Appalachian region of the USA). We also accept that the boundaries of terms are fuzzy, so that some Englishes may have overlapping memberships. The following are examples of phenomena with multiple memberships:

(a) English hybrids – e.g. the mixed variety of English and Malay, described by Baskaran (1994);
(b) decreolising English Creoles – e.g. the continuum between Creole and Caribbean English in Jamaica, described by de Camp (1971);
(c) underworld slang – e.g. the grafting of an 'antilanguage' lexicon onto English grammar in Elizabethan cant, as described by Halliday (1978).

To return to question (ii), overlaps certainly develop amongst some categories identified within the ELC as English spreads geographically and enters new domains of use. The distinction between ESL and EFL is cast in terms of the presence or absence of a 'sizeable number' of L1 English speakers capable of exerting influence on the L2 in a territory. As it is not possible to specify such a critical mass, this must be taken as a soft boundary. Even if a critical mass were roughly specifiable, it would have to be tempered by factoring in more sociolinguistic concepts like interaction between speakers and the accessibility of L1 speakers. South Africa counts largely as an ESL rather than EFL territory, yet in the apartheid era, Black people were rigidly segregated from Whites with obvious consequences for the acquisition of English. Although ESL was the general outcome of contact in South Africa, it is a moot question whether in some parts of the country English was till recently virtually a foreign language. In their description of English in East Africa, Hancock and Angogo (1982:307–8) differentiate between non-native English spoken fluently as a second language and non-native English spoken imperfectly as a foreign language within the same territory. This shows that the apartheid South African case is perhaps not all that special. It also shows the overlapping nature of the categories. Should we then change our definitions to allow ESL to operate even in EFL territories (to describe the competence of, say, a few speakers who have been to an English-speaking country) and to allow EFL pockets in an ESL territory? In this vein Kachru's (1992:55) distinction between 'institutionalised' and 'performance' varieties is a useful one. Briefly, an institutionalised English is one that has been introduced formally in a territory via education and is used in some civil, administrative and governmental functions. A performance variety is one which does not have this backing and is reliant on ad hoc skills of communication that individuals may pick up via EFL education or via brief contacts with tourists, traders, etc. Performance varieties include EFLs, jargons, rudimentary pidgins and so forth.[2]

---

[2] Again things are far from watertight: a pidgin may expand and become institutionalised (the most famous case being that of Tok Pisin, an English-based pidgin

Another indication of overlapping memberships concerns the intermediate status of 'Protectorates' in the former British empire – territories that were not fully colonised but which did receive educational and other infrastructural support from Britain to wrest them away from the influence of rival imperialists. Territories such as Egypt and the southern African kingdom of Lesotho may well have a status intermediate between ESL and EFL territories. The spread of English in Europe in more recent times calls into question whether territories like Holland and Scandinavia are still EFL or whether they are moving towards ESL. Over a decade ago Robert Phillipson (1992:24–5) remarked that 'in the Nordic countries (Scandinavia and Finland), a shift is under way from EFL to ESL, and this has implications for school teaching and for society as a whole' – see further Chapter 7.

Notions like 'immigrant English' are also dependent on sociohistorical factors. This is not a term that is commonly used in the literature, where writers simply use the general label ESL. In our view, though, there is a difference between 'narrow' ESL, in which the L2 speakers are in a majority (and for which educated L2 speakers become the embodiment of a norm), and an 'immigrant English', where L2 speakers are in a minority and constantly exposed to the norms of the target language (TL), despite retaining a distinct social dialect themselves. The abbreviation TL is a useful one for English as L1, since it makes it possible to avoid the specifics of whether the target is standard English or a regional or social dialect, or whether British, American or other norms are involved. Another useful term for more or less the same concept is 'superstrate' language, which stresses issues of power and accessibility. Whilst 'TL' implies a second-language-acquisition perspective in which the target is more or less available (inside or outside of classrooms), 'superstrate' leaves it open whether the dominant colonial language is accessible to new learners or not. In Pidgin and Creole studies 'superstrate' contrasts with 'substrate(s)', the original language(s) of the group of speakers who are in a subordinate position in terms of power and status. In the study of pidgins and Creoles it is argued that though English often was a source of vocabulary (as 'lexifier' language), it was not really the target of acquisition, since on many plantations slaves were interested in developing a medium of inter-ethnic communication, rather than mastering the colonial language. The balance between English and the mother tongue in the immigrant English

in Papua New Guinea which underwent expansion and is now one of three official languages of the country). Hence the qualification 'rudimentary' is necessary to apply to (non-expanded) pidgins that are performance varieties.

context is not as clearly defined as in an ESL territory. The L2 status of an immigrant English may change within a generation or more, if conditions promoting assimilation to a superstrate form of English exist. Special conditions like the intention to return to the homeland or a heightened sense of ethnicity may run counter to this tendency. ESL is essentially an abbreviation for the acquisition of English under conditions of additive bilingualism (Lambert 1978), i.e. the addition of a socially relevant language to a community's repertoire. Immigrant Englishes (and language-shift Englishes) are frequently implicated in subtractive bilingualism, that is unstable bilingualism resulting in the gradual loss of a community's erstwhile language.

Finally – regarding question (iii) – there are indeed overlaps between a language-shift English and a social dialect. Yesterday's language-shift English may become tomorrow's social dialect (more specifically an ethnic dialect or 'ethnolect'). The former term (language-shift English) is desirable and necessary if one is interested in the process of shift and acquisition, rather than the ultimate 'social dialect' product. We leave it open whether language shift is reversible (Fishman 1991) – that is, in the above typology, if a language-shift English could revert to ESL, from being a social dialect under changing demographic or sociopolitical conditions. We return to the issue of 'models' of World Englishes in 1.5, in which we delineate ways in which different scholars have tried to show the relationship between these varieties in historical, political and structural terms.

1.2.1   Other distinctions made in the literature

The term 'non-native' is sometimes used in connection with the competence of ESL speakers. This has proved controversial and sparked an important debate about what it means to be a 'native speaker' (see section 1.6). Kachru (1983b:2–3) used the term 'nativised' to stress the adaptations that English has undergone in ESL territories, making it culturally and referentially appropriate in its new contexts. An example of this process is the use of new kinship terms via borrowing or other forms of adaptation like calquing, to satisfy the needs of politeness or respect. Thus new terms like *cousin-brother* may appear for a male first-cousin (in *inter alia* Indian English, Australian Aboriginal English and varieties of African English, e.g. those of Zimbabwe and South Africa). Similarly *big mother* occurs in the same varieties for 'one's mother's elder sister'. These neologisms denote a closer relationship than the superstrate forms *cousin* and *aunt* respectively. The term 'nativised' also suggests (though Kachru is less explicit about this) that though English may not be technically a native language in such territories, the degree of fluency amongst many speakers in certain domains makes it almost a native language. The term 'indigenised' is sometimes used as a synonym for *nativised*. However, we would like to suggest that a distinction be drawn between the two terms. 'Indigenisation' refers to the acculturation of the TL to localised phenomena, be they cultural, topographic or even linguistic (in terms of local grammatical, lexical and discourse norms). In this way the TL becomes part of the linguistic ecology of a particular area – see Chapter 4 in relation to lexis. Nativisation is a psycholinguistic process referring to the ways that English, whilst not the 'chronological' first language of speakers, is used like a native language, in at least some domains. This would bring the term 'nativisation' much more in line with acquisition and Creole studies where it essentially means 'formation of an L1'.

Some scholars find it necessary to draw a distinction between EFL communication involving a non-native speaker and a native speaker (characterising this as EFL proper) and that involving non-native speakers, typically from different territories. This is termed 'English as a Lingua Franca' – see Knapp (1991) and James (2000) for Europe. In this book, however, our main focus will be on 'EFL varieties' rather than on the different types of interactional contexts that their speakers might become involved in (see Meierkord 2004). *English as an International Language* (EIL) is also sometimes used as a general term or in a more specific sense for the use of English between speakers from different countries who do not have English as a mother tongue.

With all the nuances of similarity, overlap and differences within the ELC, it is little wonder that the very handy term *English as an Additional Language* (EAL) may be used when finer differences are unimportant; i.e. when a distinction is intended between ENL and other varieties. EAL has the further advantage of not discriminating between a chronologically second, third, etc. language. Indeed, current linguistics attaches little importance to whether an additional language is learnt as a second, or third or fourth, etc. language, though this position has not undergone rigorous scrutiny (see Cenoz and Jessner 2000).

Finally, the term 'New English' is a common one that is used in the field (and one which could well have been the title of this book). Platt, Weber and Ho (1984:2–3) used the term to denote a variety of English with the following characteristics:

(a) It has developed through the education system, rather than as a first language of the home.
(b) It has developed in an area where a native variety of English was not spoken by a majority of the population.

(c) It is used for a range of functions (e.g. letter writing, government communications, literature, as a lingua franca amongst some people and in formal contexts).
(d) It has become indigenised, by developing a subset of rules different from metropolitan varieties.

In this usage, by virtue of excluding many of the categories set up in section 1.1, 'New English' is almost synonymous with 'ESL'. However, it excludes L2 varieties of American Indian English (Leap 1993) and Black English of South Africa (Magura 1984), which owe their existence to a numerically and/or socially dominant English-speaking sector in the USA and South Africa respectively. Platt, Weber and Ho's characterisation may accordingly be thought of as 'narrow ESL'. The term 'narrow ESL' involves a sharp distinction between itself and what we have called 'immigrant Englishes', 'language-shift Englishes' and EFLs. Todd (1985) argues that Platt, Weber and Ho's characterisation overlooks the similarities between narrow ESL and varieties like American Indian English and Black South African English. Though these varieties exist in territories where English is dominant, the history of racial and tribal segregation has tended to neutralise condition (b) in Platt, Weber and Ho's formulation. In this book we accordingly adopt a broader conception of New Englishes (involving 'wide ESL'). To summarise the terminology used in this book: *ELC* is the entire set of Englishes; *World Englishes* represents all varieties except the L1 varieties of places like the UK and USA (prototypically EFL and wide ESL varieties); *New Englishes* covers wide ESL varieties and language-shift varieties.

1.3 LANGUAGE SPREAD: INTEGRATING NEW ENGLISHES INTO THE HISTORY OF THE ENGLISH LANGUAGE COMPLEX

The typology outlined above makes it possible to broaden the history of English to take into account multilingual developments. It also makes it possible to see New Englishes as less dissimilar from L1 varieties, in terms of their historical development.

1.3.1 The Old English period

English ultimately derives from a number of Germanic dialects, three of which – those of the Angles, Jutes and Saxons, as is well known – crossed the North Sea from north-western Europe in AD *c.* 450. We might term this migration/invasion 'the first crossing', which ultimately resulted in a merger producing what linguists now label 'Anglo Saxon' or 'Old English'.[3] In this period (450 to 1100) a number of phenomena existed that we might mistakenly think of as post-colonial and post-modern: English was fragmented, had multiple norms, varied considerably, was used in multilingual settings and evinced a fair degree of borrowing in contact with other languages. That is, traditional histories testify to the koineisation (or dialect unification) of the Germanic varieties on English soil, thus yielding 'English' (on koines and koineisation see Siegel 1985). English existed in a multilingual setting amidst Celtic languages (forerunners of Cornish, Welsh, Irish, Manx and Scots Gaelic). There may well have been cases of bilingualism as English gradually spread amongst the Celtic populace, though there is no clear textual evidence for this. There was also in all likelihood contact since AD 43 with Latin, which enjoyed prestige in British cities during the Roman period, and later, in the context of the Roman Catholic Church. Extensive influence from Old Norse (forerunner of Danish and Norwegian) occurred with the Viking invasions and settlement of the eighth to the eleventh centuries. Fisiak (1995:58) suggests that towards the year 1000 there were signs of a written standard emerging out of the monasteries in and around Winchester 'which was written and read from Canterbury to York'. In the light of Crystal's (2004:54–6) account entitled 'the rise and fall of West Saxon' it is tempting to characterise the fate of West Saxon as 'the first decline' (of a Standard English variety).

In terms of our ELC typology the following phenomena are likely to have existed in the Old English period: regional dialects, ethnic dialects (initially amongst the different Germanic tribes), social dialects (presumably between kings and lords as against the serfs) and an incipient standard. The extent of Celtic–English bilingualism in this period is, as indicated above, unclear, and can best be described as incipient, unlike English–Norse bilingualism, which was more extensive. However, in subsequent centuries gradual bilingualism and shift did occur. We may therefore speak of language-shift Englishes (with Celtic or Scandinavian substrates) in the post-Old English period. These would have involved a degree of ESL in generations prior to shift. The notion of EFL would not have made sense at the time (Latin being the real language of status and power in Europe), and there is no evidence of pidgin and Creole Englishes in this period.

---

[3] The early presence of the Jutes (inhabitants of Jutland) is now in doubt; and the invasions may have included Franks and Frisians (Fisiak 1995:38).

1.3.2 The Middle English period

The early part of this period (c. 1100 to 1500) was dominated by the linguistic consequences of the Norman Conquest, with French being the language of the new upper classes and English being associated with their subjects. In the course of time there was convergence between the two languages, one assumes after a period of bilingualism, amongst segments of the populace (see Crystal 2004:124–5). This convergence, admittedly, shows up much more in English than in Anglo-Norman. The radical differences between Old and Middle English has given rise to considerable debate over the reasons for this change. One line of reasoning holds that Middle English could be said to be a Creole (Domingue 1975; Bailey and Maroldt 1977), in so far as a former Germanic language emerged in the post-Conquest period as a Germanic–Romance hybrid. Whilst the consensus these days seems to be that it is not a Creole on most conceptions of creoleness (see Thomason and Kaufman 1988:306–15), we could just as well ask whether Middle English at some stage involved some mutual influence between traditional English and a language-shift variety (Norman English). The on-going bilingualism made the contact situation fairly complex.

This is also the period of the 'second crossing' of English with the conquest of Ireland by Henry II in 1164. This brought French (of the nobility) and English (of their soldiers and retainers) to Ireland. However, English did not really spread in Ireland at this time; rather the colonisers became bilingual (and eventually shifted to Irish).

1.3.3 Early modern English

In this period (c. 1500–1700) a new Standard English emerged. On considering a variety of views on the topic, Fisiak (1995:81–7) concludes that a written standard arose in the fifteenth century but that this had no spoken correlate. The standardisation of the pronunciation of English began in the sixteenth century but was not completed until the eighteenth (Dobson 1955; Strang 1970:161). The growth of a standard (written and oral) was a slow and unplanned event. English was after all – like many vernacular languages of Europe – still vying for status with French and Latin at the time. However, once the ideology of a standard (see Milroy and Milroy 1991:22–8) came into force, and with the increasing role of print and (much later) radio broadcasting, Standard English has almost come to have a life and power of its own. While the standard was once based on spoken (regional) dialects, the ideology of standardisation has overturned that relationship, presenting the standard as the primordial entity from which other dialects deviate. This centralising ideology has important ramifications for the status of new varieties of English that developed or were developing beyond the south of England and beyond the British Isles. However, as Crystal (2004:514–34) stresses, the technology and cultural practices of the post-modern era seem to support an opposing tendency towards decentralising the norms of English.

1.3.4 Modern English, exploration and colonisation: the period of spread (1500 onwards—) ▬▬▬ ▬▬

Within the United Kingdom, English spread further by conquest (a kind of internal colonisation) into Wales, Scotland and (for a second time) Ireland. In Ireland, English became entrenched in the seventeenth century with new English migrations and economic control that displaced the Irish from three provinces. Initially a form of ESL, Irish English (aka Hiberno English) gradually became a language-shift English, from the eighteenth century on – see Hickey (2004b). It is an important language in English studies for structural and historical reasons. It furnishes us with a clear-cut example of a language-shift English, in which a host of substrate features has survived, some to become part of an informal standard. Moreover, in the age of empire, many Irish citizens (speaking Irish and/or Hiberno English) went abroad in search of work, forming, in many instances, a more accessible informal model of English than that of the colonial masters.

The imposition of English in Wales was begun in the Norman period in the twelfth century and was formalised by the Tudors in the sixteenth century. However, it was only in the nineteenth century that English really spread, with industrialisation and the immigration of English speakers. English in Scotland also has a two-pronged history. By the seventh century Northumbrian English was taken up north by the Anglo-Saxons, giving rise to Scots, an L1 variety. Scots was once a national language but after union with England in 1707 was reduced in status to a social and regional dialect of English. There are still vigorous movements aimed at recognising and promoting it as a separate language. By contrast English in the Scottish Highlands started off as an L2, introduced from England around the middle of the eighteenth century, which gradually replaced Gaelic. It was apparently more influenced by standard varieties of Scottish English through books and imported schoolteachers than by the Scots and Scots English of the neighbouring territory (Romaine 1982:67).

In the last 500 years voyages of exploration have taken European languages to all corners of the earth. Political and military encounters resulted in the spread of Portuguese, Spanish, English, French and German. As far as English is concerned we might refer to this as the 'third crossing'. US English has, of course, since undergone a substantial rise to occupy the position of co-standard with southern British English. The reluctant admission of a co-partner in the standard stakes makes it only a slight exaggeration to conceive of this process as a 'second decline' (of a standard variety, southern British English). This time, unlike the 'first decline' (of West Saxon in the tenth century), the standard variety is not given up (in fact it continues to prosper). The decline is in its potential sovereignty over a large territory, the USA. Furthermore, globalisation seems to be propelling US English into a position as a potential rival to standard southern British English over other EFL territories like Japan and China.

The historians' distinction between 'colonies of settlement' and 'colonies of exploitation' is of some significance in the history of Englishes (Mufwene 2001:8, 204–6). The former resulted in what are sometimes called 'transplanted varieties' of English in the United States, Canada, Australia, New Zealand, South Africa and islands like St. Helena and the Falklands. Colonies of exploitation frequently started off as trading outposts with small numbers of traders who did not have the intention of long-term settlement, as in parts of Africa and Asia. In such situations 'fort pidgins' frequently arose. These colonies were typically appropriated in the second half of the nine-teenth century and expanded into exploitation colonies. It was in these colonies that the prototypical 'English as second language' emerged. A related factor is whether large-scale population displacements occurred, with the dispersal or decimation of indigenous peoples and the re-peopling of colonies with multilingual slave or inden-tured forms of labour. In these circumstances new (Creole) languages emerged, based only partly on the colonial language. A problem with the distinction between 'colony of settlement' and 'colony of exploita-tion' is that it is unclear what constitutes a critical mass before a colony can be said to be 'settled'. Moreover, as happened in some Caribbean islands, an initial European settlement could be disrupted for one reason or another and move elsewhere or back to Europe. But their linguistic legacies could remain. Finally, there were territories that were never formally colonised but had 'protectorate' status within the empire. Such protectorates included African countries like Botswana, Lesotho, Swaziland and Egypt, and Middle Eastern countries like Saudi Arabia and Iraq. In these countries English plays a role in administra-tion and education that is reminiscent of the colonies. As suggested earlier, there is a case for considering the English of these territories as intermediate between prototypical ESL and prototypical EFL. As far as EFL territories are concerned, it is customary to cite them as cases where the English language spread, rather than its speakers. In a globalising world with countries like China and those of the former Soviet Union embracing English influence and teachers from the West, we are witnessing a 'fourth crossing' of a post-colonial type.

1.4 THE SPREAD OF ENGLISH IN FORMER BRITISH COLONIES

We now focus more concretely on some of the movements of speakers and carriers of English, as well as on subsequent agencies that enhanced that spread.

1.4.1 English in colonial history

Crystal (1997:7) concludes that 'the history of a global language can be traced through the successful expeditions of its soldier/sailor speakers. And English . . . has been no exception.' It is therefore necessary to look at the introduction of English in colonies before classrooms were built.

According to Spencer (1971:8), English was probably first heard in Africa in the 1530s when William Hawkins the Elder passed there on his way to Brazil. This would have been a form of Elizabethan English. A regular trade in spices, ivory and slaves began in the mid 1500s when British ships sailed along the Guinea coast (Schmied 1991:6). European forts were built along the West African coast. The earliest form of a European language used there would have been pidgin Portuguese. As British supremacy in trade gradually grew, English became established. During this time West Africans were taken in small numbers to Europe to be trained as interpreters. An account in Hakluyt (1598, Vol. VI), cited by Spencer (1971:8), suggests that by 1555 five West Africans had been taken to England for over a year for this purpose. It is of some importance linguistically that in Africa as elsewhere, the earliest contacts between English speakers and the locals were informal and sporadic. There was no expectation of a permanent settlement or of colonisation (and therefore formal education) until centuries later. In this first phase pidgins and 'broken English' (i.e. early fossilised interlanguages) were the outcomes of contact. These would not necessarily be ephemeral: West African pidgin English whose roots lie in the seventeenth and eighteenth centuries is today more widespread (in the Cameroons, Ghana and Nigeria) than is English as a second language. Pidgin English was not the only code used, as the African interpreters returning from training in England would probably have used

ESL rather than pidgin. Two later influential varieties in West Africa (from about 1787 onwards) were the forms of Creole English spoken by manumitted slaves who were repatriated from Britain, North America and the Caribbean. Krio was the English Creole of slaves freed from Britain who were returned to Sierra Leone, where they were joined by slaves released from Nova Scotia and Jamaica. Liberia was established in 1821 as an African homeland for freed slaves from the USA. The Creole English that the returnees brought with them was most likely related to African American Vernacular English (Hancock and Kobbah 1975:248, cited by Todd 1982:284). Today, American rather than British forms of English continue to dominate in Liberia (see Singler 2004). Todd (1982) describes four types of English in West Africa today: pidgin; ESL; Standard West African English (mostly oriented to the UK, with the exception of places like Liberia) and francophone West African English.

The history of English in the USA goes back to 1607 with the successful (second) expedition that established the colony of Jamestown in Virginia. US English developed out of both Standard British English of the time and a variety of dialects from the motherland; as well as from the ESL of settlers who later arrived from Europe. Our concern in this book is not the distinctiveness of American English; rather it is with the impact of English on other peoples of North America. More especially, the rise of ESL, in former times, among native Americans and of the creole-like African American English (AAE), is of interest to World English studies. The former arose gradually and took root from a variety of sources:

(a) initial pidgins used in European–Indian contact,
(b) on-reservation schools from the 1860s, and more importantly,
(c) off-reservation boarding schools set up for Tribes from 1879 onwards (Leap 1993:155–7).[4]

The development of AAE is a matter of greater debate: is it a decreolised variety – i.e. former Creole (with a plantation pidgin even further in its past) or is it a variety that resembles a Creole whilst leaning somewhat to ESL models in its genesis, and having a large residue of the syntax of now archaic British English dialects? The former explanation probably has more adherents (see Rickford 1999; Singler 2004); though the latter view is being pursued by, *inter alia*, Poplack (2000), and Poplack and Tagliamonte (1991). This is a complex matter which we

---

[4] We follow Leap's use of capitals on the word *Tribes* in conformity with the preferences of people so designated.

cannot resolve here. However, because AAE has generally been studied within the frameworks of Creole studies, it will not feature as prominently in this book, where the main emphasis is on ESL.

In the early seventeenth century English was also carried to the Caribbean, becoming a serious rival to the already established Portuguese and Spanish. Early settlements at St Kitts (1624) and Barbados (1627) initially established English dialects on the islands. With the growth of a plantation economy (especially a sugar industry), the importation of African slaves resulted in the emergence of pidgins and Creoles based on English and African languages. It is still a matter of debate whether Creoles were formed anew on each island, or whether the early settlements formed the basis for the English-based Creoles. It is also debated whether Creoles necessarily evolved out of an earlier pidgin stage (Baker 1995; 2000). Since pidgin and Creole languages are studied as a field in their own right, they will not feature prominently in this book, except in Chapter 5, when we examine some similarities between Creoles and New Englishes.

In 1600 Queen Elizabeth I granted a charter to the merchants of London who formed the East India Company. As in Africa it was the traders who first introduced English in India. Kachru (1983b:19–21) identifies three stages in which English was introduced in India: (a) a missionary phase that began around 1614; (b) a phase of 'local demand' from leaders; and (c) the educational phase that began with formal colonisation in 1765. Perhaps we should identify a prefatory 'reconnaissance and trade period' prior to these three stages.

This history was replicated in other parts of South and South-East Asia, with the proviso that some of the earliest teachers of English and clerks in places like Singapore, Malaysia, Brunei, Hong Kong and Fiji were South Asians (from India or Ceylon/Sri Lanka) in the employ of the British-administered government of India and Ceylon (Platt and Weber 1980:23; Gupta 1994:44; McArthur 2003b:21). McArthur also notes the continuing influence of South Asian teachers in the Middle East.

Australia was settled in 1788, and unlike the colonies in Africa and Asia the European settlers came to dominate numerically. As in the USA, the aboriginal population greatly declined in the aftermath of colonisation. A consequence of the social segregation and exclusion that followed is the eventual rise of a distinctive Aboriginal English. Eagleson (1982:432) stresses that Creole exists side by side in Aboriginal communities with other forms of English: pidgin, 'broken' English, non-standard sociolect and standard forms of English.

English settlement in East Africa was rather more like that of India than West Africa. English ships began making trips along the east coast of Africa by the end of the sixteenth century, proving to be forerunners of the British East Africa Company. An alliance was formed with the British government in India in 1810, resulting in Mombasa becoming a protectorate of the Crown. In West Africa local people had very little exposure to native speakers of English (the mosquito has something to do with this), giving prominence to Pidgin English. In East Africa, by contrast, 'native speakers were present in considerable numbers, had great influence in government and filled a higher percentage of teaching posts' (Hancock and Angogo 1982:306).

South Africa followed a slightly different route, being intermediate between the Australian and the Indian or East African outcomes. That is to say, the settlement was larger than in India and East Africa but not as numerically dominant as in Australia. The significance of this is that English is a prominent language in formal spheres (and this has not changed much in the post-apartheid era, 1994–), though the local languages (like Zulu and Sotho) remain numerically dominant and viable modes of communication amongst large parts of the populace.

What generalisations can be drawn from these different, yet not dissimilar, colonial histories? Where contact was via trading ships, rather than large-scale settlement, pidgins tended to arise. Where large-scale population displacement and mixing of speakers of different languages occurred (as in slavery), pidgins or jargons gave rise to Creoles. Under colonisation as a formal process involving government and administration, ESL varieties emerged. Some indigenous elites with a good education in English and with opportunities of contacts with administrators (social networks, albeit of a restricted nature) would use the colonial language like native speakers. It might be necessary to stress that sociolinguists do not attach any stigma to the development of one type of language over another. Whether speakers come up with a pidgin, EFL, ESL or ENL depends on factors such as the following: (a) the relative number of speakers of the different languages, including the TL; (b) the social relations between them; (c) the duration of the contact; and (d) educational opportunities in the TL.

The age of formal empire in Africa began in 1885, making English an official language of certain territories. However, by force of circumstances English would coexist with local languages in administration – there was frequently a degree of complementarity in official institutions of state. For East Africa, Mazrui and Mazrui (1998:143) put it as follows:

> If the English language dominated at higher levels of colonial administration, it is the African languages which prevailed in the lower administrative echelons.... If the body that made the law, the legislative council, was the domain of the English language, the institutions charged with the enforcement of the law, like the police, the prisons and the army, were heavily dependent on the local lingua franca, Kiswahili.

In the educational sphere this complementary relationship was especially noticeable in primary education. English was associated with new knowledge, and sometimes came to be synonymous with academic and technical knowledge. Local languages became associated with traditional culture and, in the education sphere, were considered but a gateway to the acquisition of English. This relationship between the languages was part of a wider dialectic between tradition and modernisation, which the British encapsulated as their 'dual mandate' (Mazrui and Mazrui 1998:143) – the introduction of modern, Western ideas and technology alongside a continuation of local culture and identity. This mandate differed from that of the French, for example, whose ideal was to transform the locals into 'Frenchmen' and 'Frenchwomen'.

It has proved difficult for post-colonial policy makers to dislodge in parents' and pupils' minds what the novelist Chinua Achebe (1975:xiv) called 'the fatalistic logic of the unassailable position of English'. The English language remains one of the most enduring legacies of Africa's and Asia's experience with British colonialism. One reason for the hegemony of English is that it became a symbol of a new developing elite in colonial times as well as a medium of the anti-colonial struggles. Mazrui and Mazrui (1998:145) argue that one of the African nationalists' demands to the colonial office concerned greater access to English: 'the colonial office found itself pressured by African nationalists to move faster than it was prepared to do in the introduction of English in schools'. Some intellectuals were not ignorant of the contradictions of using a colonial language in the struggle for freedom. Perhaps the most articulate of the critics of English was the first anti-colonist, Mahatma Gandhi. He had earlier chastised the elites of India for being 'drunk with the wine of English' and for thinking that 'we cannot acquire the spirit of freedom without the music of the English words ringing in our ears and sounding through our lips' (*Young India*, 2/2/1921). On the whole, though, post-colonial movements have found it hard to shake off the use of the erstwhile colonial language.

The nexus of colonial policy, local attitudes and practical considerations established what might be termed a 'colonial habitus' (after
Bourdieu 1991). In the colonial linguistic market bilingualism involving English and a major regional language (e.g. Kiswahili in East Africa,
Hindi-Urdu in India, Malay in Malaysia) was the chief desideratum. The
establishment of English in Singapore and Malaysia, described by Platt
(1983: 388), is not atypical of the way the colonial linguistic habitus
was formed:

1. The English-medium schools did not teach local languages. If any
   other language was taught at all, it was typically Latin.
2. The use of English was strongly encouraged both in and out of
   the classroom and, in fact, there were often sanctions in the
   form of small fines imposed on pupils using another language
   at school.
3. Headmasters and headmistresses, and often senior staff, were
   usually from Britain.
4. Although most pupils were Chinese, there were also Indians and
   Eurasians. It is likely that junior pupils used Bazaar Malay [a
   pidgin] at first in inter-ethnic communication, but soon found
   English an appropriate language for the expression of more complicated ideas.
5. For almost all pupils, English was the only language in which
   they were literate.

However, the presence of non-English–medium schools should not be
ignored. Brutt-Griffler (2000:191–5) gives statistics to show that in certain British colonies (like Ceylon (now Sri Lanka), the Federated Malay
States and the Unfederated Malay States) vernacular schools outnumbered English-medium schools. But as high-status jobs for local people
required 'colonial bilingualism', the demand for English swiftly grew.

Success in learning English within particular territories was not uniform, but depended on circumstances. Second Language Acquisition
(SLA) studies place a great deal of emphasis on 'instrumental' versus
'integrational' motivation (Gardner and Lambert 1972) to explain why
some speakers do better than others in mastering a second language.
Broadly speaking it was posited that a purely instrumental motivation
in learning a TL (e.g. a certificate or a job) was less likely to ensure
success (measured in terms of closeness of the outcome of learning to
the TL) than an integrative motivation (wanting to associate with TL
speakers and having positive attitudes to their culture). This explanation seems to be based on specific studies of people learning English in

an Anglophone environment. That is, it applies to immigrant Englishes rather than ESL (in the way we differentiated them earlier). The colonial situation demands a bit more care, since the number of TL speakers was always small and shrank even further after decolonisation. The learning of English took place largely within the classroom, rather than via direct access to TL speakers, a process labelled 'macroacquisition' by Brutt-Griffler (2000). This meant that motivation as conceived in the Gardner and Lambert model would always tend to the instrumental rather than the integrational. However, matters are not as simple as this. Firstly, learning English as an additional language conferred a new identity on learners: it signalled entry into a world of change and modernity, with emerging opportunities. Secondly, even if the initial impulse for learning English was largely instrumental, schooling sometimes fostered a new integrationism – not with TL speakers, but amongst pupils of different linguistic backgrounds, especially in urban centres. Clearly the issue of motivation is more nuanced in colonial and post-colonial settings than in Gardner and Lambert's immigrant English environment.

Given the association of English with the backing of empire, the value of education, the uses of literacy and the vocational market, it is not surprising that the ideology associated with the standard should come into force. American ideas concerning the autonomy of their form of English (see Kahane 1992) did not influence the emerging Englishes elsewhere. In many colonies the number of locals with a mastery of English was generally much smaller than those still learning it. If a local form of English was recognised, it was typically formulated within the 'problem' paradigm – of errors, interference, miscommunication and demeaning of the Queen's language. The hegemony of the standard allowed no other way of conceptualising the emergent Englishes; there was no way of romanticising them in the way that turned rural dialects in the UK into objects of preservation. In the post-colonial period, when governments and writers continued to use English confidently, it still took a great deal of persistence to convince linguists and educationists that the post-colonial grammars, lexicons and phonologies were worthy of study and not some deviation to be scrubbed away. Much of the credit for this persistence is due to Braj Kachru, who was influenced by the British linguists J. R. Firth and M. A. K. Halliday in paying attention to the social contexts of post-colonial English. Kachru has argued vociferously since the 1960s for the recognition of post-colonial Englishes, firstly as worthy objects of empirical study and secondly as appropriate forms of language for use in education. However, he has also been sensitive to attitudes of speakers of these varieties and of educational officials towards these varieties. Whilst the metropolitan standard commands what Labov (1972) called 'overt prestige', local forms of English do command a measure of 'covert prestige'.

Although the formal age of empire has declined, the sun has not set on the English language. This time the spread of English has been due mainly to the power and prestige of the US economy, technology and culture (of which Hollywood and American English are a vital part) in the years following the Second World War. The phenomenon of globalisation has made English a part of the linguistic ecology of most nations. The demand for English outstrips the supply of native-speaker teachers and EFL is a major export industry for the metropolises. We call this the fourth crossing of English, this time involving the movement of the language (via EFL materials, radio, television and the media generally) rather than of large numbers of speakers from the metropolis, as was the case under colonialism. Plüddeman (in press) has characterised the effects of globalisation as causing large numbers of people (in South Africa, but also places like China, Brazil, etc.) to be 'English-seeking', rather than 'English-speaking'. This dichotomy captures the difference between the desirability of English in the global economy and the difficulties of learning a language to which one has limited access and even less access to interactions with fluent speakers. As Neville Alexander (2000) warns, if English seems unassailable, it often seems unattainable too.

1.4.2 Agencies of spread

Thus far we have concentrated on the early period of contacts which led to English gaining a foothold in many parts of the world. Once the informal empire of sailors, traders, adventurers and missionaries turned into a formal colony, educational and other agencies focused on the formal propagation of English. Important work in this field comes from Robert Phillipson's (1992) book *Linguistic Imperialism* which analyses the forces responsible for the promulgation of English in the colonial and post-colonial era. His main thesis is that, apart from the earliest period, the spread of English has not been left to chance; rather language teaching has played a major part in this success (1992:6). Moreover, if English had official status in the empire, its power did not wane with the end of colonisation. More money has been spent since then on consolidating the position of the language. Phillipson (1992:7) cites Troike (1977) who points to the enormous amounts of government and private foundation funds spent between 1950 and 1970 'perhaps the most ever spent in history in support of the propagation of a language'. The primary agent of propagation is undoubtedly the British Council, inaugurated in 1935 by the British Government, which funds it to popularise not just the language, but British literature, arts, political philosophy and science. A range of activities and opportunities followed – such as the establishment of cultural centres, anglophile societies, scholarships for study in Britain, support for British schools abroad, book donations and exhibitions, theatre performances and so forth (1992:139). Phillipson is highly critical of the idea that English is the natural choice for a world language, that 'market forces' (of demand and supply) determine its popularity and that its spread over vast territories is for the good of the countries concerned. His main concern is that policies of the British Council foster linguicism – the devaluing and ultimate attenuation of the local languages. For Phillipson (1992:151) the spread of English serves British interests:

> It may... prove something of a shock to members of the ELT [English Language Teaching] profession, who regard themselves as being concerned exclusively with cultural, intellectual, liberal or non-political pursuits, to realize that the foundations of the academic and professional world in which they operate were laid by a Conservative British Cabinet which was preoccupied with the Cold War and the security of worldwide British investments.

The British Council's counterpart across the Atlantic was the United States Information Agency (USIA), which formed part of the American Embassy. This body, now defunct, was till 1999 responsible not just for the spread of American English in areas of US influence (e.g. the Phillipines) but within areas where British English once held sway. There are still other US agencies involved in teaching English worldwide: the Peace Corps and the Agency for International Development. Phillipson (1992:153) also cites the role of the World Bank and the IMF in emphasising English in the educational systems of developing countries to further the goals of national development. Phillipson and a host of other scholars (e.g. Tollefson 1991, Pennycook 1994; Heugh 2002) suggest that English-only or English-mainly educational policies are doomed to failure and serve only to widen the gap between the core and periphery in world politics, and the haves and have-nots within the periphery.

Scholars working within the 'World Englishes' paradigm typically support the goals of multilingualism. They are critical of Western studies on second-language acquisition that assume that the goal of learning English is to imitate the native speaker perfectly (see Sridhar and Sridhar 1986). They would see this assumption as a ramification of linguistic imperialism within academia. Whilst being interested in the linguistic and sociolinguistic aspects of the spread of English, these scholars insist on placing English within its proper multicultural ethos. World Englishes scholars stress the multiple norms character-istic of English grammar and discourse relative to different contexts. The idea that the grammar of English emanates from the royal court of London has long been questioned in Linguistics and is being pushed to its limits in World English studies.

Phillipson is sometimes described as a 'conspiracy theorist' (see, e.g., Davies 1996), i.e. being of the view that inequality and domination of some powers over others is a deliberate and planned process. Such critics would argue that power is less centralised than this in the modern world: that following Foucault (1972), power is everywhere and unavoidable, it is not restricted to a few elites or political leaders. Moreover, Brutt-Griffler (2000:86–105) provides extensive evidence that in the era of British colonialism far from being foisted on a reluctant populace, English was frequently withheld from it. Some would argue that, similarly, Phillipson's view of present-day agencies like the British Council is particularly uncharitable, as the work of the British Council is of benefit to (and desired by) local communities lacking educational opportunities. The desire amongst sociolinguists for a balance between propagating English (or Englishes) and being sensitive to the position of local languages (and, by implication, cultures and economies) is expressed in an anecdote by David Crystal, by no means a conspiracy theorist.

> Even a statement recognizing the value of competing linguistic standards is too much for some. I was a member of the panel which discussed English language issues at the ... launch of David Graddol's book *The Future of English?* (1997), and I hinted at this view in a contribution I made there. Afterwards, at the buffet, someone came up and asked me if my notion of linguistic tolerance of English diversity extended to such things as the errors foreigners made. I said it all depended on what you mean by an error. *I am knowing*, for example, is not allowed in traditional standard English, but it is normal in some parts of the world, such as the Indian subcontinent (and also, incidentally, in some British dialects). Would you correct a Frenchman who said *I am knowing*, then, he asked? It all depends, I said. Not if he was learning Indian English. My interlocutor's face told me that the concept of a Frenchman wanting to learn Indian English was, at the very least, novel.
>   There was a pause. Then he said, 'Are you saying that ... we should be letting our teachers teach Indian English, and not British English?'
>   'If the occasion warranted it, yes,' I said.

'I don't like the sound of that,' he said, and he literally fled from me, upsetting a glass of wine in the process. He didn't hear me add: 'Or even other languages.' Crystal (2001:61)[5]

The idea of a regionally influential (even if not officially standard) variety of an ESL broached by Crystal is not that far-fetched. Some South-East Asian families having EFL background (from, e.g., Thailand) prefer to send their children to study English (ESL) in places like New Delhi rather than in a Western metropolis, citing reasons of (a) relative cost-saving; (b) cultural appropriateness ('Asian' rather than 'Western' values); (c) geographical proximity; and (d) a higher quality of English education than is possible in an EFL country.

1.5 MODELS OF ENGLISH

At roughly the same time three scholars came up with rather similar models which aimed to characterise World Englishes within one conceptual set. Tom McArthur's 'wheel model' (Figure 1.1) appeared in *English Today* in July 1987. McArthur's wheel conceives of a central variety called 'World Standard English' which is obviously an idealisation, and perhaps best represented as 'written international English', though there are slight differences between written British and American norms. The next circle round the hub is made of regional standards or standards that are emerging. Finally, the outer layer comprises localised varieties which may have similarities with the regional standards or emerging standards.

The model is neat, though – not surprisingly – it raises problems we have cited before. The second circle has geographic coherence but conflates three very different types: ENL, ESL and EFL. Some of the ENLs have a crystallised norm (UK and USA), but others are ambivalent between a local (endogenous) versus an externally based (exogenous) standard – e.g. South Africa and Australia. ESLs may have standard or emerging standard varieties, but these are grammatically more stigmatised than ENLs in South Africa and Australia. The main problem with this layer is whether EFLs can be said to have 'standardising' forms or not. (This recalls the distinction between 'performance' and 'institutionalised' varieties.) Also missing in this layer are the multitude of Englishes in Europe, which with the rise of the European Union (EU) are becoming more visible than they used to be (see Cenoz and Jessner 2000). Finally, the outside layer includes pidgins, Creoles

---

[5] In fairness to the organisation concerned we have omitted its name.

Figure 1.1 Tom McArthur's Circle of World English (from McArthur 1987:97)

and L2 Englishes. Most scholars would argue that English pidgins and Creoles do not belong unambiguously to one family: rather they have overlapping multiple memberships.

Some of these criticisms are met, not necessarily intentionally, in a model (see Figure 1.2) presented by Manfred Görlach at about the same time (1988). Görlach's and McArthur's models are reasonably similar. Both exclude English varieties in Europe. As Görlach does not include EFLs at all, his model is more consistent (though less complete). Outside the circle are mixed varieties (pidgins, Creoles and mixed languages involving English), which we have argued are better characterised as having partial membership in the ELC.

Braj Kachru's model (see Figure 1.3), which appeared in *English Today* in 1988, conceptualises Englishes more broadly and differently. The

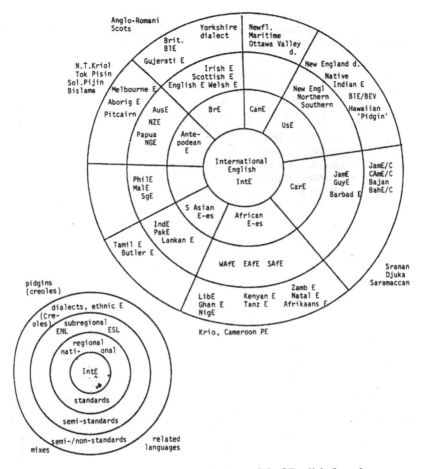

Figure 1.2 Manfred Görlach's Circle model of English (based on Görlach 1990)

circles are no longer concentric; there is no centre holding it all together. Inner Circle varieties come closest to constituting such a centre but are conceived of as non-monolithic – they are influential ENLs which are 'norm providing'. The Outer Circle comprises ESLs which have their own spoken norms but tend to rely on the Outer Circle for models of formal written English especially. The Expanding Circle comprises EFLs which have not developed internal norms and accordingly rely on external norms. Whilst seeming to be based on geography, Kachru's model is actually based on history and politics. It has the advantage of not treating English in say the Phillipines and the

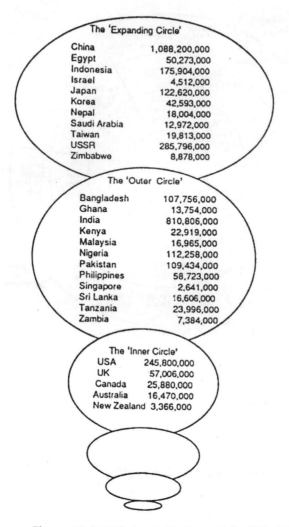

The 'Expanding Circle'	
China	1,088,200,000
Egypt	50,273,000
Indonesia	175,904,000
Israel	4,512,000
Japan	122,620,000
Korea	42,593,000
Nepal	18,004,000
Saudi Arabia	12,972,000
Taiwan	19,813,000
USSR	285,796,000
Zimbabwe	8,878,000

The 'Outer Circle'	
Bangladesh	107,756,000
Ghana	13,754,000
India	810,806,000
Kenya	22,919,000
Malaysia	16,965,000
Nigeria	112,258,000
Pakistan	109,434,000
Philippines	58,723,000
Singapore	2,641,000
Sri Lanka	16,606,000
Tanzania	23,996,000
Zambia	7,384,000

The 'Inner Circle'	
USA	245,800,000
UK	57,006,000
Canada	25,880,000
Australia	16,470,000
New Zealand	3,366,000

Figure 1.3 Braj Kachru's Circles model of World Englishes (from Kachru 1988:5)

UK as 'on the same layer', which the other two models do (Phillipines English – an ESL falls within the second circle of both McArthur's
and Görlach's models, as does 'British English'). However this political
explicitness comes at a cost, in so far as Kachru does not overtly position social and ethnic varieties within 'Inner Circle countries'. Where,
for example, does Chicano English of the USA fit? Although Kachru
also avoids placing Euro-Englishes within his framework, they would

fit quite easily into his scheme (as expanding Englishes) rather than in the other two models.[6] None of the models are able to do justice to the intricacies of specific countries. Take, for example, South Africa, where the settler population has either ENL or is Afrikaans-speaking, whilst a large segment of the indigenous populace use ESL.

Such nuances have led Bruthiaux (2003) to argue that the time has come for a less historical and a more synchronic model which recognises differences between English in different territories, according to criteria such as the following:

(a) Geopolitical power and size of population (e.g. USA vs New Zealand)
(b) Multicultural versus monocultural ethos (e.g. Singapore vs Hong Kong)
(c) Administrative and public roles for English in certain territories, without formal colonisation (e.g. sheikdoms of the Middle East like Oman and Qatar, which were not colonies but British 'Protectorates')
(d) Internal differentiation (e.g. two varieties of English in Panama; several varieties of English in South Africa; many sociolects within a recognised variety like 'Singapore English')
(e) Variation in details of linguistic competence pertaining to factors like speech versus writing ability; comprehension versus production and so forth.

Historical models can also be found for the historical development of World Englishes in the work of Moag (1992) and Schneider (2003). We focus on Schneider's development of the earlier models into a five-step characterisation of the spread of English. Schneider tries to avoid a purely geographic and historical approach evident in the 'circles' models and incorporates sociolinguistic concepts pertaining to acts of identity (Le Page and Tabouret-Keller 1985). He argues that despite obvious differences, transplanted Englishes throughout the world were shaped by fundamentally uniform sociolinguistic and language-contact processes. Identity construction is a central part of this process, arising from mutual accommodation between indigenous populations and immigrant groups. Schneider makes the following proposals:

(a) In the process of the English language being uprooted and relocated in colonial and post-colonial history New Englishes have emerged by undergoing a fundamentally uniform process which

---

[6] Kachru's placement of Zimbabwe (formerly Rhodesia) is an error, as this is (like South Africa) an Inner and Outer Circle country, not an Expanding Circle one.

can be described as a progression of five characteristic stages: foundation, exonormative stabilisation, nativisation, endonormative stabilisation and differentiation.

(b) The participant groups experience this emergence in complementary ways, from the perspective of the colonisers or that of the colonised, with these developmental strands getting more closely intertwined and their linguistic correlates, in an on-going process of mutual linguistic accommodation, approximating each other in the course of time.

(c) The stages and strands of this process are ultimately caused by and signify reconstructions of group identities of all participating communities, with respect to the erstwhile source society of the colonising group, to one another, and to the land which they jointly inhabit.

Schneider outlines the following phases in the spread of English:

Phase 1 – Foundation: This is the initial stage of the introduction of English to a new territory over an extended period of time. The motivations may be trade or long-term settlement. Two linguistic processes are operative at this stage: (a) language contact between English and indigenous languages; (b) contact between different dialects of English of the settlers which eventually results in a new stable dialect (a *koine*, see Trudgill 1986). At this stage bilingualism is marginal. A few members of the local populace may play an important role as interpreters, translators and guides. Borrowings are limited to lexical items; with local place names and terms for local fauna and flora being adopted by the English.

Phase 2 – Exonormative stabilisation: At this stage the settler communities tended to stabilise politically, under British rule. English increases in prominence and though the colloquial English is a colonial koine, the speakers look to England for their formal norms. Local vocabulary continues to be adopted. Bilingualism increases amongst the indigenous population through education and increased contacts with English settlers. Knowledge of English becomes an asset, and a new indigenous elite develops, based on, *inter alia*, contacts with settlers and knowledge of English.

Phase 3 – Nativisation: According to Schneider this is the stage at which a transition occurs as the English settler population starts to accept a new identity based on present and local realities, rather than sole allegiance to the 'mother country'. By this time the indigenous strand has also stabilised an L2 system that is a synthesis of substrate effects, interlanguage processes and features adopted from the settlers' koiné English. A 'complaint tradition' develops at this stage as educationists and others point to the differences between the local forms of English and the more prestigious metropolitan norms. Nevertheless neologisms stabilise as English is made to adapt to local sociopolitical and cultural practices.

Phase 4 – Endonormative stabilisation: This stage is characterised by the gradual acceptance of local norms, supported by a new locally rooted linguistic self-confidence. By this time political events have made it clear that the settler and indigenous strands are inextricably bound in a sense of nationhood independent of Britain. Acceptance of local English(es) expresses this new identity. National dictionaries are enthusiastically supported, at least for new lexis (and not always for localised grammar). Literary creativity in the local English begins to flourish.

Phase 5 – Differentiation: At this stage there is a change in the dynamics of identity as the young nation sees itself as less defined by its differences from the former colonial power as a composite of subgroups defined on regional, social and ethnic lines. Coupled with the simple effects of time in effecting language change (with the aid of social differentiation) the new English koine starts to show greater differentiation.

Schneider provides the following examples illustrating phases 2 to 5 (he does not exemplify phase 1, though one can think of it in terms of EFL countries like China, where more than trade relations with the West have long been discouraged, though this has changed since the late twentieth century).

Phase 2 example – Fiji: Fiji was a British colony between 1874 and 1970 (after which it became independent). The number of European residents has never been large. The main population groups are the indigenous Fijians and the Indian Fijians (whose ancestors were brought from India by the British in the nineteenth and twenteeth centuries). The onset of phase 2 according to Schneider begins with New Zealand influence in the 1930s as an attempt to form a bond between the two countries. English is today used as a 'de facto official language' (Schneider 2003, quoting Tent and Mugler 1996:251). Bilingualism is fairly widespread, though the motive to acquire English is currently instrumental rather than integrative (in terms of bringing local groups of people together). With political polarisation of the two main groups of the country, there is no attempt yet at a joint national identity that would probably require taking English beyond phase 2. Schneider argues that apart from vocabulary related to the local environment and culture, and a few grammatical localisms, there is little nativisation.

Phase 3 example – Hong Kong: Like Fiji, Hong Kong is characterised by a very small percentage of native speakers and people of British descent, though stronger colonial rule in the recent past resulted in a more advanced phase. More particularly, Schneider cites its former politically stable status as a British Crown colony in Asia, an unchallenged exonormative orientation in language teaching and usage, the spread of elite bilingualism, the development of an identity among British representatives in an Asian outpost, and among the local Chinese as people with British cultural contacts and experience. The subsequent Joint British-Sino Declaration, which resulted in the handing over of the island to China in 1997 also led to a change from an 'us' versus 'them' colonially based differentiation among inhabitants to a special Hong Kong identity. Applied linguists like Bolton (2000) argue that there is now a distinct form of Hong Kong English (in addition to L1 Hong Kong English). This local English has a recognisable phonology that is positively evaluated as a source of identification (Bolton 2000:277–8) and is evolving some distinctive grammatical rules.

Phase 4 example – Singapore: Unlike the territories described in phases 2 and 3, the evolution of English in Singapore is a product of a language policy specifically espousing 'English-based bilingualism'. The growth of Singapore follows the establishment of a trading post in 1819, followed by large-scale importation of labourers, traders, travellers and colonial agents. By the late nineteenth century a small British ruling class coexisted with British subjects of Chinese, Indian and Malay ancestry, resulting in a cultural blend of Europe and Asia. A decolonisation movement, which began in the 1950s and 1960s, saw the island gain independence in 1965. Education policy fostered ethnicity-based bilingualism (English plus Mandarin, Malay or Tamil) meant to enhance the Asian-Western blend: 'every child is educated in English as "first language" and his/her ethnic language out of the other three official languages as a "mother-tongue second-language"' (Foley 1988:130–1). English is thus the common bond, but it has acquired a distinct local identity. As we shall see in Chapters 2 and 4, it is replete not just with local vocabulary but with a syntax that owes much to the home languages.

Phase 5 example – Australia and New Zealand: Initially a colonial koine marked by a high degree of homegeneity and local toponyms, but very little overt prestige, Australian and New Zealand English has, in Schneider's model, come full circle. At first linguistic allegiance was unambiguously towards standard British norms. A growing sense of difference from the metropolis was exacerbated by second World War experience in which Australia was left unprotected against a Japanese attack in 1942. In Schneider's model this is referred to as 'event X' – a formative event which was pivotal in the construction of a new sense of identity, partly based on the need for self-sufficiency, rather than uncritical reliance on the mother country. (In New Zealand this was the economic and political consequences of British entry into the European Union in 1973, which left New Zealand bereft of its prime export market.) Phase 4 followed, with the claim to homogeneity (i.e. claims to a unique linguistic identity) and the beginnings of codification, as evident in the Macquarrie Dictionary in Australia (Mitchell and Delbridge 1981) and the *Dictionary of New Zealand English on Historical Principles* (Orsman 1997). Schneider argues that the on-going birth of new dialects in these territories is the sign of their having reached the end of the cycle (phase 5).

Schneider intends his model to apply to all varieties of extraterritorial and new Englishes. The model also predicts that different territories are likely to proceed (given current world trends) from phase n to $n + 1$, where n denotes any current phase from 1 to 4. The model is interesting in that it does not differentiate between extraterritorial varieties and ESLs. It is a useful co-ordinated way of looking at the spread of English. But, again, there are several questions it raises. Firstly, the incorporation of 'dominion' countries like Australia and New Zealand in a model that deals mostly with ESL countries like Fiji seems unwarranted. The conditions surrounding the installation of dominions seems quite different from that of colonies and protectorates. Secondly, identity is conceived very much as a 'public' concept in terms of nationhood. Schneider downplays other aspects of identity like class and status, which in the Australian and other cases resulted in an early opposition between vernacular and standard English; and later a continuum between 'general', 'cultivated' and 'broad' colonial L1 Englishes (see Mitchell and Delbridge 1965). Thirdly, positing 'event X' seems to give too much due to a particular political phenomenon. Whereas this might have implications for the acceptance or rejection of an external standard, it is questionable how significant an influence such an event could have on vernacular usage. Fourthly, the model has a predictive aspect – that a variety at phase n is likely to proceed to phase $n + 1$ (and not skip a stage in between). This remains to be tested by cases other than those described by Schneider: it seems possible to us that a territory could move from phase 3 to 5, bypassing phase 4. This would be a territory in which English became nativised and subsequently differentiated into sub-dialects, without there being a commonly accepted endonormative standard. Varieties of English in West Africa appear to follow this route, (see Gut 2004 for Nigeria). Finally,

Schneider's model grew out of an analysis of the Asia–Pacific region; it is not clear if the model applies as clearly to countries in Africa and South Asia. One could argue that for India the era of identity construction vis-à-vis the colonising power has long gelled; and that the position of English is now driven by other dynamics. These include factors like elite formation. Class is noticeably missing from Schneider's model (and in fact from many of the 'circles' models); yet there is a large gap between the middle-class varieties of New Englishes and their jargon, pidgin or basilectal counterparts (the term 'basilectal' is discussed in Chapter 2). Nevertheless Schneider's model offers a research framework for 'placing' and analysing developments in individual territories; it is truly 'dynamic'.

1.6   A CONTROVERSY IN WORLD ENGLISH STUDIES – THE NATIVE SPEAKER

The distinction between a native and non–native speaker of a language – long taken for granted in Linguistics – is being increasingly called into question in World English research. Traditionally a native speaker is assumed to be one who has learnt a language from birth without formal instruction. By contrast a non-native speaker of a language has learnt it as a second (or later) language some time after being initiated into his/her native language and does not display the same automatic fluency in the non-native language as in the native language. Paradis (1998:207) describes a speaker's native language as 'the dialect acquired from the crib ... acquired incidentally, stored implicitly, and available for automatic use'.

Several commentators have pointed out that such definitions of a native speaker seem to be premised on the norms of monolingual societies, whereas in fact the world is largely multilingual. In some multilingual societies a child may be said to have several native languages, with the order of acquisition not being an indicator of ability. Multilingual speakers may switch languages according to situation in a way that monolingual speakers switch styles of the same language 'natively' (Scotton 1985). For many New English speakers monolingualism is the marked case, a special case outside of the multilingual prototype. Today's ideal speaker lives in a heterogeneous society (stratified along increasingly globalised lines) and has to negotiate interactions with different people representing all sorts of power and solidary positions on a regular basis. What is this ideal speaker a native speaker of, but a polyphony of codes/languages working cumulatively (and sometimes complementarily), rather than a single, first-learned code? These codes are appropriate to different functions or criss-crossing of functions (one can, e.g., discuss politics informally with a friend, or debate it formally with an opponent).

For Singh (1998:26) the grammatical deviations found amongst fluent speakers of 'New Englishes' or 'World Englishes' (WEs) are not qualitatively different from differences between dialect and standard English or between one historical stage of standard English and another. In mathematical formulation Singh (p. 61) argues that: (a) there is no structural feature α such that all 'non-native' varieties of English have α and no 'native' variety does; and (b) there is no structural feature β such that no 'native' variety of English has β but some 'non-native' varieties of English do. Complementary to this argument is Mufwene's (1998) insistence that language as a system is partly inherited and partly being made by its speakers, and that monolingual native speakers have no more authority than their (fluent) multilingual counterparts, especially in the modern world.

Still, few WE scholars would argue that there is no difference between ENL and ESL; the acquisitional contexts, they would insist, *are* different. Ho and Platt (1993:4) argued that a crucial difference between native speakers of English in a metropolitan context and 'New English' speakers of a territory like Singapore is based on stylistic behaviour. The most fluent, educated speakers of Singapore English still preserve earlier-learnt (or basilectal) forms and actively use them in interaction with less educated speakers or those who are still learning English.[7] ENL speakers do not deploy early-learnt forms in this way.

The debate over the native speaker is not a purely 'academic' one: it raises important questions about norms and about who the most appropriate teachers in ESL countries are; we postpone discussion of it till Chapter 7 on pedagogical issues.

1.7 CONCLUSION

This chapter has provided an introductory overview of the spread of English and the multifaceted nature of the ELC. Some of these issues raised by the globalisation of English will be examined in greater detail

---

[7] Of course, one could argue that native speakers of English do the same when talking to children or foreigners. Platt, Weber and Ho suggest that 'downshifting' is more pervasive and a feature of ordinary interaction (rather than limited to special registers) in Singapore.

in Chapter 7 (in sections on pedagogy and language endangerment). In the next three chapters we will switch focus somewhat to examine the linguistic features of WEs, especially recurring features found in the Outer Circle, and ways of describing, analysing and understanding them.

STUDY QUESTIONS

1. Clarify the differences (and mention overlaps) between the following: ENL, L1, TL, L2; EFL, ESL, immigrant English; performance variety, institutionalised variety.
2. Discuss the terms 'Inner Circle', 'Outer Circle' and 'Expanding Circle', with three examples of countries belonging to each category.
3. Review the difference we propose between narrow ESL and wide ESL.
4. Contrast Platt, Weber and Ho's (1984) narrow definition of New English with wider interpretations of the term.
5. Review Schneider's five-stage model of New English development and place the following countries within his model: the United States, Nigeria, India.

Further reading
All works mentioned here are fully referenced in the bibliography.

For a wide historical and geographical coverage of English, see Bailey and Görlach's *English as a World Language* (1982), and Kachru's two books, *The Other Tongue* (2nd edn. 1992) and *The Alchemy of English* (1986). An updated and more detailed account of syntax and phonology of these varieties can be found in the *Handbook of Varieties of English* (2004), Vol. I on phonology, ed. Schneider *et al.*; Vol. II on morphology and syntax, ed. Kortmann *et al.*; Vol. III is a CD Rom, with maps, phonetic examples and opportunities for students and researchers to do their own interactive comparisons of individual features in different parts of the world. A good introduction to the field, aimed at a slightly lower level than the present text, is Melchers and Shaw's *World Englishes* (2003), and Schneider's *Postcolonial Englishes* (2006). A useful workbook is *World Englishes: A Resource Book for Students* by Jenkins (2003). The three significant journals in the field are *English Today*, aimed at a 'popular' readership, and the more specialised *World Englishes* and *English World-Wide*.

2 Structural features of New Englishes I: morphology and phrasal syntax

This chapter provides an overview of the main syntactic and morphological characteristics of New Englishes (i.e. mainly 'Outer Circle' varieties). The main focus will fall upon their recurrent features, though some rarer constructions, limited to one or two varieties, will also be discussed where relevant.

2.1 A NOTE ON METHOD

Our focus in this chapter is largely descriptive, seeking to establish similarities amongst the recurrent features of New Englishes. In Chapter 6 we examine the broader questions raised by these similarities and the attempts that have been made to tie them together within particular analytic and theoretical frameworks. We begin with an excursus on methodology.

This chapter, like the rest of the book, is reliant upon individual descriptions of World Englishes occurring in journals, monographs devoted to individual countries and overviews found in handbooks. Ideally, before linguistic generalisations can be made, we should be sure that we are comparing varieties and sub-varieties that are indeed comparable. Broadly speaking this means being mindful of the ESL–EFL distinction, as well as of the somewhat special status of what we called 'language-shift varieties' (see section 1.2). It also means comparing appropriate subgroups of speakers, paying attention to differences between users still learning the local variety of English and those who are competent users who have already acquired it. This distinction is perhaps not as clear-cut as it may first appear, given the principle of lectal shifting. This principle is ultimately traceable to David de Camp's (1971) description of Jamaican Creole, vis-à-vis its relation to its superstrate, English. Instead of individuals switching from the one system to another, a 'societal' continuum had developed between the 'deepest' Creole (or basilect) and the most standard form on the island (the acrolect), with the majority of speakers located somewhere between these two extremes (the mesolect, or more appropriately, mesolects). Individual speakers were competent in not just one part of the continuum, but in a slice of it, which they deployed in appropriate contexts, taking into consideration contextual factors like the status of the interlocutor, the formality of the situation, the purpose of the communication, etc. Several commentators (Platt, Weber and Ho 1984; Mesthrie 1992a; Chew 1995) have argued for a similar situation in New Englishes, where speakers may be described as basilectal, mesolectal or acrolectal according to their norms in spontaneous speech. It has been noted that in many New Englishes speakers who might be described as (for example) upper mesolectal 'backslide' (i.e. drop back) to a lower mesolectal (or even basilectal) style when speaking informally to a basilectal speaker. This principle applies in L1 situations too, when speakers of a dialect shed some of its features in conversation with strangers but use 'broader' dialect features in informal speech to close friends. However, what is noteworthy in the New English situation is that in 'dropping back' people deploy features from an earlier stage of acquisition. For example, in one of Mesthrie's (1992a:60) interviews involving South African Indian English (henceforth *IndSAf Eng*) speakers, a high-school English teacher whose general speech norm was upper-mesolectal dropped back in conversation with his wife (thinking he was out of range of the tape recorder) as follows:

1. *Wife:*   You bought cheese, Farouk? (= 'Did you buy cheese, Farouk?')
   Husband: No', but lot butter I bought. (= 'No, though I did buy a lot of
                     butter') (No' = [noʊ])

This single utterance contained several items that the speaker himself might heavily stigmatise in a classroom context: topicalisation (with the object *lot butter* taking up pre-subject (topic) position; *lot* for 'a lot of' (or *much* in classroom English) and the basilectal pronunciation [nɔː] for acrolectal [noʊ] and [lɔːt] for acrolectal [lɒt]. On the basis of experience with Singapore English (henceforth *Sgp Eng*), Chew (1995:165) cautions that there might be limits to such backsliding: 'it is unlikely that a Singaporean would mistake an educated [Singaporean] English speaker speaking informally for an uneducated speaker'.

Sometimes, analysts prefer to use the terms *basilang*, *mesolang* and *acrolang*, rather than *basilect*, *mesolect* and *acrolect*, to emphasise that they are dealing with developing competence in an L2 (as with say an isolated immigrant learning English), rather than the L1 competence usually implied by terms like 'basilect', etc. The principle of lectal shifting makes it very important to gather data within comparable situations, as we suggest below. Other sociolinguistic aspects pertaining to 'register' are also methodologically important. Comparative work should ideally not mix spoken and written data. Unfortunately individual case studies do not always adhere to this desideratum. In some cases authors of articles are probably correct in suggesting that certain features from written sources (newspaper articles, students' essays, conversation in a novel) are regular features of a particular variety. However, writing has its own conventions, some of which have little connection with features of speech. Moreover, we rarely have information on the editing process accompanying the written efforts cited. The work of creative writers particularly needs to be cited with care, as they are usually concerned with creating a general effect via language, rather than using constructions with sociolinguistic veracity. Even the best intentioned authors may be susceptible to linguistic stereotyping. We take, as an example, an excerpt from a recent novel, *The Wedding* by Imraan Coovadia, which uses IndSAf Eng dialect in highly creative ways. One of the features, reduplication, is used as follows:

> 'Just think,' he'd told Shireen 'when that aunt of yours dies away and we can sell her rings off, we can cut that chicken, serve chicken *biryani,* chicken cutlets, chicken curry, *masala* chicken, what.'
> 'Ha!' Shireen replied. 'That chicken! That one useless skinny-skinny chicken. Not enough on it for one good breast.' (p. 39)

The example of reduplication (*skinny-skinny chicken*) in the above passage does not accord with spoken IndSAf Eng norms. Despite the author's feel for the dialect and his transformation of it into a creative medium, his collocation of reduplicated adjectives with singular nouns counts as poetic (or grammatical) licence. Data gathered from large samples of actual speech (Mesthrie 1992a) show a constraint against the use of reduplication in this context. Reduplication is largely distributive, with a slight connotation of pejoration or exaggeration (the connotation is captured by the author, but not the grammar). Thus *big-big fellows*; but not *(one) big-big fellow* is possible in IndSAf Eng, and such poeticisms as *blue, blue day* (with 'comma' intonation and singular head noun) are not used.

Sometimes, even though a piece of creative writing may be written in English, its syntax and discourse patterns may be intended to reflect not the local variety of English, but the first language of the community concerned (famous examples are Raja Rao's novel, *Kanthapura* and Gabriel Okara's *The Voice*, reflecting, via very creative English, the idioms of Kannada (a language of South India) and Ijaw (a language of West Africa), respectively). But these tell us very little about the spoken English of those communities. Literary effects within New Englishes are covered in Chapter 5.

This is not to suggest that written data are unimportant: for earlier periods concerning the genesis of New Englishes written data may be all that analysts have to go on, and can provide valuable snippets of information for the linguist. Thus non-literary, written sources like ships' logs, court records, missionary diaries, boarding school records and the like can be as valuable to the linguist as to the historian. And, obviously, for educational and literacy studies of World Englishes, student writing and revisions are the core material of analysis.

For contemporary studies, though, spoken data are a sine qua non, which should ideally be gathered along principles well established in Variationist Sociolinguistics. That is, fieldwork should be undertaken with a reliable judgement sample of the community concerned, culminating in informal tape-recorded interviews. These should stress the topics of a controversial, but not taboo, nature that elicit extended conversation. Such topics usually centre around local practices; including possibly Labov's (1972:209) well-known 'danger-of-death' module. The advantage of the 'Labovian' methodology is that it provides comparable data gathered under roughly the same conditions. Some successful studies within the WE paradigm have indeed utilised this methodology (Mesthrie 1992a; Ho and Platt 1993; Sharma 2005b). There is an important caveat, however, since the aim of urban dialectology is to study the vernacular, i.e. the least formal L1 variety that speakers use. The obvious question is whether the same techniques should apply to WEs which are not generally L1s and which are seldom appropriate in the most informal local context. A related question is whether speakers should use only English in a WE interview. It might be sociolinguistically artificial to expect English to be the only language used if the interviewer and interviewee share the same background. Bilingual behaviour including mixing and switching should be encouraged where natural and expected. On the other hand, an interviewer who is an outsider may well elicit only English conversation. Overall there seems to be no reason why the approach by 'variationist' interviewers would be inappropriate for WE research. However, discussions around more 'serious topics' like school, university and local politics are likely to be more prominent in WE contexts than in urban dialectology.

These days Corpus Linguistics is a growing field, utilising the convenience of the computer to collect and analyse larger samples of spoken and written data than is manageable within the traditional sociolinguistic interview-based survey. As such Corpus Linguistics is an important complement to, and ally of, WE studies. However, it is not immune to some of the concerns raised above regarding register, style and intention.

The data we draw on in this chapter do not always meet the ideal requirements we would like for comparative sociolinguistics. Where a local feature occurs, it is not always clear from our sources how frequent it is, and what its relations to more standard or colloquial 'L1' constructions are. These are aspects that we hope future scholars in the field will be more explicit about. A final note is that we use Standard English (henceforth *Std Eng*) in a non-prescriptive way in this book, taking it as an easy reference point to explain the meanings of phrases that are unfamiliar outside a particular WE variety. This use of a standard English sentence as a metalinguistic 'gloss' should not be taken to mean that this is the only correct or appropriate form that speakers should aim for. Furthermore, in this metalinguistic function it does not matter whether the standard is based on British or American norms. (Of course there are differences in detail between the two standards, but they do not impact much upon the issues raised in this book.) In practice the meanings given represent a widely understood and accepted written international English norm.

2.2 A NOTE ON TERMINOLOGY AND VARIETIES STUDIED

In this section we provide a fairly traditional overview of the main features reported in New English studies. More theoretical generalisations are made in Chapter 6.

2.2.1 Varieties compared in this section

Our focus in Chapters 2 and 3 will fall on linguistic characteristics of the New Englishes, rather than the EFLs of the 'Outer Circle'. Furthermore, as noted in that chapter we take a relatively broad view of the term 'New English'. We include prototypical varieties like Indian or Nigerian English, which are largely L2s in countries having few L1 speakers of British English left. We also include varieties like Black South African English (*BlSAf Eng*) or individual varieties of (native) American Indian English (*AmInd Eng*), which exist amidst a sizeable L1 populace, with a long tradition of L1 usage. We also include varieties which have recently undergone language shift (IndSAf Eng) or are in the process of doing so like Sgp Eng. We need to motivate why we include Irish Eng (*Ir Eng*) in our discussions, since at one level it can be considered an L1 variety on a par with other regional dialects in Britain, and since it formed part of the superstrate in the colonies historically. More relevantly, its origins are, in fact, as an L2, under a kind of internal colonisation described in Chapter 1. As Hickey (2004b:92) puts it, '[t]he fact that the majority of the Irish acquired English in an unguided manner as adults had consequences for the nature of Irish English'. This is what we termed a 'language-shift variety', in which an L2 stabilised as an L1, without significant contact with L1 speakers. In Kachru's terms Ireland is part of the Inner Circle. We suggest that it could equally be treated as Outer Circle (see its intermediate status, described in section 1.3.4. as 'a second crossing'). We therefore treat Ir Eng as appropriate to 'New English' studies, especially where it 'behaves' rather similarly in terms of linguistic features to other varieties cited in this chapter. In a review of a book on Irish English, King (2001:109) affirms that Ir Eng is 'a laboratory of special interest and inestimable value to the student of World Englishes. Ir Eng offers history and an exactitude of knowledge and linguistic detail that few other varieties of non-standard English can claim.'

In this chapter we do not focus on pidgin and Creole Englishes, since their history and linguistic status belongs to a different wing of Contact Linguistics. For this reason we have excluded the well-studied African American English variety, which many (but not all) scholars take to have a Creole ancestry. Likewise, Aboriginal English appears to have derived from pre-existing pidgins of the country, especially New South Wales pidgin (Malcolm 2004:657). The variety today has been restructured towards English rather than Creole and hence shares some significant similarities with New Englishes. While it is tempting to describe such features in this chapter, on the whole it makes greater sense to characterise them from the perspective of Creole studies (which Malcolm in fact does). For different reasons Expanding Circle Englishes (or EFL varieties) are not generally discussed in this chapter, except to show their difference from prototypical Outer Circle varieties. This is so since EFLs do not typically display a focusing of linguistic features (on the notions of focusing and diffusion see Le Page and Tabouret-Keller 1985). Such varieties are discussed in Chapter 7 in connection with the sociolinguistic issues relating to their use. Finally, the New English varieties we do focus on are ones well described from South Asia, South-East Asia, sub-Saharan Africa, the USA (American Indian English) and Ir Eng. Only occasionally do we draw on varieties outside this pool.

2.2.2 Further terminology

Most writers tend to ascribe WE features to either substrate or superstrate influences. The former is an old term in Historical Linguistics signalling the influence of a language formerly spoken by a community upon their current language (or that of their descendants). Thus, it is speculated that the counting system of French comes not directly from its ancestor, Latin, but from a Celtic language or languages no longer spoken in France (Fox and Wood 1968:21). Implicit in the formulation is the idea that the feature was originally used by bilingual speakers of a Celtic variety and of Vulgar Latin/Old French, and was passed on to all speakers, even though the Celtic language largely ceased to exist there. In the WE context the term substrate does not necessarily imply the demise of the 'donor' language. For example, the relevant substrate languages in Singapore are Chinese, Malay and Tamil, which are still used to varying degrees. 'Superstrate' refers to the language that is spreading; it is usually a language of power and influence that replaces other languages. The superstrate language in WE studies, rather obviously, is English. However, this is not as vacuous an assertion as may first seem. Since English varies enormously over space (e.g. American vs British English and specific regional and social dialects within these) and time (e.g. early modern English vs present-day English), it is important to be clear about which form of the superstrate is relevant to specific issues in WE studies. Of particular interest are occasional features that may no longer be part of contemporary standard English but which may have been at the time of colonisation or first contacts (see section 6.5.1 for a discussion of unstressed *do* in some WE varieties). Secondly, although the superstrate is prototypically the modern standard (or early modern standard) language introduced via the school system, some features of a New English may come not from the standard but from an influential regional variety. We mentioned Irish English in this regard in section 1.3.4.

A third term used in Contact Linguistics is 'adstrate'; which refers to the influence of one language on another which has equal status. Thus in a territory like the Cameroons, English and French may have roughly equal status and be considered for certain purposes to be adstrates vis-à-vis each other. A feature of Cameroon English deriving from French influence would be considered an adstrate feature[1] – e.g. *They love themselves* (< *ils s'aiment* 'they love each other' – Todd 1982:285).

Before turning to the features of WEs, some discussion of the terms 'error' and 'feature' is necessary. In the following sections some of the morphological features exemplified might be considered errors or mistakes by the narrow norms of formal written standard English or even informal, spoken Std Eng. Kachru (1983b) drew a distinction between

---

[1] For speakers 'on the ground' they may well be described as co-superstrates.

'mistake' and 'deviation'. The first is a feature that arises out of a slip of the tongue or out of ignorance of a rule in the dialect concerned. All L1 speakers make mistakes sometimes – these are usually slips of the tongue. L2 speakers in addition may use a form that reveals their uncertainty about the rules of the TL (or the version of the TL as developed by more competent L2 speakers of their variety). An example of such a mistake or 'one-off error' would be a speaker saying *I is,* where most speakers of the same L2 variety say *I am* or *I'm.* However, if there were a sub-variety of some L2 whose speakers regularly said *I is* in a specific context, it would no longer count as a mistake. (We know of no such sub-variety.)

Hypercorrections at an individual level also count as mistakes. As in L1 usage, hypercorrections usually arise when some speakers try and correct a regular feature of their dialect because they perceive it to be unprestigious, but in so doing do not necessarily attain the prestige form aimed at. Some analysts refer to this as 'qualitative hypercorrection' to distinguish it from the 'quantitative hypercorrection', prominent in Labov's model of sociolinguistic variation – see Janda and Auger (1992). An example of such qualitative hypercorrection occurs in Ind-SAf Eng, where a regular construction attracts the copula *be* to the *wh*-word as in (2a) in contrast to the Std Eng form (2b).

2a.	Do you know when's the plane going to land?
2b.	Do you know when the plane's going to land?
2c.	Do you know when's the plane's going to land?

In trying to 'correct' their usual rule for copula attraction to *wh-*, some (mesolectal) speakers produce an anomalous (2c), which has both the non-Standard Eng form *'s* attached to *wh-* as well as the Std Eng form *'s* attached to NP. At an individual level this counts as a mistake, as it is not characteristic of the dialect concerned. However, if a sufficient number of speakers produce sentences like (2c), then what started off as a hypercorrection can itself become a (variable) feature of a sub-variety. This is not currently the case in IndSAf Eng.

A 'deviation' according to Kachru (1983b:2) is a feature that counts as a mistake from the viewpoint of Std Eng, but which is a regular feature of the New English, used by all, or at least a majority of, speakers. Thus the form *theses* (i.e. [θi:si:z] is the favoured form in several New Englishes (even amongst many educated speakers) for both singular and plural. It therefore can justifiably be considered a feature of the variety concerned, even if it is prescriptively corrected to *thesis* in formal contexts (like a PhD dissertation!). In the next section we will be describing 'deviations' not 'mistakes': however, we prefer the term 'feature' (meaning 'regular and widely, informally accepted feature') to 'deviation'. The latter term can be misconstrued psychologically and already seems to have run afoul of semantic derogation. Some features are indeed historical errors, in that they show incomplete application of a superstrate rule. But, as we suggest in this chapter and the next, not all features of New Englishes are like this:

(a) They may be dialect features of the superstrate, which have survived despite the norms of classroom English – e.g. *to fright for X* 'to be afraid of X' in IndSAf Eng may well have come from Scots usage.

(b) They may be features of early modern Std Eng surviving in a particular colony, but lost to the metropolis. E.g. the early modern Eng sense of *furlong* survives in Indian English (*Ind Eng*), whilst being restricted only to the register of horse-racing in modern English.

(c) They may be innovations within the New English without an equivalent form in the TL, e.g. the form *who-all* (the pl. form of interrogative *who* in Ind Eng).[2] In the rest of this chapter we describe features of spoken WEs that are used in a range of contexts by a range of speakers, pertaining to the Noun Phrase, Verb Phrase and some function words other than nouns and verbs.

2.3 THE NOUN PHRASE

2.3.1 Articles

WEs tend to use articles in slightly different ways from the TL. The indefinite article *a* may be (variably) deleted or replaced by the form *one*. *The* is likewise variable, alternating with Φ. Platt, Weber and Ho (1984:52–9) provide the following examples from Sgp Eng:

3. I want to buy bag.
4. There! Here got one stall selling soup noodles.
5. I didn(t) buy the dress, lah. (*lah* – an exclamatory tag; see section 5.3.1).

Traditional prescriptive analysis would view the use of the article in the above sentences as unsystematic and evidence of a failure to master the TL system. However, Platt, Weber and Ho (1984) propose

---

[2] In fact *who-all* and *what-all* are found in Ulster and Midland US English (Montgomery 2004:318). We believe its existence in India to be an independent development, however.

that Sgp Eng speakers are using a different cognitive subsystem here. In this they follow a distinction made by Bickerton (1981), in another context, between 'specific/non-specific' on the one hand and 'known to hearer/unknown to hearer' on the other. In his study of Creole languages Bickerton proposed that the prototypical specific/non-specific system uses zero for non-specific; an indefinite article (e.g. *wan/one*) for asserted-specific noun phrase (henceforth *NP*); and a definite article (e.g. *the*) for presupposed-specific NP. Following this proposal Platt, Weber and Ho (1984:54) analyse the NP *bag* in (3) above as non-specific, the speaker presumably being unconcerned about the particular type of bag s/he was going to buy.[3] In (4) the speaker asserts the existence of a specific stall that the interlocutor does not know about ('specific' and 'unknown' to hearer is marked by unstressed *one*). In (5) the article *the* marks the following noun as specific and previously known to the listener (or as given in the conversation). Platt, Weber and Ho claim further that this distinction underlies similar examples to be found in other WEs in places such as India (Agnihotri 1991); West Africa (Kirk-Greene 1971:133); East Africa (Schmied 1991:71); Papua New Guinea (Smith 1978:40) and Hong Kong (Platt 1982:410). Using data from Ind Eng, Sharma (2005a) expands the category of 'known to hearer' into a scale of assumed familiarity with the NP being delineated. The more familiar the NP or the more obvious from being previously mentioned or other discourse cues, the more likely it is to be omitted.

There are some overlaps between the two systems 'specific/known to hearer' versus 'definite/indefinite' (see Bickerton 1981:245–50; Platt, Weber and Ho 1984:52–4). Platt, Weber and Ho attempt to explain the variation as a competition between two systems in WEs, since the latter is taught at school. This is obviously a testable hypothesis. Data from early learners of a WE suggest that learners use a non-superstrate system early on; and that the superstrate system gradually emerges; initially in competition with the non-superstrate system. One such study is that of Ionin, Ko and Wexler (2004) who use the framework of Universal Grammar (UG; Chomsky 1981) to analyse learner data from Korean English. They argue that article use by Korean ESL learners is neither random nor due to L1 transfer effects, but is in fact sensitive to UG-provided semantic universals. Learners initially fluctuate between the two possibilities (specific versus definite) until the input leads them to the choice of the appropriate one, which, in the case of English, is the definiteness value. In cases like this, we can also expect complications

---

[3] Platt, Weber and Ho's (1984:56) remark that 'it is irrelevant whether he wants to buy one only or another for his friend' is not over-clear in this regard.

arising from the two competing systems becoming stylistically differentiated: the first as informal, the second as the formal norm. Other recent studies on articles in ESL and EFL contexts include Huebner (1983), Thomas (1989) and Robertson (2000).

The role of the substrate is relevant to discussions of article usage: indeed many (but not all) of the substrate languages concerned do not use articles. Languages such as Hindi, Chinese and Zulu compensate for the absence of the superstrate category of article by use of context and by strategies such as topicalisation or the strategic use of demonstratives (see Leap 1993:55–8 for American Indian languages; Platt, Weber and Ho 1984:58–9 for Singaporean languages). However, as with the study by Ionin, Ko and Wexler (2004) cited above, it is becoming clear that few WEs are tied down by the stranglehold of their substrates. Sand (2004) uses evidence from the *International Corpus of English* to provide a nuanced, quantitatively robust, comparative analysis of article use in New Englishes. She compares the use of indefinite and definite articles in native varieties of English (e.g. British and New Zealand Englishes) and three different WEs (Indian English, Singaporean English and Kenyan English). The most interesting finding in her study is that the use of articles in all three WEs, irrespective of their substrate (presence or absence of articles), is variable, the variability being keyed to the text type. In the spoken text types (spontaneous conversations), the use is lowest in the informal spoken genre (linked perhaps weakly to substrate influence) and highest in the 'public dialogues' and 'monologues'. In the written text types, the most homogeneous text category is 'informational writing', which indicates that the 'stylistic and pragmatic conventions of this type are valid internationally' (Sand 2004:288). Other written text categories appear more heterogeneous with respect to definite article use in new Englishes, and as such no generalisation can be made.

The distribution across New Englishes for indefinite articles also shows no substrate influence and much less text-type-specific variation. In fact, as Sand (2004: 294) observes, the variability 'must be chiefly due to individual speakers' or writers' level of competence or stylistic preference'.

A comparison of some articles across WEs might sharpen our understanding of article systems and of the ESL/EFL/language-shift variety distinction. As examples of EFL article systems we draw on Swann and Smith (1987) which describes 'learner English' from many parts of the world, with the aim of offering teachers a 'guide to interference and other problems'. In that volume Coe (1987:83–4) reports the following characteristics of Spanish and Catalan learners of English:

(a) The definite article is used with generic (= non-specific) nouns which may be either mass nouns or plural count nouns:

> 6. The food is more important than the art.
> 7. Do you like the big dogs? (meaning: 'big dogs in general'?)

(b) The definite article is used with possessive pronouns:

> 8. That is the yours and this is the mine.

(c) Singular non-specific expressions need no article:

> 9. Do you have car?
> 10. Her sister is dentist.

(d) *One* may be used as an indefinite article:

> 11. We used to live in one flat; now we live in one house.

(e) Indefinite articles may be used in a plural form (on analogy of Spanish and Catalan):

> 12. I have ones nice American friends.

Whilst (c) and (d) are similar to the typical New English features reported by Platt, Weber and Ho (1984), the others are specific to Spanish EFL. That EFLs are less of a unified group than New Englishes for article usage can be seen from the following description of Chinese EFL articles (Chang 1987:231). Unlike Spanish, Chinese has no articles at all.

(a) Article omission:

> 13. Let's make fire.
> 14. I can play piano.

(b) Article insertion:

> 15. He finished the school last year.
> 16. He was in a pain.

(c) Interchangeability of articles:

> 17. Xiao Ying is a tallest girl in the class.
> 18. He smashed the vase in the rage.

As detailed information about the source of these examples, their frequency and so forth is not given, it would be premature to make too many generalisations about the differences between article usage in New English and EFL varieties. However, the EFL examples above do appear to be characteristic of learner varieties, rather than stable systems.

As yet another subtype within WEs, we turn to Irish English, a language-shift variety, which has no fewer than seventeen functions of *the* (Filppula 1999:56) in addition to the standard expression of definiteness. Some of these additional functions occur in dialects of British English, including other 'Celtic Englishes'. We exemplify the full list to demonstrate that a New English (in this case a language-shift variety) can have a stable non-standard system.

(a) Plural count nouns with generic reference:

> 19. Do they keep the goats?

(b) Non-count abstract nouns and concrete mass nouns:

> 20. And the money used to flow around Ringsend at that time.

(c) Quantifying expressions involving *most, both, half* and *all*:

> 21. And the both of them is dead.

(d) The numerals *one* and *two* in the senses 'same' and 'both' respectively:

> 22. But the two parishes were the one ... (= 'Both parishes are the same')

(e) Names of languages and branches of learning:

> 23. Whoever is speaking the Irish, might as well be, as the saying says, speaking Dutch ...

(f) Physical sensations or states:

> 24. The tiredness left him ...

(g) Names of diseases and ailments:

> 25. ... the time the polio came into this country now, that's about ten, twenty year ago ...

(h) Names of social and 'domestic' institutions:

> 26. I left the school in early age ...

(i) Names of geographical areas and localities, public institutions, buildings, monuments, and streets:

> 27. We's had a habit of playing football outside the George's Church.

(j) Expressions involving reference to body parts or items of clothing:

> 28. ... a crowd of birds come and they nearly took the head off him ...

(k) Terms for members of the family:

> 29.   When we went over, me and the missus...

(l) Terms for parts of the day, week or year:

> 30.   Well, the Wednesday was nearly a special day.

(m) Names of festive days or seasons:

> 31.   You see, they chased him up here the St Stephen's Day...

(n) Expressions involving the -ing form of verbs, used to refer to trades and professional or general activities:

> 32.   But America is a better country in that line of the labouring.

(o) Names of persons when qualified by an adjective or a title:

> 33.   I knew the Sister Dominica fairly well.

(p) Reference to means of transport:

> 34.   They'll come out there on the bus to where I'm telling you ... (Std Eng: 'by bus')

(q) Sentences containing nouns with a strong emotional colour:

> 35.   You are the pig, says I. (= 'You are a pig')

There appear to be two different classes of New Englishes in respect of article usage: those that use non-zero forms of articles more frequently than Std Eng (Irish and other Celtic Englishes) and those that use them less frequently (many varieties in Asia and Africa). A similar dichotomy appears to hold for fluent EFL users, again probably relatable to the article system of specific substrate languages.

2.3.2 Number

All studies of individual WEs indicate a great deal of variability in the marking of noun plurals. The following tendencies are reported:

(a) *Non-use of plural -s where expected in the superstrate*: This may be due to genuine variability (i.e. to having its roots in the stabilising of earlier learner patterns – as in (36); or to simplification of consonant clusters – as in (37); or to a tendency not to mark plurality in the phrase more than once, as when the noun is preceded by a numeral or other quantifier, as in (38).

> 36.   One of the worksheet ... (Lakota English; Leap 1993:53, citing Flannigan 1984)
> 37.   I know people who speak with those accent (Sgp Eng; Platt, Weber and Ho 1984:48)

> 38. There's two way of talking (Lakota English, Leap 1993:53, citing Flannigan 1984).

More detailed work needs to be done with individual varieties to ascertain the variable rules governing plural -*s* usage. The other striking New English innovation in pluralisation involves irregular nouns, in (b)–(d) below.

(b) *Regularisation of zero plurals and other exceptions of English*: e.g. *sheeps; oxens; childrens*. These forms occur among basilectal and lower mesolectal speakers of, *inter alia*, IndSAf Eng. Note that this regularisation might appear to contradict the absence of -*s* with regular nouns. Again, this is an area where more systematic analysis and reporting are awaited. The paradox will probably be resolved once we examine the behaviour of individual speakers or subgroups of speakers. It is likely that such regularisation is an intermediate stage (showing overgeneralisation or hypercorrection) between minimal marking of plurality and the acquisition of the full TL system taking cognisance of exceptions (with some speakers fossilised in between).

(c) *Other irregular 'foreign' forms:* The form *theses* for both sg. and pl. is very common in varieties of Asian and African English. We trust that this has not been formed on analogy of *faeces*, which has no singular form! We are less interested in prescriptive shibboleths of higher education like *datum – data; phenomenon – phenomena; cherub – cherubim*.

(d) *Phonological regularisation:* Std Eng has a small set of nouns (*knife, roof, hoof*, etc.) in which final fricatives are voiced together with plural -*s*. This set is exceptional in disallowing a straightforward voicing assimilation of the final -*s* with the root-final *f*. Instead it arbitrarily treats the final consonant of the root as voiced [v] in the plural, triggering a voiced plural suffix [z]. This rule is – unsurprisingly – not used in some New Englishes: thus IndSAf Eng has *roofs; hoofs* and *knives* [ru:fs], [hu:fs], [naɪfs] respectively, except in careful or acrolectal speech.

(e) *Treatment of mass nouns as count nouns:* Almost every study of individual WE varieties in Africa and Asia reports frequent examples like *furnitures, equipments, staffs, fruits, accommodations*, and less common ones like *offsprings, underwears, paraphenalias*, etc. Leap (1993:54) observes that American Indian speakers of all background languages add plural markers to mass nouns: *alphabets, homeworks*, etc. As Platt, Weber and Ho (1984) suggest, this may be a kind of regularisation as many mass nouns of Std Eng double up in other contexts as idiomatic or grammatical count nouns:

water but *Waters of Babylon*; *fruit* but *fruits of the earth*; *How much
experience do you have?* versus *How many experiences with the occult did
you have?* In many New Englishes these have a singular form preceded by an indefinite article: thus for some speakers *a furniture*,
a staff and *an equipment* are equivalent to 'a piece of furniture',
'a member of staff', 'an item of equipment'. There is thus some
semantic simplification vis-à-vis the TL.

Sometimes there are other motivations: certain nouns which are
treated as semantically sg. in the superstrate may have pl. (or perhaps
dual) status in New Englishes: thus East Africa and Singapore have
bums, *bottoms* and *laps* (Hancock and Angogo 1982:316; Platt, Weber and
Ho 1984:52). Hancock and Angogo (1982) add the form *noses* from East
Africa, with *nose* treated as equivalent to the (dual/pl.) Std Eng form
nostrils. To this list we may perhaps add *bosoms*. Sey (1973:28) claims that
though regularisations, like *staffs*, are common in Ghanaian English
(*Ghan Eng*) they do not apply to truly uncountable nouns like *petrol*, *mud*
and *gold* which do not have equivalents like *petrols*, *muds*, *golds*,
even in New Englishes. This suggests that the underlying cognitive
distinction is made, at least for Ghan Eng, but has a different cut-off
point on the count/non-count axis.

If we try and account for plural variation in WEs, it is clear that
there must be substratal, superstratal and other factors at work. Some
substrates do not use suffixes for plurals: Chinese marks plurality by
a free morpheme meaning 'multitude' only when necessary. Malay
marks the plural by reduplication of the noun if there is no numeri-
cal or similar indication of plurality. The majority of WE substrates do,
however, have plural affixes, though they might not map exactly onto
the TL system. In view of the irregularities within the superstrate system this is not surprising. In Chapter 6 we consider proposals taken
from language-processing theorists, who stress the selective production of such markers in second language acquisition.

Turning to pronouns and demonstratives we find some evidence
of variation in number. Although most WEs regularly distinguish
between the pronouns *it* and *them* and the demonstratives *this* and
these and *that* and *those*, in actual usage there is some syncretism (use
of singular for plural especially). Leap (1993:57) provides an example
from American Indian English of the San Juan Pueblo:

39.   This worms, they get into your body.

For IndSAf Eng Mesthrie (1992b:129–30) reports that whereas *those*
is frequently used (81.4 per cent *those* vs 18.6 per cent plural *that* in

a sample of 150 speakers), *these* is much more frequently conflated with *this* (the respective figures are 49.4 per cent *these* vs 50.6 per cent plural *this*). The partial phonetic similarities between [d̪ɪs] and [d̪iːz] might well play a role in this syncretism.

Finally we hypothesise that whereas inanimate *it* and *they* are frequently distinguished for number in WEs in referential usage, they are less frequently distinguished in anaphoric usage across clauses, even amongst acrolectal speakers. Sentence (40) is from Baskaran (2004:1075) on Malaysian English (*Mal Eng*):

40.   Those books are very informative. It can be obtained at Dillon's.

However, this process does not apply to animate nouns, for which the plural anaphoric pronoun *they* is common.

2.3.3 Gender

Gender is not the pervasive structural or pragmatic category in English as it is in languages like Hindi and French. English nouns no longer fall into morphological classes on the basis of gender; and adjectives do not show agreement with nouns. Male speakers do not use a different set of verb endings from female speakers (as in Hindi). However, there are two areas where gender does operate in Std Eng, if only partially. Pronoun co-reference does show sensitivity to the 'male–female–inanimate' trichotomy; and certain nouns traditionally allow a male–female distinction by use of the marked form *-ess*. The latter tradition has been severely called into question by the feminist movement and may well be an endangered suffix. Gender has proved – despite its minor role in English – susceptible to variation in New Englishes. Some varieties use gender in pronouns differently. Platt, Weber and Ho (1984:61–2) report that in some New Englishes where the background languages do not make a distinction between *he*, *she* and *it*, pronouns 'are often used indiscriminately'. They offer the following examples:

41.   My husband who was in England, she was by then my fiancé. (East Africa)
42.   My mother, he live in kampong.[4] (Malaysia)

Since Bantu languages do not make sex-based distinctions with pronouns, and the spoken forms of the Chinese languages of Singapore and Malaysia do not differentiate gender in 3rd person pronouns (Platt,

---

[4] *Kampong* refers to a fenced or fortified village, a district of a city or a collection of buildings (borrowed into English as *compound*).

Weber and Ho 1984:62), substrate influences may well be at work here. Schmied (1991:71) argues for phonological simplification as a further confounding factor in the case of *he* versus *she*; he suggests that the difference between [hi:] and [ʃi:] is not salient enough, though this is open to acoustic investigation.

Mesthrie (2000) studied pronoun gender patterns amongst Black South African English speakers, as it had been previously observed that basilang L2 speakers do use pronoun gender variably, rather like (41) and (42) above. (*Basilang* – as mentioned in section 2.1 – is the term preferred to *basilect*, in a context of unstable, early interlanguage use.) Whilst substrate influence is a likely influence here, Mesthrie cautions that direct transfer from languages like Xhosa should not be automatically assumed. The crucial difference is that whereas Xhosa has one 3rd person sg. pronoun form for the categories of gender and case, basilang L2 speakers either start with a two-way distinction or quickly progress to a two-way distinction for subject pronouns. That is, *he* is the basic form for human referents and *it* is used for inanimates. There were no instances of *she* in Mesthrie's early basilang data. On the other hand basilang speakers do occasionally conflate sg. and pl. (*he* or *it* for 'they'), whereas Xhosa regularly distinguishes sg. pronoun from pl. None of these facts suggest a substrate stranglehold on the grammar of pronouns: rather, substrate influence is of a general and indirect nature.

Finally, some analysts report a cultural effect in the use of *-ess* with nouns that do not require it in Std Eng. Platt, Weber and Ho (1984:96) cite Mehrotra's (1982:160) example of *teacheress* 'female teacher' in Ind Eng, where gender specification is important for cultural reasons. We might add *butleress* in Ind Eng for 'a female butler' (or household servant, whose chief function is cooking). These examples are structurally unsurprising, as they make use of a pattern established in traditional English.

2.3.4 Possession

Not much discussion of variability in the marking of possession occurs in the New English literature. Platt, Weber and Ho (1984:61) suggest that possessive *-s* is 'not often used' in the New Englishes. This suggestion does not appear to be supported in the literature and Platt's examples involve West Indian English (where Creole might be a formative influence) or involve irregular nouns (*women, children*). The following constructions are from primary school learners in West Africa of Hausa background – (43) is from Bokamba (1992:133); (44) is from Kirk-Greene (1971:136):

> 43. I met the teacher our new. ('I met our new teacher')
> 44. That your brother, will he come? ('Will that brother of yours come?')

Whereas (43) replicates the Hausa pattern of 'demonstrative – noun – possessive', (44) has the order 'demonstrative – possessive – noun'. In other parts of Africa postposed possessives follow the Bantu pattern of noun – possessive – pronoun: *father for me* 'my father' and *country for him* 'his country' are basilang examples from BlSAf Eng. This Bantu pattern happens to follow the marked possessive order of Std Eng of the type 'that book of mine'; 'the hat of John's'. However, the case marking is different and, for some speakers, the choice of possessive preposition as well. Amongst basilang speakers double postposed genitives may also occur (Mesthrie 2001:94):

> 45. It's *bakkie* for brother for me. ('It's my brother's van'; *bakkie* = 'light pick-up truck')

2.3.5 Pronouns

Pronoun gender has already been covered in section 2.3.3. Some innovations in 2nd person pl. pronouns are reported in New Englishes:

(a) the pronoun paradigm is regularised by the formation of a specific 2nd person pl. form. In IndSAf Eng this is *y'all*; which appears to be an independent form, not having links to southern US English. It has a genitive form *yall's*. An alternative form *you-people* (genitive: *you people's*) exists in this dialect, probably carried over from Ind Eng. In some varieties like Cape Flats English (henceforth, *CFl Eng*), spoken by people referred to as 'Coloured' (as opposed to 'Black') in and around Cape Town, the form is *yous(e)*, phonetically [ju:s]. This form, which also occurs sporadically in White South African Eng, appears to be a British dialect survival: the form is reported in Scots and Irish Eng, Australian Eng as well as English in Liverpool and Tyneside.

(b) Pronoun deletion: English is not a pro-drop language; pronouns may not be deleted except in certain narrative contexts, as in the sixth and seventh sentences in (46), taken from a Woody Allen comic sketch:

> 46. ... The moose is next to me. My host comes to the door. 'Hello', I say, 'You know the Solomons.' We enter. The moose mingles. Φ did very well. Φ scored. Some guy was trying to sell him insurance for an hour and a half ...

In contrast, deletions are quite common in some WEs and are not
necessarily governed by discourse effects. Leap (1993:60) reports on
subject and object deletions in Mohave English (based on Penfield-
Jasper 1980:137):

47.   Φ shot himself.
48.   But then Φ woke him up.
49.   They just put Φ between your teeth.

Platt, Weber and Ho (1984:117–18) cite similar deletions in a range
of WEs (India, Sri Lanka, Singapore and parts of Africa). (50) is from
Sgp Eng (Wee 2004:1062):

50.   Φ must buy for him; otherwise he not happy. ('We must buy...')

A related phenomenon is the use of *is* instead of *it is*. Platt, Weber
and Ho (1984:118) provide examples such as the following:

51.   Is very nice food. (Uganda)
52.   But when I move into the flat, is OK. (Phillipines)
53.   Here is not allowed to stop the car. (Hong Kong)

It is difficult to decide whether this is a grammatical deletion of the
pronoun *it*; or a phonological cluster reduction of *it's* to *is*. Platt, Weber
and Ho argue for the former rather than the latter citing the fact
that in their data people who use *is* for *it's* do not frequently exhibit
consonant cluster reduction elsewhere and that substrate languages
like Hokkien permit zero pronouns.

2.4   THE VERB PHRASE

2.4.1 Tense

The basic tenses (past, present and future) are encoded in New
Englishes, with minor differences from Std Eng.

(a) The past tense suffix is variable and may be replaced in certain
contexts by zero marking. These contexts may include the past in narratives (i.e. the Conversational Historic Present), as in some L1 varieties
of English:

54.   We stay there whole afternoon and we catch one small fish. (Sgp Eng; Platt,
      Weber and Ho 1984:69; Past tense reference; narrative)

Sometimes the use of adverbials that establish past tense reference makes it unnecessary to mark tense on the verb:

> 55. Last time she come on Thursday. (Sgp Eng; Platt, Weber and Ho 1984:70)

Likewise, in some varieties if a main clause verb is in the past tense, subsequent subordinate clause verbs might be unmarked.

> 56. We stayed in Kotzebue for a few days, then we start coming up the Noatak River. (Kotzebue (American Indian) English; Vandergriff 1982:136)

Sometimes, what appears to be zero tense marking might be a phonological effect involving consonant cluster simplification. In (57) below it is likely that the -*d* past tense ending is dropped before the initial /t/ of the next word.

> 57. I move to hostel. (Ind Eng; Platt, Weber and Ho 1984: 69)

In some varieties the marking of the past is related to the semantics of the verb. Leap (1993:63) argues that for Isletan English (of central New Mexico) such marking depends on whether the action of the verb is distributive, delimited or continuous. Distributive references identify activities that occur only during particular periods but may occur within any number of such periods. These typically take zero marking in the past. Delimited references identify actions that occur only within a particular, definable time frame and will not be repeated, as such, once the time has come to an end. These typically take past tense suffixes. Continuous references do not involve any temporal restriction or interruption. They are included here for reasons of completeness, even though – as an aspectual category – they do not determine past tense forms alone. Leap's examples are as follows:

> 58. The girl run up to me and she said . . . (*run* – distributive; *said* – delimited)
> 59. So him and his boys come over and asked them what they are doin'. . . (*come* – distributive; *asked* – delimited; *doin'* – continuous)

Leap argues that for other varieties of American Indian English, different semantic/pragmatic constraints apply, depending (as with Isletan English) on the particularities of the ancestral language structures. Research on tense clearly is a difficult area as there are many possible explanations for the same phenomenon. For example, consonant cluster simplification, as in (57), may be as viable an explanation as the operation of other grammatical constraints.

(b) The future tense evokes fewer comments in New English descriptions than the past. In some varieties overlap between present and future is possible:

60. I think I go and make one new dress for Chinese New Year. (Sgp Eng; Platt, Weber and Ho 1984:74).
61. I take it later. ('I'll take it later' – CFl Eng)

Again it is difficult to decide if this is present marking (with zero) or whether it is a phonological effect - with *will* (in its reduced cliticised form [l]) being deleted before the initial consonant in *go* and *take*. Substrate influence cannot be ruled out here, since Afrikaans – like German – expresses (61) as present rather than future tense.

Shall and *shan't* are seldom discussed in the New English literature; and we suspect that they are infrequent in colloquial speech. *Shall* does occur in Nigerian English (henceforth *Nig Eng*, Jowitt 1991), where it appears to be influenced by formal English of the classroom. In Ind Eng *shall* is not used in declaratives: *I shall do it* and *I shan't do it* do not occur in informal speech. However, *shall* may occur optionally in 1st person interrogatives (*Shall I do it now?*).

(c) Present: From what we have said above it is clear that the relation between (unmarked) present and (marked) past varies amongst New Englishes and between New and other Englishes. Further issues relating to the present are discussed under 'number' and 'aspect' below. Issues of speaker competence are not always addressed in the descriptions available.

Influenced by the work of Bickerton (1975) on Creole tense and aspect marking, Ho and Platt (1993:74–141) examined past tense marking of 150 Sgp Eng speakers of Chinese background, They studied 8,725 verbs which would be marked for past tense in formal Std Eng. They classified speakers under five educational levels; and verbs by three semantic categories and four phonetic types. The semantic categories were punctual (e.g. *cough, hit, jump*), non-punctual (e.g. *push, fall, roll*) and stative (e.g. *know, want, need*). Punctual verbs involve a single point of time (i.e. are non-durative in nature); non-punctual have inherent duration (and are typically made up of habitual and iterative verbs). Stativeness is a subclass of non-punctual verbs involving states rather than action; and – as is well known – Std Eng does not use *be + -ing* with stative verbs. The phonetic types identified by Ho and Platt were as follows:

(a) strong verbs (which involve vowel change like *fall – fell*) and irregular verbs (*go – went*);
(b) verbs which take [ed]: *want – wanted*
(c) verbs ending in a vowel and taking [d] (*follow – followed* [fɔloʊd])
(d) verbs ending in a consonant, whose past form involves a consonant cluster: *pick – picked* [pɪkt].

Table 2.1. *Past marking of verbs by
phonetic type in Singapore English*
(based on Ho and Platt 1993)

Vowel change verbs:	57.3%
t/d + [ed] verbs:	40.6%
Verbs ending in vowel + [d]:	36.2%
Consonant cluster verbs:	3.9%

Ho and Platt (1993) found a differential pattern of past marking depending on verb types. Punctual verbs are more frequently marked than non-punctual verbs for past tense (56.2 per cent vs 23.2 per cent). Within the non-punctual class past statives were marked 36.9 per cent of the time as opposed to 14.7 per cent for non-statives. For the phonetic types the marking is given in Table 2.1 above.

There are some difficulties reported in this study; notably the problems of classifying verbs unambiguously into one semantic category or another. The authors give a detailed exemplification of the effect of educational level on the acquisition of past marking, surveying an array of individual verbs in this regard (see Ho and Platt 1993: 74–141).

2.4.2 Aspect

New Englishes show greater divergence from Std Eng in aspectual than in tense distinctions.

(a) Perfective *have* + EN of Std Eng is replaced in a number of varieties, often with a slight change in semantics. In Std Eng perfective aspect signifies an action that is – relative to the time of speaking – recently completed and which sets up a statement in the time frame currently in focus:

> 62. I've seen the movie and I think it's great. ('*ve* signifies present perfect relevant to the present tense verb in following clause)
> 63. I'd just eaten my food and was about to get up from the table when I heard someone screaming … ('*d* signifies past perfect, relevant to past tense of verbs in following clauses

Whilst many New English speakers are comfortable with this usage, substitute markers like *already* or *finish(ed)* are also in use. Williams (1987:184) gives the following example from Sgp Eng and Mal Eng, where *already* marks completion of activity.

64. He already go home. (= 'He's gone home')

In CFl Eng *already* usually occurs in sentence-final position and signifies either completive aspect or that an activity has occurred once in the past:

65. The people died already. (= 'The people are dead/ have died')
66. My husband went to Durban already. (= 'My husband has been to Durban / once went to Durban / *has gone to Durban)
67. I wanted to give it to you yesterday already. (= 'I had wanted to give it to you yesterday')

Whilst past tense in this variety is marked by a standard suffix, aspect is not generally marked by *have* + Past Participle. In informal style this gap is filled by *already* in mesolectal speech especially. Bao (2005, discussed further in 6.2.2), proposes a substrate explanation for this feature from Chinese. Williams (1987:184) provides examples of how completive *already* can occur with the more standard adverbial *already*, thus suggesting that its completive function is being grammaticalised in Sgp Eng:

68. Malaysia already got breakdance already. (= 'Malaysia already has the breakdance')

Platt, Weber and Ho (1984:71) give an alternative, more colloquial, form with *finish*:

69. You eat finish, go out and play. (= 'When you've finished eating, go out and play')

In basilectal IndSAf Eng *finish* is used preverbally to indicate completive aspect:

70. I finish clean the window. (= 'I've cleaned the window')

Finish usually occurs with the zero marked verb (infinitive). However, in more formal styles speakers might add a past ending to *finish* and/or a participle *-ing* to the main verb.

71a. I finished clean the window.
71b. I finish cleaning the window.
71c. I finished cleaning the window.

These count as hypercorrections in IndSAf Eng, occurring in a predictable part of the speech continuum (the mesolect). These constructions aim at, but do not replicate, the Std Eng norm *I've cleaned the window.* Instead they mediate between the basilectal form (in 70) and the acrolectal or standard form.

Another feature associated with New Englishes is the use of *have* with extended temporal contexts.

> 72. I have read this book last month. (Ind Eng; Verma 1982, cited by Williams 1987:183)
> 73. It has been established many years ago. (Ghan Eng; Tingley 1981, cited by Williams 1987:183)
> 74. Rajesh had bought this for me. (= 'Rajesh (once) bought this for me'; IndSAf Eng)

In (74) above no continuing impact of *had* is indicated. It is possible that these are unstable forms occurring as a kind of hypercorrection, as speakers move from a system that marks tense overtly and perfective aspect by adverbials to the target tense/perfective system aspect of Std Eng. Part of the reconstitution is the overgeneralisation of the HAVE morpheme. On the other hand, if the examples in (72) and (73) are as stable as the authors suggest, we would be dealing with an aspectual innovation.

Bao (2005:239) discusses yet another perfective innovation in Sgp Eng: the use of aspectual *ever*, as in (75) and (76):

> 75. I ever see the movie. (= 'I have seen the movie')
> 76. This share ever hit forty dollars. (= 'This share was once forty dollars')

Whereas *ever* and *already* share the semantics of completion, *ever* focuses more on the experience of the event, as in (75). Sentence (76) differs from the Std Eng semantics of 'relevant to the present', as the implication is that the price is no longer forty dollars.

(b) Past habitual: Some interesting variation occurs involving Std Eng *used to*. In Singapore and Malaysia the form *use(d) to* signifies past habitual extending into the present (i.e. non-completive):

> 77. My mother, she use to go to Pulau Tikus market. (implying 'she still does so'; Platt, Weber and Ho 1984:71)

In IndSAf Eng the form *should* is the usual marker of past habitual:

> 78. We should go to the river every day in summer. (= 'We used to go ...')

It is difficult to say whether *should* is based on analogy with the narrative and slightly literary form *would* or whether it is based on a reinterpretation of colloquial/fast speech phonetics of *used to* [stu:] or [stə]. The Std Eng obligative sense of *should* is rare in IndSAf Eng: speakers who habitually use *should* for 'used to' usually substitute *must* for obligation. IndSAf Eng also has 'extended' habituals formed by *an' stay* and *an' leave* :

79. They only shout and stay. (= 'They're always shouting')
80. She filled the bottle and left it. (= 'She filled the bottle completely')

Irish English has a special perfect form with *be* + *after* + V-*ing* that has come to be known as the *after* perfect or the 'hot-news perfect' (Harris 1984). According to Filppula (1999:99) the construction refers to an event or activity in the more or less recent past, whose effects persist some way or the other into the present:

81. An' there was a house you're after passin', there was fifteen, sixteen children in [the house]. (Filppula 1999: 99)

For other perfective innovations in Ir Eng see section 3.2.1 (a).

2.4.3 Modality

There is little to report in this category, which deals with the expression of mood, i.e. the speaker's orientation and attitude towards the action of the verb. The modals of Std Eng are in use in most varieties of WEs, with slight differences in semantics. In some varieties *would* takes over the sense of *will*. (82) below is from Ghan Eng (Huber and Dako 2004:856):

82. We hereby wish to inform you that the meeting would take place on Thursday.

In some New Englishes modal *'d* (the reduced, cliticised form of *would*) is deleted, as in (83), especially if adverbials like *rather* make the modality clear.

83. I better leave now. (Ghan Eng; Platt, Weber and Ho 1984:75)
84. I rather go by plane. (Mal Eng; Platt, Weber and Ho 1984:75)

Would is traditionally a hypothetical in Std Eng, but in many New English contexts is better described as a declarative softener, as in (82). Other examples occur in CFl Eng, IndSAf Eng, Phillipines English (henceforth *Phl Eng*), etc. The familiar question of whether we are simply dealing with a phonological reduction before an initial consonant arises. Examples that go against a phonological explanation come from Ghan Eng (Sey 1973:34–5):

> 85. I will like to go right now.
> 86. I will like to see him.

Here *will* replaces *would*, and consonant cluster reduction does not operate. *Will* for 'would' and *can* for 'could' in certain contexts occurs in BlSAf Eng, Nig Eng, Ghan Eng, IndSAf Eng and Mal Eng (Mesthrie 2004a:1134). In several African varieties of L2 English *can* co-occurs with the apparently equivalent phrase *be able*; (87) is from BlSAf Eng:

> 87. I can be able to go. (Gough and de Klerk 2002:363)

The negative *can't be able* is also possible. A similar construction occurs in Ute English (of Utah). Leap (1993:107), who provides the example below, argues that it has special stylistic status in that it is used more in out-group than in-group communication.

> 88. Can you be able to do that?

The expression of politeness can result in differences between some WEs and Std Eng. The form *may* appears to be generalised as polite permissive modal in BlSAf Eng to contexts beyond the first person:

> 89. May you please look at this message and respond. ('Could you please...')

The use of *may* in (89) could have originated as a hypercorrection, with the prescriptivists' insistence that schoolchildren use *May I go?* instead of *Can I go?* resulting in over-generalisation to second person usage as well. See further sections 5.1 and 5.4 on pragmatics and politeness. Bhatt (2004:1022) gives a similar example of polite obligation from Ind Eng:

> 90. These mistakes may please be corrected. ('These mistakes should please be corrected')

This time an additional influence from substrates like Hindi is possible, with *may* serving to compensate for the lack of honorifics in English that one finds in Hindi (in pronoun choice, verb-endings, etc.).

2.4.4 Number

Number is a rather impoverished category in the Std Eng verb phrase, and even more so in regional dialects. Most discussions of number

in fact fall under present tense, since the -s ending simultaneously
marks 3rd person sg. and present tense. No other person-related ending
occurs for regular verbs. It is not surprising that this defective category
is subject to variation in many New Englishes. Alternation of 3rd person sg. with zero forms are reported for Nig Eng (Jowitt 1991:117); varieties of East African English (henceforth *EAf Eng*, Schmied 1991:65–6);
varieties of AmInd Eng (Leap 1993:62; though some varieties go the
other way, as we note below); Ind Eng (Platt, Weber and Ho 1984:67);
IndSAf Eng (Mesthrie 1992a:130); BlSAf Eng (Gough and de Klerk
2002:362), Phl Eng (Gonzalez 1983:163); Sgp Eng (Wee 2004:1059) and
CFl Eng (McCormick 1995:205).

> 91.   He go to school. (Phl Eng; Gonzalez 1983:163)

A more interesting treatment of number occurs in a few varieties
which use zero for sg. and -s for pl. Leap (1993:72–3) claims that for
Isletan English subject–verb concord is reworked in this way. Thus (92)
to (94) have inflected verbs which concord with their plural subjects:[5]

> 92.   There are some parties that goes on over there.
> 93.   Some peoples from the outside comes in.
> 94.   All the dances that goes on like that occur in the spring.
> 95.   The women has no voice to vote.

On the other hand (96) to (100) show zero marking on verbs in concord
with the singular subjects:

> 96.   Maybe the governor go to these parents' homes.
> 97.   About a dollar a day serve out your term.
> 98.   This traditional Indian ritual take place in June.
> 99.   By this time, this one side that are fast have overlapped.
> 100. The governor don't take the case.

A similar tendency has been reported for CFl Eng of Cape Town
(McCormick 1995:205); though the data seem genuinely variable:

> 101.   They drink and they makes a lot of noise. (McCormick 1995: 205)

In such varieties a symmetry is achieved between noun and verb marking: for sg. nouns and sg. verbs there is zero marking; pl. nouns and
pl. verbs take an -s inflection. We therefore label this system -s plural
symmetry'. The caveat must again be sounded that descriptions of this

---

[5] Leap (1993:73) suggests that for distributive reference both subject and verb take
zero marking. The data, however, suggest that this is not mandatory – i.e. the rule
coexists with more standard options.

symmetry have not been undertaken quantitatively. Case histories of individual speakers will reveal whether a degree of hypercorrection is involved in the addition of -*s* to plural verbs; whilst the possibility of competition between two different systems (the TL system and -*s* plural symmetry) makes analysis all the more challenging. '*S* plural symmetry' may well derive from, or be influenced historically, by what has come to be called 'the Northern Subject Rule' (Ihalainen 1994; McCafferty 2004). This rule, associated with Scots, and northern British English, assigns -*s* to verbs with full NP plural subjects (hence *The boys eats*). For plural pronoun subjects zero is used, except if the verb is separated from the pronoun (hence *They eat* versus *They eat and leaves without paying*). This system has been transported from the north of Britain to Ireland, and thence to places like the US Midland (Montgomery 2004:318–19).

2.4.5 Stative vs non-stative

The distinction between stative and non-stative or dynamic verbs is frequently overridden by New English speakers. Briefly, in Std Eng verbs denoting actions allow the present progressive form in *be* + -*ing*; while verbs denoting states rather than actions do not. In almost all New English varieties, however, stative verbs are allowed to take *be* + -*ing*:

102. I am having a cold. (BlSAf Eng; also Sgp Eng; Platt, Weber and Ho 1984:72)
103. She is owning two luxury apartments. (Mal Eng; Baskaran 2004:1078)
104. I am smelling something. (Nig Eng; Jowitt 1991:114)

It is not clear why this tendency should be quite so pervasive in the New Englishes. Distinctions between stative and non-stative do not always have the same force in the substrate languages as in English. Certain idiomatic examples which do allow *be* + -*ing* with Std Eng verbs that are protypically stative are a confounding factor:

105. I am loving every minute of it.
106. We are having a good time.

Examples like the worldwide McDonald's advertisement of 2005 *I'm loving it*, which plays on this New English stative fluidity, may well reinforce such usage. Another confounding factor for ESL learners is the fact that most verbs may be used as statives or as progressives in Std Eng (*I speak English* versus *I'm speaking English right now*). Substrate influence may also account for some of the examples – see Makalela (2004:358-9) for Sepedi, one of the substrate languages for BlSAf Eng and Kachru (1983a:75) for Hindi.

2.4.6 Forms of *be* ▬▬▬▬▬▬▬▬▬▬▬▬▬▬▬▬▬▬▬▬

As one of the most irregular verbs of English, and one of the most used, the verb *be* deserves separate treatment. As an auxiliary it undergoes some modification in number in WEs, since the variety of forms *am – are – is; was – were; be* give difficulty to early learners, not just by their variety but by their unrelated surface forms. Varieties reporting unsystematic variability or regularisation include Navajo English (Cook and Sharp 1966, cited by Leap 1993:71); CFl Eng, IndSAf Eng; etc. Some forms of auxiliary *be* may be deleted, though no variety has been reported to do this consistently.

(a) **Copular *be***: Absence of copular *be* in present tense contexts is reported in a number of varieties.

> 107. The house Φ very nice. (Sgp Eng; Wee 2004:1060)
> 108. She Φ a Red Corn people. (Isletan English; Leap 1993:70)
> 109. My brother that. ('That's my brother'; IndSAf Eng)

Copula deletion in New Englishes needs to be studied more carefully for individual varieties, from a variationist perspective. For IndSAf Eng, e.g., deletion is not possible with first and third person sg. (**I Φ a farmer*; **She Φ clever*); deletion with other forms may well be phonologically motivated. Thus, in *You're my nephew* the form *'re* would normally be [ə] in this non-rhotic dialect; which may itself be deleted in fast speech. Other examples may well follow Std Eng informal, telegraphic style (*Nice food, this.*)

A variationist analysis for copula deletion in Sgp Eng is provided by Ho and Platt (1993), which we shall cite in some detail for its methodological clarity in Chapter 3.

(b) **Habitual *be***: Habitual *be* as an invariant or uninflected form denoting habitual aspect is well known in some English dialects and Creoles (Holm 1988:159–61). The best-known varieties are perhaps Ir Eng and AfAm Eng:

> 110. A lot of them be interested in football matches. (Ir Eng; Filppula 1999:136)
> 111. Even when I be round there with friends, I be scared. (AfAm Eng; Rickford 1999:190)

Amongst New Englishes other than Irish Eng invariant *be* has been reported in IndSAf Eng (Mesthrie 1992:116–17):

112. Spar's tomatoes be nice. (= 'Tomatoes from Spar (a chain store) are usually nice')
113. Whenever we go there they be playing.

The use of habitual *be* is, however, not very common in IndSAf Eng, co-varying with other (inflected) forms of copular *be* in the stative and with forms like *will* (or *'ll*) + *be* + V-*ing* for non-statives. However (113) cannot be said to result from phonological factors (consonant-cluster simplification in a phrase like *they'll be*), since deletion of future *'ll* before initial consonants does not occur in the dialect.

Invariant *be* is not widely reported in other WEs. Ho and Platt (1993:33) provide an example that may well be relevant:

114. I was the only one to be scolded and my brothers and sisters never be scolded so that I always objected.

It is unclear whether this is an instance of a more general invariant habitual *be* or a result of more specific facts about negation of passive verbs with *never*. Note that the form *used to* would be inapplicable in (114), as its usual semantics in Sgp Eng is 'used to and still do', as in (77) above. The appearance of invariant *be* in IndSAf Eng and Sgp Eng might well be an example of Irish English influence.

(c) **Passive *be*:** In some varieties passive *be* is deleted, with the verb occurring in either stem or passive form. In the latter case it is likely that we are dealing with genuine passives:

115. As soon as children are about 4 or 3 they Φ sent to Kinder. (Ghan Eng; Platt, Weber and Ho 1984:79)
116. The private schools Φ mostly run by religious orders. (Phl Eng; Platt, Weber and Ho 1984:79)

Other examples provided by Platt, Weber and Ho may well involve topicalisation (with active semantics; rather than the passive they assume them to be).

117. Pack your toy(s)! This room must Φ clean before Chinese New Year. (Sgp Eng; Platt, Weber and Ho 1984:79)

In (117) a passive interpretation is valid, provided *clean* is passive (with *clean* being derived from *cleaned* by final consonant-cluster reduction). In the absence of such information an alternative possibility is that *this room* functions as topic with *You must clean before Chinese New Year* as comment, with pro-drop (which is recoverable from the imperative

of the preceding sentence). The structure would then be: *This room –
Φ must clean before Chinese New Year.* Indeed, subsequent discussion
in Platt, Weber and Ho (1984:80) makes it clear that such topicalised patterns with active verbs frequently replace conventional
passives.

(d) Existential *be* versus *get*:   In some varieties existential *be* is
replaced by *got,* especially in the phrase *there is/exists*:

> 118. Here got very many people. (= 'There are many people here' – Sgp Eng;
>   Wee 2004:1060)
> 119. Got one ghost over there (= 'There's a ghost over there' – IndSAf Eng
>   basilect)

2.4.7 Unstressed *do*

Some varieties do not use *do*-support in questions, except in formal
and careful speech. Such absence of dummy *do* is reported in Ind Eng,
Pakistani English (henceforth *Pak Eng*) and IndSAf Eng.

> 120. She gave you the book? (informal IndSAf Eng)
> 121. Did she give you the book? (formal IndSAf Eng)

In contrast to this usage, several varieties introduce unstressed *do* as
an alternative periphrastic way of marking past tense in indicative
clauses:

> 122. She did take the book. (Swaziland Eng; Arua 1998:144)
> 123. He did eat his food. (CFl Eng; McCormick 1995:206)
> 124. They did trot down there the other day. (Ir Eng; Filppula 1999:154)
> 125. I did go to town yesterday. (EAf Eng of Swahili speakers; Grant 1987:201)

In (122)–(125) *did* is unstressed and does not carry the counter-
presupposition pragmatics of Std Eng ('I assert X though you might
assume "not X"'). It is commonly assumed that unstressed *do* is a feature of language learning, with *did* being a transparent way of marking
the past (by a free morpheme). It is claimed that *did* is a form parallel
to a free or bound morpheme in substrate languages that preceded the
verb (*ge-* in Afrikaans, *li-* in Kiswahili). This may be a partial explanation. In Chapter 6, however, we consider an alternative historical explanation, since this construction was once part of Std Eng. It is now a relic
form in south-western dialects in England, where it marks the habitual present or past. In Irish English unstressed *do* usually co-occurs

with *be*, but may sometimes occur on its own: 'the function of *did* appears to be one of merely marking the tense rather than adding anything to the aspectual meaning of the verb phrase' (Filppula 1999:154). Though Ir Eng is an influential source for a similar construction in AfAm Eng, the combination of *do* + *be* is not reported in many New Englishes.

2.4.8 Novel verb forms

Finally in this section on the Verb Phrase we outline some innovations that suggest the difficulties that first or subsequent generations of learners of English in colonial settings have had in mastering entries relating to verbs in the Std Eng mental lexicon.

(a) New compound verbs: In Indian English and its South African offshoot the verb *by-heart* is used by pupils and teachers alike, for 'to learn off by heart':

126. Don't by-heart your work.
127. She was by-hearting her work. (= 'She was learning her work off by heart')

In IndSAf Eng basilect related forms *to look-after* and *to back-answer* ('to retort, answer back') occur, which like *by-heart* are treated as compounds:

128. He look-aftered his children very well.
129. He's always back-answering me.

(b) Change of part of speech: The use of *on* and *off* as verbs (for 'to switch on' and 'to switch off') has been reported in Sgp Eng and Mal Eng (Hickey 2004b:570); IndSAf Eng and Ind Eng:

130. I told her to on the stove, but she offed it. (IndSAf Eng)

(c) Verb categorization: A striking feature of New Englishes is the way verbs select phrasal and prepositional elements in ways that differ from Std Eng. The distinction between phrasal and prepositional verbs hinges on whether they allow particle movement or not. Phrasal verbs allow particle movement as in *picked the paper up* as an alternative to *picked up the paper*. Prepositional verbs do not (*got up at nine*, rather than *got at nine up). Platt, Weber and Ho (1984:81–5) outline six categories, for which we supply new examples from different territories:

(i) Phrasal verbs used without a particle: e.g. *pick* for *pick up* (EAf Eng; WAf Eng; Sgp Eng); *crop* for *crop up*.

(ii) Phrasal verbs used with a different particle from Std Eng: e.g. *throw out* (one's hands) for *throw up* (Sgp Eng); *dish out* (food) for *dish up* (IndSAf Eng); *put off* for *put out* (the gas) (Ghan Eng; Huber and Dako 2004:854).

(iii) Non-phrasal verbs used with particle: e.g. *voice out* (one's opinion) for *voice* (WAf Eng; Sgp Eng); *pick up a quarrel* for *pick a quarrel* (EAf Eng).

(iv) Prepositional verbs used without a preposition: e.g. *apply* for *apply for* (Ind Eng); *provide* for *provide with* (EAf Eng).

(v) Prepositional verbs used with a different preposition: e.g. *result into* for *result in* (WAf Eng); *good in* (arithmetic) for *good at* (IndSAf Eng); *congratulate for* for *congratulate on* (EAf Eng).

(vi) Non-prepositional verbs used with preposition: e.g. *discuss about* for *discuss* (WAf Eng; Sgp Eng; IndSAf Eng;); *emphasise on* for *emphasise* (Sgp Eng; IndSAf Eng).

Motivations for these differences are analogy (*voice out* on the basis of *speak out*); 'near misses' (i.e. minute differences from Std Eng; e.g. *take out* (one's shirt) for *take off*), and transparency (e.g. *vomit out* for *vomit*). Most interestingly for linguistic theory is the set of verbs that retain the same preposition associated with their corresponding nouns: *discuss about* (cf. *discussion about*); *emphasise on* (cf. *emphasis on*). Schmied (2004:68) provides the following examples from East Africa: *advocating for*; *demand for*; *stress on*; *mention about* and *attend to* (for *advocating*; *demand*; *stress* (v.); *mention* and *attend* respectively). In this regard New Englishes have made their lexical entries more transparent; verbs match nouns where possible for subcategorization. Simo Bobda (1994) labelled processes like these 'logicalisation'. Hartford (1996) uses the cognitive grammar framework, following Langacker (1983), to analyse the occurrence of forms like *discuss about, explain about* and *narrate about*. She proposes that New Englishes reanalyse the clausal semantics in which these verbs appear, so that the meanings are coded in a regular way. These 'disquisition' verbs appear in clauses that are lower in transitivity (having low object-affectedness). As such the insertion of prepositions such as *about* accurately reflects its transitivity status vis-à-vis other clauses that are higher on the transitivity scale (e.g. those that appear with V + *up*, as in *He ate up the apple*).

2.5   OTHER FUNCTION WORDS

2.5.1   Prepositions

Some studies, unsurprisingly, report variability in preposition use. Some of this has been discussed under verb categorization. African and American Indian varieties of English seem to exhibit a particularly wide variability. The following examples are from Leap (1993:74), who cites studies of different AmInd communities:

131. He got fired of the church. (Mohave Eng; Penfield-Jasper 1980:145)
132. They were at fishing.
133. Ricky got in such a hurry on his zipper.[6] (Papago Eng; Bayles and Harris 1982:17)

Navajo English examples include *go to downtown*; *at store*; *all kinds from birds* (Cook and Sharp 1966:28).

Sometimes preposition absence is striking:

134. He lives Φ that second house.
135. I was Φ California. (Mohave Eng; Penfield-Jasper 1980:144)
136. I color Φ this. (Φ = 'with')
137. You wanna go Φ bathroom?
138. They live Φ New York. (Lakota Eng; Flannigan 1984a:92)

And, finally, some varieties tolerate 'double prepositions':

139. During at that time ...
140. I get on in Head Start.[7] (Mohave Eng; Penfield-Jasper 1980:145)

In some varieties prepositions (or preposition-like elements) follow the NP, making them postpositions: *the chalkboard under* (Navajo Eng; Cook and Sharp 1966:28).

Quasi-postpositions were also noted in basilectal IndSAf Eng by Mesthrie (1987): *night time* ('at night'); *Telugu way* ('in Telugu'); *Fountain Head side* ('at/towards Fountain Head'); *morning part* ('in the morning'). These are influenced by the structure of the substrate languages (Tamil, Telugu, Hindi) in which postpositions are common. However, they are outnumbered by 'regular' prepositions in all varieties of IndSAf Eng. Schmied (1991:67–9) supplies examples of preposition variation in African varieties of English with forms like *participation with* (for *in*); *attached with* (for *to*), *switch out* (for *off*) and *deprived from* (for *of*).

2.5.2 Conjunctions

(a) Correlative *so*: A tendency to use *so* with clauses having a causal or temporal relation at the beginning of both clauses has been noted in several varieties of English:

141. *So* when I was a baby, *so* my father-an'-them shifted to Sezela. (IndSAf Eng; Mesthrie 1992a:198)
142. *So* we had about two rooms each, *so* we stayed. (BlSAf Eng)
143. Q: When did you learn Mandarin?
     A: *So* when I completed my primary education, *so* I just take some night classes of that Mandarin, that's right. (Sgp Eng; Platt, Weber and Ho 1984:126).

In this usage, *so* does not really invite a comment from the interlocutor, nor does it always involve a didactic exposition as one expects in Std Eng. Rather, it seems a device to introduce and keep track of clauses that have a causal or temporal relation.

(b) Conjunction balance: Williams (1987:189) notes that relations like 'supposition' and 'contrast' are often marked in each clause:

144. *Though* the farmer works hard, *but* he cannot produce enough. (India; Nihalani, Tongue and Hosali 1977:177)
145. *Although* he is rich, *but* he is stingy. (Nig Eng; Alo and Mesthrie 2004: 819)
146. *But* I don't know it well, *but* I like it. (BlSAf Eng)

Examples with *but* in both clauses of (146) are similar to correlative *so*, apart from the adversative semantics of *but*.

(c) Double conjunctions: There are a few examples of double conjunctions occurring within the same clause: *supposing if* ('if' in Sgp Eng and IndSAf Eng); *if supposing* (in Singapore for *if* or *supposing*); *because why* ('because' in BlSAf Eng and IndSAf Eng); *if at all* (in BlSAf Eng for 'if') . In some varieties conjunctions are deleted when context makes the clausal relations clear. This, of course, contradicts the rather neat correlative and conjunction balance identified above.

147. Stay longer, they have to over-charge. (= 'If you stay longer, they have to charge more' – Sgp Eng; Platt, Weber and Ho 1984:125)
148. Born over there, I'm brought up over there. (= 'I was born and brought up over there' – IndSAf Eng basilect; Mesthrie 1992: 197)

How these sentences relate to (144) to (146), where conjunctions are maximally present is worthy of investigation using a large corpus. We suspect that speakers begin with zero marking and then mark one or both clauses with a conjunction. In this analysis double conjunctions would be a form of hypercorrection. Some speakers possibly fossilise at this stage, while others go on to acquire the TL convention of single marking.

(d) Clause-final conjunctions: These are a possibility in IndSAf Eng basilect. Mesthrie (1992:108) provides examples of *but* being used in clause-final position, not so much as an adversative, but as a modifier 'though, really, truly'.

> 149.   I donno the rain is pouring, *but*. (= 'I didn't really know that the rain was pouring')
> 150.   I fright for dogs, *but*, eh! (= 'I'm really afraid of dogs')

Mesthrie also discusses clause-final *too* as a conditional, 'if, even if' in the basilect:

> 151.   It can be a terrible house *too*, you have to stay in a terrible house. (= 'Even if it's a terrible house, you have to live in it')
> 152.   Very sick an' all *too*, they take them to R. K. Khan's. (= 'If they're very sick, they take them to R. K. Khan Hospital')

Such use of clause-final *but* has precedents in northern British dialects.

2.5.3   *Wh*-words

Bimorphemic equivalents of *wh*-words do occur in some New Englishes, though not as commonly as in Creoles. IndSAf Eng basilect has *what thing* 'what'; *what time* 'when'; *for what* 'why'. The forms *for what* and *what for* (both meaning 'why') also occur in Sgp Eng (Platt, Weber and Ho 1984:127). In IndSAf Eng *wh*-words can be reduplicated with the semantics 'plural/distributive' (Mesthrie 1992a:204), based on details of the syntax of the Indic substrates.

> 153.   Who-who came? (= 'Who (of several people) came?')
> 154.   What-what they said? (= 'What (different) things did they say?')

In Sri Lanka the equivalent forms are *who and who* (Kachru 1982:361), and in India *who-all*, *where-all*, etc. These are plural interrogatives and cannot be used as, say, relative clause markers. *Who-all* also occurs in Ir Eng and was thence transported to the Midlands of the USA.

(Montgomery 2004:318). It is not clear if it is related to the Ind Eng form historically. *Because-why* as a variant of *because* occurs in BlSAf Eng and IndSAf Eng.

2.6 CONCLUSION

In this chapter we covered the main features pertaining to noun and verb phrase syntax reported in WE studies. Inevitably, our coverage has been wide rather than deep. We have tried to point out areas of interest for further in-depth study and comparative analysis. In the next chapter we continue the grammatical focus by examining cross-clausal syntax and some detailed studies which have used theories and models from other branches of linguistics.

STUDY QUESTIONS

1. Review the difference between copular *be* and habitual *be*. What claims have been made about these forms in New Englishes?
2. Give some examples of verbs that are unambiguously stative in Std Eng and of some that are unambiguously non-stative. Now give some example sentences showing that the distinction between stative and non-stative is fuzzy for some verbs of Std Eng – i.e. that they may be used in a stative or progressive (non-stative) way.
3. Review the difference in Std Eng between *I have read this book* and *I read this book last month*. More generally what is the difference between the use of perfect aspect and simple past? Suggest a possible semantic or grammatical reason why some New English speakers might say *I have read this book last month*.
4. Review the difference between (dialectal) unstressed auxiliary *do* and (standard) stressed auxiliary *do*. Give some examples of *do* as a full, rather than auxiliary verb in Std Eng.
5. Review the difference between a phrasal verb and a prepositional verb in Std Eng. What innovations occur within these categories in New Englishes?

Further reading
All works mentioned here are fully referenced in the bibliography.

The first attempt to compare recurring features of the sort carried out in this chapter is in Platt, Weber and Ho's *The New Englishes* (1984). Coverage of wide territories are Schmied's *English in Africa: An Introduction* (1991), Kachru, *Asian Englishes: Beyond the Canon* (2005); Platt and Weber *English in Singapore and Malaysia,* (1980); Kachru *The Indianization of English* (1983a); Leap's *American Indian English* (1993); Tristram's *The Celtic Englishes* comes in four volumes published between 1997 and 2006. Good reference grammars for readers to look up aspects of colloquial standard English are Quirk et al. *A Communicative Grammar of English* (1972) and Huddleston and Pullum's *The Cambridge Grammar of the English Language* (2002).

3 Structural features of New Englishes II: – cross-clausal syntax and syntactic theory

3.1 INTRODUCTION

In this chapter we continue the discussions begun in the previous one, this time focusing mainly on constructions that go beyond the phrasal level. We also examine in detail analyses of such constructions from the framework of Optimality Theory and Variationist Sociolinguistics.

3.2 CROSS-CLAUSAL SYNTAX

In this section the main emphasis is on word order and syntactic constructions that result in word-order permutations: questions, passives, topicalisation, relative clauses and rank-reduction.

3.2.1 Word Order

Although all New Englishes follow a basic SVO order, some varieties prove fairly 'leaky' in allowing certain word-order principles of the substrates to filter through. Mesthrie (1987) shows how OV syntax of Indic and Dravidian languages influences a range of basilectal structures in IndSAf Eng. In more or less the same vein Leap (1993:77) posits that some varieties of American Indian English exhibit left-branching in certain constructions, rather the right-branching structure of Std Eng. Ritchie (1986) shows how certain features of Singapore English can be better characterised as following topic-comment principles rather than the relatively rigid SVO syntax of Std Eng.

(a) Declarative clauses: Mesthrie reports only a few 'one-off' examples of genuine SOV sentences in basilectal IndSAf Eng:

1. She her own house got. (= 'She's got a house of her own')

Forms like these have not really stabilised in the sociolect and are better considered a matter of ad hoc 'performance', rather than reflecting a regular rule. On the other hand, Irish Eng *has* evolved a rule for placing the main verb at the end of sentences, for the expression of 'resultative perfects':

2. He has the job done. (Hickey 1995:115)

The semantics of (2) emphasises that the state which is envisaged as the end-point of an action has indeed been reached. Hickey (1995:125) notes the difference between the following pair in Irish Eng:

3a. Have you read Finnegan's Wake?
3b. Have you Finnegan's Wake read?

In (3a) the usual Std Eng interpretation is intended ('Have you (ever) read Finnegan's Wake?'). In the second sentence of the pair the interlocutor is being asked whether he/she has completed the task of reading the book.

Leap (1993:77) gives an example of a VS structure in Yavapai English, though it is not clear how widespread this is and/whether it is restricted to *wh*-questions:

4. Where going you?

Confronted with a sentence like (4), WE studies need to consider a difference between what creolists like Mufwene (2001) call the 'pool of variants' as against the forms that are eventually selected from this pool as part of a stable Creole grammar. The pool of variants consists of elements taken from a range of sources in the early stages of Creole formation: superstrate, substrates, linguistic universals and universals of contact. When a Creole is nativised (i.e. used as a first language), some selection and restructuring takes place. Pending further information, we wonder whether forms such as *Where going you?* have passed from an antecedent pool of variants to the WE in question. An example from IndSAf Eng might clarify matters. Word-order rules are flexible in this variety. Certain orders which are permissible in one or more of the substrates may form part of the pool of variants developed by early adult learners of English. However, some of these orders are ruled out from the dialect as it subsequently stabilised. An example comes from a middle-aged Gujarati speaker forced to speak to a non-Gujarati speaker in (basilang) English. She asked haltingly *India*

like – you? (= 'Did you like India?'). This form (OV, with subject pronoun extraposed) is not acceptable within the dialect. This was vividly
demonstrated when an elderly L2 speaker, herself basilectal, later commented with great amusement on this phrase. In the basilect the form
which has stabilised from an earlier pool of variants is *India – you liked?*
(Object topic – subject pronoun – V with complex intonation). This is a
contextual and stylistic variant of *You liked India?*; *Did you like India?* is
a more formal mesolectal or acrolectal form.

(b) Questions: Questions throw up more variation in word order
than declaratives. Many New Englishes show a greater preference for
forming *yes/no* questions by a rising intonation pattern, rather than by
auxiliary inversion.

5.   She's coming tomorrow? (='Is she coming tomorrow?' – IndSAf Eng)

The application of '*do*-support' is optional in questions for many New
Englishes, especially in informal speech:

6.   She promised you? (Sgp Eng; Williams 1987:173)
7.   Anthony learned this from you or you learned this from Anthony? (Sgp Eng;
     Williams 1987:173)

In negatives *do*-support is mandatory in IndSAf Eng, often without
inversion:

8.   She doesn't help you? (IndSAf Eng)

The equivalent with *do*-support *Doesn't she help you?* would be stylistically marked as formal. For *wh*-questions, similar principles are operative, with some varieties using *do*-support variably:

9.   What time he come? (= 'What time did he come?' – Sgp Eng: Platt, Weber
     and Ho 1984:127)
10.   What he wants? (= 'What does he want?' – IndSAf Eng)

These same varieties favour non-inversion in *wh*-main clauses:

11.   What you would like to read? (Ind Eng; Kachru 1982:360)
12.   What he'll say? (IndSAf Eng)

Conversely in some varieties *do*-support and aux-inversion surface in
indirect questions:

13. I asked Hari where does he work. (Ind Eng; Verma 1982:181, in Pride 1982)
14. I'll tell you why do people use such a style of language. (BlSAf Eng)
15. Do you know what will be the price? (EAf Eng: Schmied 1991:74)

In IndSAf Eng the forms *be* and *will* are reduced and attached to *wh-*:

16. Do you know when's the plane going to land? (IndSAf Eng; Mesthrie 1992a:61)

Irish English shows some variation here. One prominent possibility is the retention of inversion in embedded clauses:

17. ...I don't know what is it at all. (Filppula 1999:168)

Indirect questions with *whether* and *if* are also variable, often lacking such subordinators, and using inverted word order:

18. I wondered was the horse well bred. (Hayden and Hartog 1909, cited by Filppula 1999:167)

The interplay (and apparent contradiction) between non-inversion in main clauses and inversion in subordinate clauses is discussed in section 3.4 from the perspective of theoretical syntax.

(c) Topicalisation: Topicalisation phenomena are common in informal Std Eng. In New Englishes they are noteworthy for several reasons: (i) the extension to a wider range of grammatical contexts; (ii) a (possibly) higher frequency of occurrence; and (iii) an extension to formal contexts. Under the broad rubric of topicalisation several subtypes can be identified on the grounds of syntax, pragmatics and intonation – see Prince (1981) for Yiddish English of the USA and general US English, Mesthrie (1992a, 1997) for IndSAf Eng and BlSAf Eng respectively.

(i) Left dislocation: This construction, which preposes a topic and supplies a comment by way of a full S, is widely reported in New Englishes:

19. The people, they got nothing to eat. (BlSAf Eng; Mesthrie 1997:132)
20. My daughter, she is attending the University of Nairobi (EAf Eng; Bokamba 1992:131)

Similar use of subject topics (with pronoun apposition) are reported for Ind Eng, Sgp Eng and Sri Lanka Eng. Mesthrie (1997) shows that the following hierarchy of functions applies in BlSAf Eng (in decreasing order of frequency):

Subject < Direct Object < Locative < Genitive < Temporals < Other.

In terms of their pragmatics the functions of left dislocation in BlSAf Eng are not qualitatively different from that of Std Eng. The construction is used to reintroduce information that has not been talked about for a while as well as to contrast noun phrases, as when 'speakers go through lists and make comments about each individual element in the list' (Finegan and Besnier 1989:227).

(ii) Fronting: The second topicalisation phenomenon of interest is fronting, in which an NP is fronted, without an overt trace in the main clause:

> 21. To my sister sometime I speak English. (Sgp Eng; Platt, Weber and Ho 1984:121)
> 22. Q: Zulu? (i.e. Do you speak Zulu as well?)
> A: Yah, and Zulu I speak. (BlSAf Eng; Mesthrie 1997:128)

Fronting differs from left dislocation in terms of intonation. Pragmatically, it puts old information first; this topic must be already evoked in the discourse or stand in a salient set-relation to something already in the discourse (Prince 1981).

(iii) Clefting: Leap (1993:77) gives examples of such movement rules which involve focusing on a variety of American Indian Englishes:

> 23. They ride bikes is what I see them do. (San Juan Tewa)
> 24. There are circle dance songs that we have. (Apache)
> 25. What he is doing there is he Ø announcing. (Lakota)
> 26. From the family is where we learn to be good. (Arapaho)

Clefting of a related sort is a well-known feature of Irish English:

> 27. It's badly she'd do it, now. (Filppula 1999:250)
> 28. I think it was painting, I was. (Filppula 1999:260)

Clearly topicalisation and focusing phenomena need to be studied carefully in context and by means that foster comparison. To this end Mesthrie (1992a:110–27; 1997) and Filppula (1999:260–70) provide some useful groundwork.

3.2.2 Relative clauses

There is a tendency for resumptive pronouns to be used in WE relative clauses:

29. The man who I saw *him* was wearing a big hat. (BlSAf Eng; Gough 1996:61)
30. The guests whom I invited *them* have arrived. (WAf Eng and EAf Eng; Bokamba 1992:131)

Resumptive pronouns also occur in L1 varieties of British and American Eng, and may appear in spoken formal English under 'discourse' conditions to help speakers keep track of NPs in deeply embedded relative clauses. More 'exotic' relatives have been reported in IndSAf Eng, Sgp Eng and Hong Kong English (henceforth *HKng Eng*). Alsagoff and Lick (1998a) describe the influence of the Chinese substrate on Sgp Eng relative clauses:

31a. The man [who sell ice-kachang] gone home already.
31b. The man [sell ice-kachang one] gone home already.
31c. The man [who sell ice-kachang one] gone home already.

Sentence (31a) is the usual Std Eng relative clause, while (31b) is an alternative realisation with the relative pronoun *one* occurring at the end of the clause. The form *one* is based on two details of Chinese (Mandarin, Hokkien, Cantonese) grammar: (a) in terms of function, it is a nominalizer, rather than the pronoun of Std Eng; (b) in terms of position, it occurs at the end rather than the beginning of the relative clause. Sentence (31c) shows a compromise construction that combines substrate and superstrate options.

Relative clauses in basilectal IndSAf Eng show a number of options (Mesthrie and Dunne 1990). The following three are the most unlike Std Eng, though they are not very commonly used: correlatives, a participial strategy and prenominal external relatives.

(a) The correlative strategy involves a relative clause placed before the head noun, introduced by *which* or *which-one*. The head noun in the main clause is pronominalised (with a pronoun or the anaphoric *one*):

32. ... which-one principal came here, she's just cheeky like the other one (= 'The principal who arrived recently is just as stern as the previous one' – IndSAf Eng; Mesthrie 1992a:75)
33. Which-one I put in the jar, that-one is good. (= 'The ones (i.e. pickles) I put in the jar are the best' – IndSAf Eng; Mesthrie 1992a:75)

(b) The participial strategy involves passive verbs in the relative clause which are compounded with the agentive noun (in genitive form). The relative clause precedes the head noun and fits in overall like an adjective:

34. That Neela's-knitted jersey is gone white. (= 'That jersey which
    Neela knitted/ knitted by Neela has gone white')
35. You can't beat Vijay's-planted tomato. (= 'You won't find better
    tomatoes than those planted by Vijay / which were planted by Vijay')

(c) The third strategy resembles the 'prenominal external' prototype
of Dravidian languages, in which a relative clause precedes the
head noun, with the relative marker being a verb suffix. As there
is no relative pronoun, there is only a single occurrence of the
noun being relativised.

36. That's all [we had] trouble. (= 'That's all the trouble we had')

This type is rather rare and may well be a relic from the 'pool
of variants' that provided input into the dialect. Other types of
relative clauses in IndSAf Eng, and statistics for their use, are
supplied in Mesthrie and Dunne (1990). Strategies typical of Std
Eng and English dialects, however, far outnumber the substrate-
influenced ones.

3.2.3 Passives

As with Std Eng, passives with *be* + past participle and agentive noun
with *by* are not common in informal speech in New Englishes. Passives
with *get* that leave agentive nouns unstated are probably more frequent
(*They got knocked down*; rather than *They were knocked down*). Bao and Wee
(1999) describe two innovations in Singapore English based on Malay
and Chinese:

37a. John (was) scolded by his boss.
37b. John kena scolded by his boss.
37c. John give his boss scold.

The first type of passive (37a) is from Std Eng, with the important
difference that passive *be* is optional. The other two are closely related
to each other (but less so to the Std Eng construction) in involving
an 'adversity' reading. In (37b) *kena* is the Malay verb 'to strike, to
come into contact with', which acts as an auxiliary in the passive
construction. Bao and Wee (1999:3) outline four properties of the *kena*-
passive that distinguish it from the Std Eng prototype:

(i) The lexical verb can be in the bare form or the past participial
    form
(ii) The agentive *by*-phrase is optional
(iii) The subject must be adversely affected
(iv) Stative verbs cannot be passivised with *kena*

The *kena* passive is unusual among New Englishes in so far as an indigenous lexeme is recruited as a grammatical marker, without calquing (i.e. being translated into English). The only other such element we are aware of is the agentive *wala* suffix in Ind Eng and Pak Eng (e.g. *laundry wala* 'laundry man', with female equivalent *-wali*). The *give*-passive of Sgp Eng has the structure NP_1-*give*-NP_2-*Verb*; where NP_1 is the Patient; and NP_2, the obligatory Agent. Sentence (37c) thus means 'John was scolded by his boss.' The surface subject of the *give*-passive is typically understood to have contributed in some way to its misfortune. Bao and Wee trace the origins of this construction to Chinese.

On variable *be*-deletion in passives in some WEs see section 2.4.6 (c).

3.2.4 Comparison

Adjectives which have irregular comparative forms may be particularly prone to innovations amongst New English speakers. In IndSAf Eng basilectal speakers produce variants like *worst* for 'worse', *more worst* for 'worse'; and *more better* for 'better'. In CFl Eng basilectal speakers occasionally produce forms like *worserer* and *betterer* for 'worse' and 'better'. This might be a general phonological property rather than double comparatives, treating the comparative suffix as [ərə], rather than [ə], hence forms like *tougherer* and *biggerer* may also be heard. As far as syntax is concerned, New Englishes provide some variations on the Std Eng pattern. In some varieties of African English the adjective is variably marked for comparative:

38. It is the youths who are skilful in performing tasks than the adults. (= '... who are more skilful than ...' – Chinebuah 1976, cited by Bokamba 1992:134)
39. He values his car than his wife. (= '... more than his wife' – Angogo and Hancock 1980:75)
40. My school was one of the radical schools that you can ever find. (= ... 'most radical'...)

Sometimes the adjective *more* does surface, though the conjunction *than* may not:

41. They would have more powder on the hand and in their faces. (= ... 'than in their faces' – Chinebuah 1976, cited by Bokamba 1992:134)

In BlSAf Eng a related construction moves the superlative adverb *most* to the position before the head noun:

42. The most thing I like is apples. (= 'The thing I like most is apples' – Adey 1977:38)

Platt, Weber and Ho (1984:122) quote a variant of the comparative in Sri Lanka, where *much* may be used instead of *more*:

> 43. The unemployment position is much severe than Singapore.

3.2.5 Tag questions

New Englishes are united in using an invariant tag, where Std Eng has a complex rule involving pronoun and auxiliary copying with negative reversal; and *do*-support if the main clause lacks an auxiliary. A commonly used tag is *isn't it*:

> 44. You are going tomorrow, isn't it? (Ind Eng; Kachru 1982:360)
> 45. He isn't going there, isn't it? (Ind Eng; Kachru 1982:360)

Isn't it is reported in Sri Lankan English (SrLnk Eng), WAf Eng, EAf Eng, Sgp Eng, Mal Eng and IndSAf Eng. In IndSAf Eng it is usually reduced to *isn't*, and may even be fronted in informal styles:

> 46. She came yesterday, isn't? (= ... 'didn't she?')
> 47. Isn't, I can colour this red? (= 'I can colour this red, can't I?')

Variants in New Englishes include *no?* (SrLnk Eng); *not so?* (WAf Eng; EAf Eng); *is it* (Sgp Eng and Mal Eng); *ah* (Sgp Eng, SrLnk Eng, IndSAf Eng, Mauritian English) and *nè* (CFl Eng and BlSAf Eng, based on Afrikaans particle *nè*). It is not clear whether the Welsh English invariant form *isn't it* served as a model for this tag, in some New Englishes at least; or whether substrate influences like the Hindi–Urdu invariant tag *na* played a role. It is also possible that once adopted, the Indian English form *isn't it* played a subsequent influential role in other WEs. Scots and Welsh invariant *eh* might also have been influential in some varieties that have *ah/eh* as alternative tags.

Singapore and Malaysian English has a related structure of the 'X or not' type (Platt, Weber and Ho 1984:130), where the speaker is expected to agree:

> 48. You come tomorrow, can or not? ('You can come tomorrow, can't you?)
> 49. All churches use the same, true or not? ('All churches use the same, don't they?')

These examples are based on the Chinese substrate.

3.2.6 Answers to *yes/no* questions

Many varieties in South Asia and Africa share a response to *yes/no* questions couched in the negative that is the opposite of Std Eng.

50. Q: Didn't you see anyone at the compound?
    A: Yes, I didn't see anyone at the compound. (EAf Eng and WAf Eng; Bokamba 1992:132)
51. Q: Didn't I see you yesterday in college?
    A: Yes, you didn't see me yesterday in college. (Ind Eng; Kachru 1982:374)
52. Q: Isn't he arriving tomorrow?
    A: No. (= 'Yes, he is' – BlSAf Eng; Mesthrie 1994:189)

The same phenomenon occurs with subordinate clauses after verbs like *hope* and *wish*:

53. A: I hope you won't have any difficulty with your fees next term.
    B: I hope so. (= 'I hope what you have said will indeed be true' – EAf Eng and WAf
        Eng; Bokamba 1992:132, citing Kirk-Greene 1971:135)

For *yes/no* questions couched in the negative there seem to be two different rules operating for Std Eng and some of the New Englishes. Std Eng relies on 'the facts of the situation' (Kachru 1982:374) in which *yes* means a positive situation holds, whilst *no* means a negative situation holds. For most South Asian and African Englishes *yes* signifies that the form of the question is in accord with the facts; *no* signifies that the form of the question is not in accord with the facts. This analysis also holds for the *yes/no* questions couched in the positive (Mesthrie 1994), so that New Englishes have one rule underlying all *yes/no* questions. This rule is different from that which underlies Std Eng questions, as the following diagram illustrates:

Std Eng *yes/no* questions:
54.

Q: Is he arriving tomorrow?

A: Yes (he is)   OR   No (he isn't)

55.

Q: Isn't he arriving tomorrow?

A: Yes (he is)   OR   No (he isn't)

African and South Asian *yes/no* questions:
56a.

Q: Is he arriving tomorrow?

A: Yes (he is)

56b.

> Q: Is he arriving tomorrow?
>
> A: No (he isn't)

56c.

> Q: Isn't he arriving tomorrow?
>
> A: Yes (he isn't)

56d.

> Q: Isn't he arriving tomorrow?
>
> A: No (he is)

Note that though both systems appear to be in agreement for positive questions (where *yes* and *no* mean the same thing respectively in each variety), under this structural analysis the resemblance is superficial. For Std Eng speakers *yes* or *no* responds to a lateral comparison within the same (response) clause; New English speakers respond to a vertical comparison between question and response clauses.

There may well be a difference in pragmatics as well. Under the present analysis a positive question in Std Eng makes no presupposition: the answer could be 'X did happen' or 'X didn't happen'. For negative questions the presupposition is 'X did not happen'. By contrast, in the New Englishes under discussion (of South Asia and Africa) – if our structural analysis is correct – then positive questions presuppose the answer 'X did happen' whilst negative questions carry the presupposition 'X did not happen'.

Filppula observes that Irish English does not differ from Std Eng in the function of forms like *yea* and *no*; however, it is noticeable that these forms tend to be avoided. Interlocutors either use a truncated NP + Aux in response (without *yes* or *no*), as in (57), or simply repeat the questioner's VP, as in (59).

57. Q: Do people eat it still?
     A: They do.
58. Q: Are you telling me their names?
     A: I amn't.
59. Q: So, you belong to that parish.
     A: Belong to that parish. (Filppula 1991:165)

In Filppula's (1999:165) database, 52.8 per cent of responses involved *yes* or *no*; whilst the rest showed an avoidance of these forms.

3.2.7 Adverb placement

The placement of adverbs is more fluid than in Std Eng. One significant tendency is for adverbs to be placed in clause-final position:

> 60. I have seen you already (Phl Eng; Gonzalez 1983, cited by Platt, Weber and Ho 1984:122)

This placement of *already* is also found in HKng Eng and CFl Eng. Similar placement occurs with adverbs like *only*, *even*, *also* and *too*. In African varieties studied by Schmidt (1991:75), adverb placement varies considerably from Std Eng, leading him to suggest that this flexibility enables emphasis and focus to be expressed more readily than in formal Std Eng.

> 61. He did not arrive in time unfortunately.
> 62. She went often to see them.
> 63. Always the tank must be clean.

Whereas these would count as marked orders in Std Eng, they are unmarked in the varieties studied by Schmidt.

3.2.8 Constructions that are not widespread

Whilst there is indeed a great deal of shared syntax between New Englishes, some constructions or processes are limited to one or a few varieties.

(a) **Rank reduction:** Kachru (1983a:40) lists this as one of the striking features of Ind Eng (e.g. *key-bunch* 'a bunch of keys'; *God-love* 'love of God'). Essentially rank-reduction involves changing a modifying PP to NP. The PP becomes a prenominal modifier or forms an endocentric compound with the head noun. An interesting example showing mirror-image word order comes from a sign posted outside a South Indian temple: *Footwear placing counter*. This sign shows a change from postnominal modification of Std Eng ('Counter for placing of footwear') to Ind Eng premodification. The lexis-generating capacity of this process is discussed further in Chapter 4 (section 4.1).

(b) **Cognate object predicates:** Isletan English frequently makes use of verb–noun complexes where Std Eng is more likely to use single verbs:

64. Lay people do not *take* actual *participation* in church functions.
65. You had to *have* a book-keeping *knowledge* to do that.
66. You *have* your *belief* in the corn.
67. They do not know how to *give* a *decision*.

In Std Eng the phrases in bold would be *participate; know bookkeeping; believe; decide* respectively. Leap (1993:96–104) argues that these 'cognate object predicates' have a basis is in Isletan Tiwa syntax. Leap (1993:99) describes these rules for Isletan English as follows (slightly adapted here):

i   Select the appropriate verb reference; locate the corresponding verb base.
ii Copy verb base into object node and assign appropriate noun affixes.
iii Replace original verb with appropriate auxiliary or 'pro-verb'.

Thus for a phrase like *take participation*, at step 1 the verb *participate* would be chosen. It is then formed into the noun *participation*. Finally the full verb *participate* is replaced by a 'vector verb' *take*. Although this syntactic account – based on early transformational-generative grammar – has become somewhat dated, it does show clearly the relations between the lexical items involved. Leap (1993:96) describes the special stylistic status of the construction as follows:

> Isletan English speakers use these constructions in informal,
> face-to-face conversations and in highly structured speech events. By
> my assessment, the constructions occur less frequently in the English
> of younger members of the pueblo (persons under 21), though the
> frequency increases as they reach adulthood and take a more active
> role in community life. It is worth noting that this is also the
> age-level at which these persons' ancestral language fluency begins to
> expand.

3.2.9 A broad dichotomy: – 'deleters' versus 'preservers'

Although there are many morphological and syntactic similarities amongst the WEs described in Chapter 2 and the present one, there are also broad dichotomies, usually dependent on the characteristic syntax of the substrate languages. One such broad dichotomy involves varieties that favour deletion of elements and those that disfavour it. In this regard the differences between Sgp Eng (especially amongst those with Chinese substrates) and African varieties of English are striking.

The following have been reported in Sgp Eng:

(a) Omission of subjects:

> 68. Φ must buy for him . . . (= '*We* must buy a present for him' – Wee
>   2004:1062)

(b) Omission of objects:

> 69. I am very interested in English. That why I must speak Φ. (Platt and
>   Weber 1980:73)

Similarly Leap (1993:60) reports a deletion pattern amongst Mohave
Eng speakers where multiple deletions of subject pronouns are per-
mitted within the same complex sentence:

> 70. I didn't know it either. Φ was playing, playing, till the bell rung, Φ open my
>   book and felt my pocket; Φ wasn't in there.

In such sentences the appropriate pronoun reference is recoverable
from context. Penfield-Jasper (cited by Leap 1993:60–1) cites the following explanations for this pattern:

  (i) Mohave equi-deletion, which allows the second or additional
      occurrence of the same noun or pronoun within the sentence
      to be deleted
 (ii) less stringent pronoun-marking conventions in casual English
      speech, as in many other Englishes
(iii) a Mohave grammatical rule that forms headless subordinate
      clauses when contextual details specify the identity of the sub-
      ject and the verb affix supplies information about the subject's
      action.

By contrast, in many African varieties the opposite word-order tendencies hold: our examples come from BlSAf Eng (Mesthrie 2006):

> 71. Come what may *come*. ('Come what may Φ')
> 72. He made me *to* do it. ('He made me Φ do it')
> 73. The fact has made me *to* conclude that my idea is sound. ('. . . made me Φ
>   conclude. . .')
> 74. As you know *that* I am from the Ciskei. ('As you know Φ I am from the
>   Ciskei)
> 75. My standard nine, I have enjoyed *it* very much (Gough and de Klerk 2002)
> 76. The man who I saw *him* was wearing a big hat. (Gough and de Klerk 2002)
> 77. As I made *it* clear before, I am going to talk about solutions, not problems.
>   ('As I made Φ clear. . .')
> 78. As *it* is the case elsewhere in Africa, much can still be done for children.
>   ('As Φ is the case . . .')

These examples show that in common with other African varieties BlSAf Eng speakers disfavour the deletion of elements like infinitive *to* (72), resumptive pronouns in relative clauses (76), dummy *it* after verbs like *make clear* (77), dummy *it* before the verb *be* (78), complementiser *that* after *as you know, as I said*, etc. Mesthrie (2006) characterises the presence of these elements as 'undeletions' and shows that a *deletion–undeletion* continuum can characterise different WEs, with BlSAf Eng at the undeleting end and Sgp Eng at the deleting end.

3.3   NEW ENGLISH SYNTAX AND SOCIOLINGUISTIC VARIATION

In this section we present an analysis of an area of New English syntax, copula deletion in Sgp Eng, that shows the potential of Variationist Theory and methods (Labov 1972a, 2001) in illuminating New English studies. Conversely New Englishes themselves have much to contribute to Variationist Theory.

It is not surprising that copula deletion occurs variably since the substrate languages (Malay, Tamil and varieties of Chinese) all tend towards copula deletion in the present tense. Ho carried out 150 interviews with speakers of Chinese background (who make up 77 per cent of the country's population). Of these 100 were selected for analysis as they fulfilled the necessary criteria of clarity of recording as well as extended speech resulting from particularly good rapport with the interviewer. Following analyses by variationists like Labov (1972b) and Baugh (1980), Ho and Platt (1993: Chapter 6) isolated several environments involved in copula variability:

- Adj = 'before Adjectives';
- V*ing* = before 'Verb + -*ing*';
- Nom = 'before Nouns and nominal groups';
- Loc = 'before Locatives';
- Cl = 'before clauses'.

They provided an implicational scale and a multivariate analysis of their data. In displaying acquisition and social patterns via an implicational scale, they used the following key: + for categorical presence; 0 for categorical absence; − for absence of relevant data; x for variable presence. As is customary in implicational scale analysis, the authors sought to find a grouping of speakers and a grouping (or hierarchy) of linguistic environments which showed an 'implicational' pattern. Exceptions to the pattern are ringed (as when a copula is expected in a particular environment for a particular speaker but is variable or

Table 3.1. *Simplified implicational scale showing copula variability in Singapore English* (based on Ho and Platt 1993:44–6)

_Adj	_Ving	_Nom	_Loc	_Cl	no. of speakers
+	+	+	+	+	3
×	+	+	+	+	12
×	×	+	+	+	20
×	×	×	+	+	23
×	×	×	×	+	32
×	×	×	×	×	7
⊗	0	×	×	×	3

absent); and the reliability of the scale measured by a simple 'scalability' formula which we describe below. Table 3.1 is a simplified version of the full scale provide by Ho and Platt.

Rather than showing the patterns of each of the 100 speakers in our simplified table we have grouped those with the same patterns together in one line and show the number of speakers of each pattern on the right. Unfortunately this means that we cannot show individual exceptions to patterns in a particular environment, which would have been ringed in the individual figure. In the first column of the last row the entire group of (three) speakers is ringed, as the speakers show variability where zeroes (categorical absence) are to be expected, if the implication pattern were indeed watertight. In the original three-page table there were forty-one such deviations and nine empty cells (signifying 'no data' for a particular environment). The scalability of the table is calculated by taking the total number of cells minus the empty cells; dividing this by the total number of cells; and expressing this ratio as a percentage. In this case the scalability was:

$$\frac{[(500 - 9) - 41] \times 100}{(500 - 9)}$$
$$= 91.7\%.$$

Such a scalability figure of over 85 per cent is considered a reliable modelling of the data. What can we conclude from Table 3.1?:

(i) There are very few zeroes – i.e. speakers who categorically delete *be* in a particular environment.
(ii) Variability is very common, but is highly structured.

Table 3.2. *Percentage scores for copula realisation by educational level and linguistic environment in Singapore English* (based on Ho and Platt 1993:44–6)

	_ Adj	_ Ving	_ Nom	_ Loc
Tertiary	94.2	91.9	97.1	95.6
A-level	92.0	91.9	96.4	96.4
O-level	85.5	87.8	93.0	92.4
Sec 1–3	69.1	65.9	89.1	80.8
Primary	59.7	58.8	79.5	66.7

Table 3.3. *Percentage scores for categorical copula realisation by educational level and linguistic environment in Singapore English* (based on Ho and Platt 1993:44–6)

	_Adj	_Ving	_Nom	_Loc	_Cl
Tertiary	10	30	55	70	80
A-level	5	35	45	70	89.5
O-level	5	25	35	45	80
Sec 1–3	0	10	25	36.8	85
Primary	0	0	15	21.1	80

(iii) A hierarchical pattern exists: *Cl* < *Loc* < *Nom* < *Ving* < *Adj*. This may be thought of as an acquisitional hierarchy, with clauses being the first environment in which the copula is acquired and Adj the last.

(iv) There is patterning according to speakers' educational histories as well; insofar as speakers at the top end of the table come from higher educational levels (tertiary, senior secondary, i.e. O and A levels) whilst speakers at the bottom of the table come from lower educational levels (secondary 1–3 and primary).

Point (iv) can be seen from the full table in Ho and Platt (1993:44–6). They also provide percentage group scores in four of the environments showing this patterning, as in Table 3.2.

Ho and Platt also provide tables correlating patterns of educational level with categorical realisation of the copula.

In Table 3.2 the percentages denote group scores for copula presence in a particular environment; in Table 3.3 they denote the percentage of speakers of each educational level who have categorical realisation of the copula in the different environments.

The importance of this kind of statistical approach is that it provides an acquisitional picture missing in other simple descriptive approaches. Moreover, it enables comparisons with other WEs. That is, by examining hierarchies of constraints for other New Englishes, it would be possible to see whether they follow the same patterning, or whether substrate influence changes the picture significantly. Ho and Platt argue strongly for Chinese substrate influence in this instance.

For the copula, matters are complicated by having to consider the preceding environment as well: from Labov's (1969) well-known analysis it is expected that phonological factors will also play a role in copula variability. To this end Ho and Platt isolated seven preceding environments: I = '1st person sg. pronoun'; 3rd sg. = 'the pronouns *he* and *she*';[1] Pn = 'Pronouns except 1st and 3rd sg.'; Nom = 'nominal groups' (e.g. *my friends*; *some of them*); Wh = '*Wh*-words and conjunction *that*'; D = 'demonstratives'; Cl _ = 'after clauses'.

This time an implicational scale with scalability of 88.3 per cent showed the following hierarchy (for details see Ho and Platt 1993:51–3):

$$Pn < Nom < I < 3sg < Wh < D < Cl$$

VARBRUL analysis is particularly useful in showing the contribution of each factor group (educational level; preceding environment; following environment) to copula usage. In VARBRUL analysis (Rand and Sankoff 1990; Robinson, Lawrence and Tagliamonte 2001) a probability or weighting associated with each relevant factor is assigned, ranging from 0 to 1. A factor assigned a value greater than 0.5 favours the rule; a value less than 0.5 disfavours it. A factor value of 1.0 does not imply 100 per cent application of the rule when the factor is present; rather, it indicates that the factor favours application more than any other in its group. (The second analysis generated by VARBRUL is an input weighting or input probability which reflects the propensity of the rule to apply on its own, apart from other linguistic and social influences.)

According to Table 3.4 two preceding environments I_ and 3sg_ and two following environments, _Nom and _Loc exert considerable influence on the presence of *be*. In contrast the other preceding environments (Pn_ and Nom_) and following environments (_Adj and _V*ing*)

---

[1] The pronoun *it* was excluded as it was not possible to work out whether the almost categorical form *is* (for *it's*) was an instance of pronoun deletion or cluster simplification.

Table 3.4. *Contribution of each factor to the occurrence of 'be' in Singapore English (input = 1.00)*

Education level		Preceding environment		Following environment	
Tertiary	0.79	I_	0.63	_Adj	0.50
A-level	0.77	3sg_	0.68	_Ving	0.49
O-level	0.65	Pn_	0.48	_Nom	0.74
Sec 1–3	0.40	Nom_	0.54	_Loc	0.62
Primary	0.30				

have a lesser effect. The educational attainment of informants is important too, as the use of *be* increases with higher levels of education.

3.4 FROM DESCRIPTION TO THEORY: AN OPTIMALITY THEORY ACCOUNT OF NEW ENGLISH SYNTACTIC VARIATION

The intention of this section is to show how certain features outlined thus far can be studied fruitfully as a unified set, rather than in isolation. Since such work is relatively new in WE studies, we go into greater analytic detail than previously. The framework for analysis is Optimality Theory, which requires some knowledge of basic syntactic concepts of modern Linguistics (e.g. of phrase structure, indexing and movement). Readers without such a background should skip the details but may wish to pay attention to the general claims being made about how differences between varieties (e.g. New Englishes and standard British or US English) can be demonstrated to involve different rankings of certain constraints. As mentioned previously in Chapter 2, many New Englishes show at least two variant representations of a range of syntactic constructions such as inversion/non-inversion in direct and indirect questions, non-null/null subjects and objects (pro–drop), etc. For the purposes of analysis we focus on two varieties of Indian English – standard and colloquial/spoken. The first is spoken by educated speakers (Kachru 1983a:77) and accords to a large extent with standard British English syntax; the second is the more indigenous variety, showing greater distance from British English norms. We will show that the differences between the two varieties are accounted for in Optimality Theory (henceforth OT) – a conceptualization of grammar that is based on a general notion of priority of syntactic constraints on well-formedness. Under this view, *linguistic competence* refers to the knowledge of what constitutes an optimal linguistic expression within a structured range of plausible alternatives, and *grammar* refers to a means of determining which of any set of structural analyses of an input is the most well formed. (It is necessary to stress that 'optimal' and 'well formed' are descriptive, not prescriptive notions.) Furthermore, *knowledge of language* under this view consists of a universal set of candidate structural descriptions, a universal set of well-formedness constraints of these structural descriptions, and a language-particular ranking of these constraints from strongest to weakest. In other words, grammars are assumed to contain ranked constraints – arranged in a strict domination hierarchy – on the well-formedness of linguistic structure. This optimality-theoretic conceptualisation (Prince and Smolensky 2004; Grimshaw 1997) captures the following linguistically significant generalisations of the syntactic behaviour of the two varieties of Indian English: (a) the spoken/colloquial variety is just as systematic and logical as the standard variety; (b) the grammars of both varieties are constrained by the same set of grammatical constraints; and (c) the differences in the two varieties is a function of how each grammar prioritises these constraints. Accordingly, the grammatical differences between the two varieties of Indian English follow as a natural consequence of the architecture of Optimality Theory: educated speakers of Indian English have alternative constraint-rankings (different grammars of Indian English) available to them.

3.4.1 Direct and indirect questions

In Standard Indian English, direct (root) questions are formed by moving the *wh*-phrase to the left-edge of the clause (Spec-CP) followed by the auxiliary verb (in Comp), in those questions where the *wh*-phrase is not a subject. Some examples are given in (79–82) below [Note: '*t*' is the original position from which the *wh*-phrase (t_i) and the auxiliary verb (t_j) move in interrogative constructions. The subscripts show the proper indexing.]

79. What$_i$ has$_j$ he t_j eaten t_i?
80. Where$_i$ has$_j$ he t_j gone t_i now?
81. [How long ago]$_i$ was$_j$ that t_j t_i?
82. When$_i$ are$_j$ you t_j coming home t_i?

Embedded indirect questions in Standard Indian English (hereafter, Std Ind Eng) also involve movement of the *wh*-phrase to the left-periphery (Spec-CP) of the embedded clause, without, however, any auxiliary verb following it (in Comp). Some examples are given in (83–86) below:

83. They know who$_i$ Vijay has invited t$_i$ tonight.
84. I wonder where$_i$ he works t$_i$.
85. I asked him what$_i$ he ate t$_i$for breakfast.
86. Do you know where$_i$ he is going t$_i$?

The well-known empirical generalisation about data such as (79–82) and (83–86) is that the rule of subject–auxiliary inversion is restricted to matrix sentences; it does not apply in embedded contexts. This rule is in fact common in other New Englishes too (see section 3.2.1).

In colloquial/informally spoken Indian English, on the other hand, direct questions are also formed by moving the *wh*-phrase to the left-periphery (Spec-CP) of the clause. However, there is no auxiliary (in Comp) following the left-moved *wh*-phrase. Some illustrative examples are given in (87–90) below:

87. What$_i$ he has eaten t$_i$?
88. Where$_i$ he has gone t$_i$ now?
89. [How long ago]$_i$ that was t$_i$?
90. When$_i$ you are coming home t$_i$?

Embedded (indirect) questions in colloquial Indian English (hereafter, colloq Ind Eng) involve *wh*-movement to the left-periphery (Spec-CP) of the embedded clause. The *wh*-phrase, surprisingly, is followed by the auxiliary verb, i.e., *wh*-movement in embedded contexts is accompanied by auxiliary verb movement (inversion) to, presumably, Comp. The relevant data are given in (91–94) below:

91. They know who$_i$ has$_j$ Vijay t$_j$ invited t$_i$ tonight.
92. I wonder where$_i$ does he work t$_i$.
93. I asked Ramesh what$_i$ did he eat t$_i$for breakfast.
94. Do you know where$_i$ is$_i$ he t$_j$going t$_i$?

It emerges from the data in (87–90) and (91–94) that in colloq Ind Eng, inversion is restricted to embedded questions; it does not apply in matrix questions. The generalisation of question-formation strategy in colloquial Indian English is the mirror opposite of the generalisation of question-formation strategy in Std Ind Eng where inversion is restricted to matrix contexts; it does not apply in embedded questions.

Furthermore, notice that the un-inverted direct questions in colloq Ind Eng discussed above, see data in (87–90), seem to behave syntactically as topicalised constructions in English, shown below in (95–98).

95. Those people$_i$, I telephoned t$_i$yesterday.
96. This coat$_i$, I will stitch t$_i$in one day.
97. All of these languages$_i$, we speak t$_i$at home.

98. His parents$_i$, she has never met t$_i$.

Taken together, the data in (87–90) and (95–98) when contrasted with the data in (87–90) present a linguistically significant generalisation: *wh*-phrases followed by an auxiliary verb (data in 87–90) yield the inversion structure – standard variety of Indian English – given in (99) below, whereas *wh*-phrases that do not have an auxiliary verb immediately following it (data in 87–90) yield the adjunction structure – colloquial variety of Indian English – given in (100) below.

99. Inversion structure

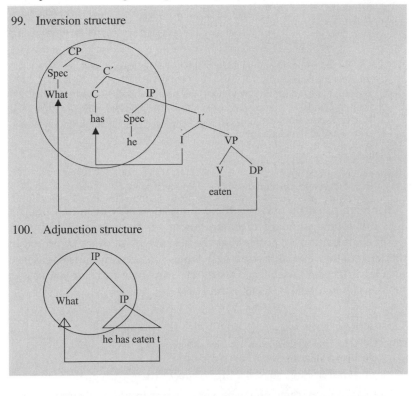

100. Adjunction structure

3.4.2 Pro-drop

The phenomenon of pro-drop has been extensively researched in the generative literature (cf. Chomsky 1981; Huang 1984; Jaeggli and Safir 1989). The generalisation is that in pro-drop languages, like Spanish and Italian, a pronoun is allowed to drop only if its reference can be recovered from the agreement marking on the finite verb. The agreement marking in pro-drop languages is presumably 'rich' enough to recover important aspects (person, number and/or gender) of the reference of the missing subject and/or object. In English, because the agreement marking is too meagre to sufficiently determine the reference of the missing subject, pro-drop is prohibited.

With respect to argument pro-drop, Std Ind Eng works like other regional standard British and American varieties: Finite clauses without subjects are disallowed, as shown in (101) and (102) below:[2]

101. *pro likes bananas.
102. *He said that pro would come tomorrow.

In colloq Ind Eng, as well as other New Englishes (see section 2.3.5) used in informal contexts, the pronoun is optionally dropped both in subject and object positions, as shown in (103–106).

103. I really wanted to read your book. Girish got pro from somewhere but he wont let me borrow pro.
104. A: He played cricket all day today – and now pro does not want to work on his homework!
     B: Our Sanjay does that too: pro plays all day long, and then pro just comes in and demands food.
105. A: Is he in his office?
     B: Sorry, pro left just now only.
106. A: You got tickets?
     B: No, pro sold pro already.

Although pro-drop usage in the colloquial variety of Indian English does not follow standard explanations of syntactic recoverability, on closer examination we notice that the absence of an overt argument in this variety becomes an option only when that argument is coindexed with an antecedent with topic status (cf. Grimshaw and Samek-Lodovici 1995), as shown below in (107) and (108).

107. A: Is he in his office?
     B: Sorry, pro left just now only.
108. A: Gautam was there with his wife shopping.
     B: Doesn't his wife work now somewhere?
     A: Yes, pro teaches at a school here locally.

The data above show that the subject argument is dropped when it has an antecedent with topic status. The generalisation, then, for pro-drop in colloquial English used in informal contexts is that pro-drop is restricted to those arguments (subject/objects) that are topic-connected.

---

[2] Cote (1996) and Mufwene (1988), among others, discuss several instances in casual speech style of (American) English where subject pro-drop is possible, e.g. *Just stopped by to say hello!, Works every time*. For an exhaustive discussion of pro-drop in conversational spoken English, see Cote (1996).

Before presenting a formal account of the syntactic variation in Indian English with respect to question formation and pro-drop, a short description of the theoretical model is presented to show how the generalisations of Indian English syntax can be theoretically encoded.

3.4.3 Optimality Theory: a description

Optimality Theory departs from the traditional frameworks in its specific proposal about the source of variation, as will become clear in a moment. Specifically, OT is about how grammars are defined by constraint hierarchies (McCarthy 1995). Universal Grammar in OT is expected to provide a finite set of potentially conflicting (violable) constraints on structural well-formedness. Languages differ from each other in terms of how each ranks the set of violable constraints. Thus, in essence, different configurations of constraint ranking yield, in principle, different grammars, as shown schematically in (109). If so, it follows that minimally different constraint-rankings will give rise to dialect variation, theoretically. Adopting OT thus provides a mechanism to account faithfully for the subtle grammatical differences between standard and colloquial varieties of Indian English.

Instead of using inviolable constraints (as in Chomsky 1981), OT uses 'violable' (soft) constraints to express empirical generalisations. These soft constraints are violable in just those contexts in which they conflict with a higher-ranked constraint. The core ideas of OT can be summed up in the following way: constraints can be violated; constraints are ranked; and the optimal form is grammatical (Grimshaw 1997).

109. Universal grammar and language variation

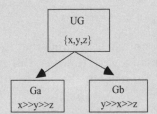

[where x, y, and z are universal constraints; UG is the Universal Grammar, Ga and Gb are grammars of two different languages (or dialects)]

The relationship between input and output in an OT-grammar is mediated by two formal mechanisms, GEN and EVAL (see Archangeli and Langendoen 1997). GEN (for Generator) uses the X-bar theoretic assumptions to generate freely all possible candidate structural descriptions for a given input. EVAL (for Evaluator) uses the language's constraint hierarchy to choose the optimal candidate. This is illustrated in (110) below. The output that has the least serious violations (= 0, in the best case scenario) is optimal, i.e. grammatical.

110. OT Grammar:

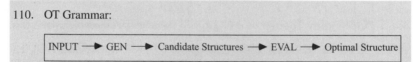

INPUT ⟶ GEN ⟶ Candidate Structures ⟶ EVAL ⟶ Optimal Structure

Let's look at an illustration of how OT accounts for language variation (cf. also Anttila 1995): Consider two grammars, Grammar A and Grammar B, both of which have three constraints {x, y, z}. Assume further, that in Grammar A these constraints are ranked in such a way that {x} dominates {y} which in turn dominates {z} [= x >> y, y >> z, x >> z]. In other words, Grammar A imposes a total order on the constraints: x >> y >> z. Now, assume that for a certain input we get two competing output candidates: *cand 1* and *cand 2*. The notation [*] in a tableau simply indicates that a candidate has violated a constraint whereas [*!] indicates that the particular violation is serious enough to disqualify that candidate from being considered optimal. Tableau 1 shows the competition between the two candidates. *Cand 1* violates the highest-ranking constraint {x}, which is lethal, indicated by '*!'. Grammar A, therefore, chooses *cand 2* straightforwardly as the optimal, grammatical, option, indicated by '⇒'.[3]

Tableau 1: output = *cand₂*:

Candidates		x	y	z
a.	*cand₁*	*!		*
b. ⇒	*cand₂*		*	*

Now consider the other grammar, Grammar B. Assume that it, too, has the same three (universal) constraints {x, y, z}. However, this grammar imposes a slightly different ordering, namely, the constraint {y} dominates {x} which in turn dominates {z}. Now for the same input as in Grammar A, we get the same two candidate-competing outputs: *cand 1* and *cand 2*. The optimal output, as shown below in Tableau

---

[3] The shaded cells in a tableau indicate their non-use in the computation of optimality. In both tableaux 1 and 2, constraint 'z' is not used to decide the optimal candidate, and thus its violations do not matter in the choice of the optimal candidate. Its role is therefore de-emphasised by shading the cells below it.

2, is *cand 1*, because in this grammar *cand 2* violates a higher ranked constraint {y}, leading to its rejection as optimal.

Tableau 2: output = $cand_1$:

Candidates		x	y	z
a.	$\Rightarrow$ $cand_1$		*	*
b.	$cand_2$	*!		*

Using this theoretical conceptualisation, we present in the next section the set of potentially conflicting linguistic constraints and show how their interactions yield well-formed utterances in the two varieties of Indian English.

3.4.4 OT-analysis of syntactic variation

The constraints that are needed to present the difference between the two varieties of Indian English are given below in (111) (following Bhatt 2000). It is worth mentioning here that these constraints are not designed to account only for the analyses of Indian English but have been independently motivated in several studies in syntactic analyses within the framework of Optimality Theory.

111. Optimality constraints:
    (a) OP-SCOPE: Operators (e.g. *wh*-phrases) must take scope over the entire proposition (= c-command VP/IP at S-Structure).
    (b) OP-SPEC: Operators must be in Specifier position.
    (c) STAY: No movement (= trace) is allowed.
    (d) OB-HD: Heads of selected projections must be filled (either by trace or overt material).
    (e) SUBJECT: The canonical subject position (= highest A-Specifier in an 'extended projection' (Grimshaw 1991)) must be filled.
    (f) DROP TOP: Leave arguments co-referent with the topic structurally unrealised.
    (g) PARSE: Parse input items.

3.4.4.1 Matrix (direct) questions

For matrix questions, we need to explain the fact that the standard variety of Indian English allows subject–verb inversion whereas the colloquial variety does not. The constraints that need to be recruited to yield direct questions are: OP-SPEC and STAY. The interaction of these two constraints in the order given in (112) yields the categorical prediction of direct questions in Std Ind Eng: the *wh*-phrase in specifier position of CP is followed by an aux in Comp.

112. Std Ind Eng: OP-SPEC >> STAY

The tableau in (113) shows a competition between two candidates, an adjunction structure and an inversion structure (recall the discussion in section 3.4.1 with respect to (99) and (100)). Both candidates violate the low-ranking constraint STAY; however, the inversion candidate structure gets two asterisks for violating STAY twice: once when the *wh*-phrase moves to the specifier position of CP and once when the modal auxiliary moves from Infl to Comp. However, STAY remains inactive on the candidate set since the adjunction structure violates OP-SPEC, a higher ranked constraint, while the inversion structure does not. The grammar of Std Ind Eng therefore chooses inversion over adjunction as more harmonic, optimal.

113. Tableau: Std Ind Eng

Candidates	OP-SPEC	STAY
adjunction [$_{IP}$What [$_{IP}$you would like to eat *t*]	*!	*
inversion ⇒ [$_{CP}$What would [$_{IP}$ you *t* like to eat *t*]]		**

Turning to the colloquial variety, recall that direct questions in colloq Ind Eng involve an adjunction structure (cf. 100 above); the *wh*-phrase adjoins to IP-Spec instead of moving to CP-Spec as it does in Std Ind Eng. It turns out that both OP-SPEC and STAY yield the adjunction structure too, albeit with a different ranking. The colloq Ind Eng grammar ranks STAY over OP-SPEC (as in (114)), which gives the desired results in (115).

114. Colloq Ind Eng: STAY >> OP-SPEC

115. Tableau: colloq Ind Eng

Candidates	STAY	OP-SPEC
adjunction ⇒ [$_{IP}$ What [$_{IP}$you would like to eat *t*]	*	*
inversion [$_{CP}$ What would [$_{IP}$ you *t* like to eat *t*]]	**!	

The tableau in (115) shows two competing candidates, both violating the highest-ranking constraint STAY. Notice, however, that the inversion structure incurs two violations of STAY – one by moving the *wh*-phrase and the other by moving the Infl/Aux to Comp – as opposed to only one violation of STAY, moving the *wh*-phrase in the adjunction structure. In this competition, inversion loses because it incurs more violations (of STAY) than adjunction.

The difference between the grammars of Std Ind Eng and colloq Ind Eng, with respect to direct question formation, reduces to different rankings of the same constraints, which is expected in OT.

3.4.4.2 Embedded (indirect) questions

The generalisation about indirect questions is as follows: Std Ind Eng does not permit inversion in indirect questions (= Non-inversion) whereas colloq Ind Eng allows inversion in indirect questions (= Inversion). This grammatical distribution of inversion in the two varieties of English under consideration can be accounted for by the interaction of three constraints, two previously recruited to account for direct questions, namely, OP-SPEC and STAY, and a new one, namely, OB-HD.

Consider first Std Ind Eng. Since Std Ind Eng does not permit inversion in indirect questions, OB-HD must have a lower prominence vis-à-vis OP-SPEC and STAY. We have already established that the grammar of Std Ind Eng ranks OP-SPEC over STAY (112, above); the relevant ranking is given in (116).

The tableau in (117) shows two competing candidates, both deferential to OP-SPEC. Since OP-SPEC cannot distinguish between the two candidates, the evaluation is passed on to the next important constraint, STAY. Again both violate STAY, but it is the inversion structure that incurs two violations of STAY as opposed to the non-inversion structure which violates STAY only once. In this competition, then, non-inverted structure is harmonic, and wins.

116. Std Ind Eng: OP-SPEC >> STAY >> OB-HD

117. Tableau: Std Ind Eng

Candidates	OP-SPEC	STAY	OB-HD
no-inversion ⇒ I wonder [cp what *e* he is eating *t*]		*	*
inversion I wonder [cp what is he *t* eating *t*]		**!	*

Turning to indirect questions in colloq Ind Eng, recall that these require inversion with *wh*-movement, i.e. the fact that the *wh*-phrase is followed by a head suggests that the movement of the *wh*-phrase is to a specifier position. The inversion facts in indirect questions in colloq

Ind Eng follow straightforwardly from a constraint hierarchy where OB-HD outranks STAY and OP-SPEC, as shown in (118).

Once again, the tableau in (119) shows two competing candidates. The optimal output, given the dominance hierarchy in (118), is the inverted structure because the non-inverted structure violates OB-HD.

118. Colloq Ind Eng: OB-HD >> STAY >> OP-SPEC

119. Tableau: colloq Ind Eng

Candidates	OB-HD	STAY	OP-SPEC
no-inversion I wonder [_CP_ what _e_ he is eating _t_]	*!	*	
inversion ⇒ I wonder [_CP_ what is he _t_ eating _t_]		**!	

With respect to indirect question formation, the difference between the grammars of Std Ind Eng and colloq Ind Eng reduces, again, to different rankings of the same constraints, which is only expected given that OT appeals to variation in ranking to provide different grammars.

3.4.4.3 Pro-drop

As cited above, Std Ind Eng, like other standard varieties of English, does not permit pro-drop. Colloq Ind Eng, on the other hand, allows pro-drop but it is restricted to those arguments (subject/objects) that are topic-connected. These different patterns of generalisation can be expressed by letting three constraints – PARSE, DROP TOPIC and SUBJECT – interact in different ways. Since Std Ind Eng does not permit argument pro-dropping, it must be the case that PARSE (an argument) and SUBJECT are ranked higher in priority than DROP TOPIC. The non-pro-drop phenomenon in Std Ind Eng follows from the dominance configuration given in (120).

As shown in tableau (121), candidate (b), which satisfies PARSE and SUBJECT is preferred over both candidate (a), which violates PARSE, and candidate (b), which violates SUBJECT. Thus the ranking PARSE above SUBJECT above DROP TOPIC yields the non-pro-drop generalisation in Std Ind Eng.

120. Std Ind Eng: PARSE >> SUBJECT >> DROP TOPIC

121. Tableau: Std Ind Eng

Candidates		PARSE	SUBJECT	DROP TOPIC
(a)	left just now only	*!	*	
(b) ⇒	he left just now only			*
(c)	left just now only he		*!	*

Turning to pro-drop in colloq Ind Eng, we find evidence of a different ranking of the three constraints. Earlier, in section 3.4.2, we provided evidence that the grammar of colloq Ind Eng does not require an overt subject (or object) when it is topic-connected, which means that the constraint DROP-TOPIC must dominate PARSE and SUBJECT. In fact, the ranking configuration in (122) gets us the desired results. In tableau (123), we find that candidate (a) is the harmonic choice since the other two candidates incur violations of the highest-ranked constraint, DROP-TOPIC.

122. Colloq Ind Eng: DROP TOPIC >> PARSE >> SUBJECT

123. Tableau: colloq Ind Eng

Candidates		DROP TOPIC	PARSE	SUBJECT
(a) ⇒	left just now only		*	*
(b)	he left just now only	*!		
(c)	left just now only he	*!		*

With respect to the phenomenon of pro-drop, the difference between the grammars of Std Ind Eng and colloq Ind Eng is reducible to different rankings of the same constraints.

To sum up, the differences between the observed patterns of generalisation in the standard and colloquial varieties of Indian English are best accounted for in a conceptualisation of grammar that is based on a general notion of priority of constraints. The grammatical constraints that govern the syntactic behaviour of the colloquial variety of Indian English spoken informally are *not* unique to it. Rather, the difference between the grammars of the two varieties of Indian English is reducible to different rankings of the same constraints, which is only expected given that OT appeals to variation in ranking to provide different grammars. It is anticipated that other sets of New English features outlined in Chapter 2 can be better understood in this way. This is very much a desideratum for future research.

3.5 CONCLUSION

This chapter has focused on cross-clausal syntax in New Englishes, again showing a high degree of structural similarity between the varieties, in respect of certain constructions. However, there is also evidence of a broad dichotomy between varieties that favour deletion (Sgp Eng being a prime example) and those that favour the retention of potentially deletable elements (African varieties of English being the best exemplars). The second half of the chapter demonstrated ways of analysing individual features in greater detail. The use of an implicational scale together with appropriate statistical techniques reveals social and structural patterning within a New English. Optimality Theory reveals the differential ranking of linguistic constraints in particular varieties.

STUDY QUESTIONS

1. Define the term resumptive pronoun, and give an example. Discuss with an example how a resumptive pronoun is different from an appositional pronoun. Give a possible New English sentence with a resumptive as well as an appositional pronoun.
2. Review the difference between answers to 'yes/no' questions in African and South Asian varieties of English on the one hand and Std Eng on the other. Do you find the pragmatic or syntactic account of this difference more compelling?
3. What are the general characteristics of tag questions in New Englishes?
4. What is an implicational scale, and how does it help to account for variation in a New English variety?
5. Explain broadly the potential of Optimality Theory to account for variation in a New English variety.

Further reading

All works mentioned here are fully referenced in the bibliography.

On the use of implicational scales and VARBRUL for Singapore English, see Ho and Platt *The Dynamics of a Contact Continuum* (1993). A good introduction to Optimality Theory is the volume edited by Dianna Archangeli and D. Terence Langendoen *Optimality Theory: An Overview* (1997), and Alan Prince and Paul Smolensky's text *Optimality Theory: Constraint Interaction in Generative Grammar* (2004).

4 More on structure: lexis and phonology

In this chapter we continue to provide an overview of characteristics of New Englishes, chiefly in the realm of lexis and phonetics and phonology.

4.1 THE VOCABULARY OF NEW ENGLISHES

This section provides a brief overview of the characteristic lexis of New Englishes, chiefly in Africa and Asia. In a sense there is little difference between vocabulary generation in individual New Englishes and metropolitan Englishes: the same processes that create new lexical items in the latter are reported in New Englishes. The interest lies more in the details. Metropolitan Englishes have long been receptive to new lexis based on the colonial experiences of the English abroad. Terms like the following now pass as international English, rather than that of a specific colonial variety:

> *bandanna* 'large coloured handkerchief or neckerchief' (from Hindi)
>
> *amok* 'rushing in a frenzy' (from Malay)
>
> *tsetse* 'bloodsucking fly which transmits sleeping sickness' (from Tswana)
>
> *zombie* 'corpse revived by witchcraft' (from Kimbunda)
>
> *safari* 'expedition to hunt or observe animals' (from Arabic via Swahili)
>
> *serendipity* 'lucky and happy outcome' (based on the Persian fairy-tale of the *Three Princes of Serendip,* an old Middle Eastern name for Sri Lanka)

The above examples count as borrowings and reflect a process of acquiring new knowledge or artefacts from other cultures. By contrast, the words to be characterised in this section are not as widely known. Some of them are specific to a particular country or region (e.g. *akara* 'beancake' in West Africa), or used in several territories without being fully international (e.g. *peon* 'a messenger' – in Ind Eng, Pak Eng, Sgp Eng and Mal Eng, based on a Portuguese term that stabilised in India). Furthermore, the term 'borrowing' for these terms is not entirely appropriate, since speakers have not been adopting a new word or acquiring a new concept. These items are therefore better characterised as 'retentions' from the ancestral languages of a territory.

Not surprisingly, vocabulary retentions in New Englishes tend to cluster in semantic fields pertaining to local customs and culture, including terms for food, clothing, music and dance. A selection of terms from different varieties is given below.

Food terms:

> *akara* 'bean cake' (Nig Eng)
> *koka sakora* 'porridge without milk' (Ghan Eng; from Akan and Hausa respectively)
> *ugali* 'staple maize food' (EAf Eng of Kenya and Tanzania)
> *posho* 'staple maize food' (EAf Eng of Uganda)
> *umqombothi* 'thick home-brewed beer' (BlSAf Eng)
> *paneer* 'cottage cheese pressed into small blocks' (Ind and Pak Eng)
> *makan* 'food' (Sgp and Mal Eng)
> *haleem* 'thick broth of meat and lentils or wheat' (Pak and Ind Eng)

Clothing:

> *akwete* 'a type of cloth' (Nig Eng)
> *mitumba* 'second-hand clothes' (EAf Eng)
> *shalwar kameez* 'baggy pants and long shirt' (Ind and Pak Eng)

Traditional medicine, music, customs etc:

> *adowa* 'Akan dance' (Ghan Eng)
> *Asaman* 'land of the dead' (Ghan Eng, from Akan)
> *marimba* 'African xylophone' (BlSAf Eng and Zimbabwean Eng)
> *bomoh* 'medicine man' (Mal Eng)
> *mela* 'fair, festival' (Ind Eng)

Political terms:

> *uhuru* 'freedom, independence' (EAf Eng)
> *nyayo* 'following in footsteps of a great leader' (EAfr Eng, especially of Kenya)[1]

---

[1] More especially, ex-president Arap Moi's following in the 'footsteps' of Jomo Kenyatta in Kenya.

ujamaa 'familyhood, African socialism' (EAf Eng, especially of Tanzania)

lekotla 'assembly of people from a village or (now) a political meeting, especially of Black groups' (BlSAf Eng)

swaraj 'self rule, independence' (Ind Eng)

bumiputra 'son of the soil, patriot' (Mal Eng)

Sometimes entire registers retain key terms from the local languages. Our first example is from the 'matrimonials' section of the *Hindustan Times* (Dec. 2003) in which families place advertisements calling for prospective brides or grooms:

Alliance invited
from Handsome boy of high status, educated business class, Delhi based family for **27 yrs, 5 ft 3 inches Slim, Wheatish, Beautiful, Non Manglik Graduate girl, well established dress designer, running her own boutique** (Wishes to continue even after marriage). Belong to respected business family [xxx] residing in Delhi. Correspond with photograph & Horoscope.

Caste No Bar
To Box no. [xxxx]
Hindustan Times
New Delhi – 110 001

[Glosses: *wheatish* 'colour of wheat, i.e. light brown rather than very dark or very fair in complexion'; *non-manglik* 'not having Mars in the relevant part of one's horoscope'; *boy* 'young man'; *caste no bar* 'caste considerations are not relevant'.][2]

The second example, taken from Kachru (1982c:362), concerns stock exchange reporting of grain prices in Ind Eng:

Urad and moong fell sharply in the grain market here today on stockists' offerings. Rice, jowar and arhar also followed suit, but barley forged ahead. (*Times of India* 23 July 1977)

[Glosses: *urad* 'black split lentils'; *moong* 'small green lentils'; *jowar* 'millet'; *arhar* 'pale green/red lentils']

The third example is from a newspaper article from Pakistan, illustrating the use of weights, measures and terms for intoxicants (Baumgardner and Kennedy 1994:184):

He said that Gujarat police recovered five maunds of charas, one kg heroin, 131 bottles of liquor, two maunds of lehan and raided

---

[2] Certain details have been omitted to ensure confidentiality.

distilleries from where five drunkards were arrested. (*The News*, Lahore, 10 Aug. 1991).

[Glosses: *maund* 'c37 kg'; *charas* 'hemp'; *lehan* 'raw materials for making liquor']

In order to work out the exact value of a *maund* the following information extracted from Baumgardner and Kennedy's (1994) article 'Measure for Measure' is necessary:

Units of measurement in Pak Eng:

ruttee/ratti	'a bean'
masha/masa	'a bean' (= *8 ruttee*)
tola	12 *masha*
chattank	5 *tola*
pao	4 *chattank*
seer	4 *pao*
dhari	5 *seer*
maund	8 *dhari* (= 37,3242 kg)

[Note: *ruttee* is used by goldsmiths; *tola* is used for spices and foods; *maund* for these as well as drugs, flour, wheat, red chilli and cotton. *Maundage* is a term for weight of such objects.]

Likewise, the numerals *lakh* '100 000' and *crore* '10 million' are extremely common in Pak and Ind Eng, forming an essential part of the numeral system. We now turn to new coinages whose roots come from English, but which are used in ways that are structurally, semantically or historically worthy of note. We repeat that these processes are not unique to New Englishes, but are rather commonly reported in the history of language change, even where contact is not involved. In terms of semantics, some words show a wider range of meanings than Std Eng. Thus kinship terms like *father* in sub-Saharan Africa take their meaning from the extended family system and refer to one's biological father, as well as his brothers. Similarly *mother* may refer to one's biological mother and her sisters. *Brother* may be extended to refer in some African societies to one's male cousins, or to males from the same village as oneself. In both Africa and Asia the terms *cousin-brother* and *cousin-sister* are in common use, for which Nihalani, Tongue and Hosali (2004:58) give the following explanation:

> Since the word 'cousin' does not contain a sex-denoting marker, where sex is important, it has to be indicated (rather awkwardly) in [Std Eng] by a phrase like 'female cousin'. Most languages in India indicate sex in the word itself, and 'cousin-brother' is an attempt to do this in Eng.

This might not be the only motivation, and the semantics of *cousin-brother* and *cousin-sister* bear further investigation, in different territories. In traditional Zulu culture of South Africa *umfowethu* referred to one's male siblings from one's 'father' (in the broad sense identified above, i.e. one's father's brother's sons as well); while *umzala* referred to a cross cousin (i.e. children of one's father's sister or mother's brother). The latter also refers to offspring of one's mother's sister. This culture-bound distinction may well underlie the distinction between *brother* and *cousin-brother* in Zulu speakers' English. Thus one's father's sons (in the broad sense of *father*) are one's *brothers*; by contrast one's father's sister's and mother's sibling's sons are one's *cousin-brothers*. However, not all speakers make this conceptual distinction; some Zulu speakers follow a pattern similar to that of Ind Eng, where *cousin-brother* refers to any male cousin.

Kinship semantics of New Englishes can be even more intricate than this. Ind Eng has terms like a *co-brother* for 'one's wife's sister's husband', and *co-daughters-in-law*, which is how women married to brothers sometimes refer to their relationship. In IndSAf Eng terms like *cousin brother-in-law* occur, though infrequently: the speaker was referring to the man who had married his *cousin-sister*.

In many varieties of African and Asian Eng *aunty* and *uncle* may be used to denote respect for an elder person, rather than a blood relationship. Where a blood relationship is involved speakers are more likely to retain the term from their local language, in addressing them. In referring to relatives in English still other neologisms might occur, such as *big mother* for 'mother's elder sister', *big father* for 'father's elder brother', etc. Such direct translations from another language are called calques or loan translations.

Staying with the concept of semantic widening, a pan-African example is the epithet *sorry*, which denotes general sympathy for another's misfortune, rather than an admission of culpability. Huber and Dako (2004:863) give the example from Ghan Eng of a tour guide saying *I'm sorry to tell you that the slaves were kept in a dungeon*, even though the misfortune applies to a third party, rather than speaker or addressee.

The opposite, restriction of meaning, is less common. In IndSAf Eng *raw* has narrowed from 'inexperienced, crude' to just 'crude, vulgar'; and *fowl* for older speakers refers to a domestic hen, rather than a generic category. Semantic shift in New Englishes often involves a subtle change of meaning compared to Std Eng, though the standard meaning may also be retained. A *hotel* in East Africa and parts of India may refer to a public place to eat, rather than necessarily a place to stay. There is no clash between the Std Eng meaning and the local meaning, since the context clarifies which meaning is relevant. These meanings may be depicted in terms of semantic features as follows:[3]

$$
hotel_1 \quad\quad\quad\quad hotel_2
$$

$$
\begin{bmatrix} + \text{local} \\ + \text{eating house} \\ +/ - \text{ place to stay} \end{bmatrix}
\quad\quad
\begin{bmatrix} - \text{local} \\ +/ - \text{ eating house} \\ + \text{place to stay} \end{bmatrix}
$$

Similar semantic shifts occur with words like *travel* 'to be away' (in Nig Eng; Bamgbose 1992a:152) and *stranger* 'guest' (in Sierra Leone Eng; Pemagbi 1989, cited by Gramley 2001:142).

Sometimes cultural restraints result in euphemisms such as the following: *late* (predicative and attributive adj.) 'deceased' (*My aunt is late*) in varieties of African and Asian English; *teasing* 'harassing a girl' (Ind and Pak Eng); and *interfere* 'to molest' (IndSAf Eng). Cultural traditions result in neologisms like *veg* versus *non-veg* in Ind Eng, with a reversal of markedness: vegetarian food is the unmarked norm; and *non-veg* (i.e. 'meat') the marked term.

Other characteristics of New Englishes pertain to stylistic choices. Several researchers have noted that New Englishes tend to use what count as formal terms of Std Eng where an L1 speaker might opt for a colloquial equivalent. For example Kachru (1983a:39) characterises Ind Eng as 'bookish' even in informal usage (1983:39), citing Goffin's (1934) examples of *demise* for 'death' and *pain in one's bosom* for 'pain in one's chest'. We may term this 'register shift', which clearly reflects the influence of written norms upon speech. Baskaran provides examples from Mal Eng like *furnish* where L1 speakers would prefer *provide* or *send*; or *witness* for *see*. It is not necessarily the case that New Englishes are being more formal when they use such terms; they appear so only to outsiders expecting metropolitan norms. Goffin (1934), cited by Kachru (1983a:39), notes a further tendency in Ind Eng towards polite diction and a moralistic tone. R. M. W. Dixon (personal communication, cited by Das Gupta 1986:740) observed that Ind Eng used the Romance verbs *inform*, *request* and *require* where native speakers use their Anglo-Saxon equivalents *tell*, *ask* and *need*. However, Ind Eng gives the Romance verbs many of the syntactic properties of the Anglo-Saxon equivalents: *Please inform him to come*; *Do you require to read this now?* Not all New Englishes have these characteristics; by contrast IndSAf Eng and Sgp Eng sound

---

[3] The feature [local] here refers to whether the establishment is typically frequented by locals or tourists. In semantic feature theory a feature with +/− is technically omitted from a feature list. However, it has been retained here, for clarity of presentation of the difference in meaning.

hyper-colloquial, even in contexts demanding a measure of formalese (see Mesthrie 1992a: 22).

Closely related to the seemingly bookish property of some Englishes is the preservation of forms that have become archaisms in metropolitan Englishes. This characterisation also views things from the perspectives of the metropolis: objectively speaking, it is the metropolitan varieties that have innovated, whilst the New English may have done nothing remarkable. Some of the 'bookish' examples cited above (*demise* and *bosom*) also fall under this category of archaism. Several examples are given in Nihalani, Tongue and Hosali (2004) like *abode* for 'home', *abscond* for 'flee, be missing', *furlong* (an eighth of a mile, now restricted to horse-racing in British Eng). Genuine archaisms (not involving register shift) include *stepney* in Ind Eng for a spare wheel (the term possibly originates from a street name in Glamorgan, Wales – OED) and *bogie* for a railway coach or carriage (now unknown in the UK, except as a technical railway term). Likewise the colonial term *station* for a soldiers' or civilians' outpost refers to a place of work, even a city or town in Ind Eng (Nihalani, Tongue and Hosali 2004) and WAf Eng (Gramley 2001:135). The term *tavern* persists in BlSAf Eng for 'a licensed informal drinking place', whereas the word is slightly archaic in L1 Englishes, including other South African varieties. McCormick (2004:1003) notes that *thrice* occurs as a colloquial term in CFl Eng, not restricted to literary texts or folk-tales as in Std Eng.

However, as living rather than fossilised systems, New Englishes generate new colloquialisms too. Neologisms in New Englishes can be very expressive: *bottom power* 'undue influence of females using sex' (Alo and Mesthrie 2004:826) and *not on seat* 'not available in one's office' (Bamgbose 1971:44) are both from Nig Eng. In Mal Eng the adjective *accidented* describes damage undergone by a car in an accident. The pun between *dent* and *accident* is probably unintended.[4] Numbers can used in a humorous or cryptic sense:

> *number 10* 'a person with a police record' – i.e. referring to section 110 of Criminal Code procedure (Ind Eng; Hankin 1994).
> *item 13* 'refreshment' – i.e. an item not on a business agenda (Ghan Eng; Huber 2004:864)
> *four twenty* 'a cheat, swindler' (Sgp Eng; Pride 1982:160–2)
> *26* 'member of hardened prison gang' (BlSAf Eng and CFl Eng).

Some neologisms pertain to time:

---

[4] These are from two different sources: *dent* is of Germanic orgins (from *dint* 'blow'), *accident* from Romance sources (the Latin root *cado-* 'to fall').

next tomorrow 'day after tomorrow' (Nig Eng, calqued on Yoruba idiom)

last two weeks 'two weeks' ago' (Ghan Eng; Huber and Dako 2004:865)

last of last week/month/year 'the week/month/year before last' (BlSAf Eng)

next two weeks 'in two weeks' time' (Ghan Eng; Huber and Dako 2004:865)

next of next week/month/year 'the week/month/year after next' (BlSAf Eng)

last before week 'the week before last' (IndSAf Eng)

Alo and Mesthrie (2004:825) provide colloquial euphemisms from the semantic field of bribery and corruption in Nig Eng:

X can deliver 'fix/ rig an election'
X understands 'is ready to offer a bribe'
an arrangement 'preferential treatment/ special arrangement'
to add sugar to the tea 'to offer a bribe'

We do not mean to suggest that Nig Eng alone is prone to such anti-language: *tea* in fact is a widely known euphemism in East Africa; and all languages have their underworld euphemisms. Finally idioms and proverbs can express local wisdom:

a crocodile in a loin cloth 'a hypocrite' (Ind Eng; Kachru 1983a:39)
to want mutton curry and rice everyday 'to have unrealistic expectations' (IndSAf Eng)
to take in 'to become pregnant' (Nig Eng; Bamgbose 1992a:156)

Manfred Görlach (1995) coined the term 'heteronym' for words pertaining to the same (or very similar) concepts in different territories in which a language is spoken. His primary interest was in the L1 varieties, with the primary division being between the UK and USA (*petrol* vs *gasoline*, etc.), and some interesting vacillation between other territories. For New Englishes research has still to be conducted on the status of heteronyms; whether, e.g., *truck* and *lorry* coexist (as they do in South Africa, because of British colonialism and subsequent American global influence). We note that in Ind Eng the preferred term is *mobile phone* (as in the UK), but New Englishes in South Africa (and L1 Eng there) favour the US-based term *cellphone*. The neologism *handy* occurs in Germany.

Finally, the grammatical form of lexical items has been commented on by many researchers. Reduplication has been noted as a common feature of Asian and African varieties of English, on account of substrate tendencies. However, their functions are not identical in all varieties. Bokamba (1992:138–40) notes a common tendency in sub-Saharan African Eng to reduplicate adjectives to form adverbs: *quick-quick* 'quickly'; *small-small* 'in small doses'; *slow-slow* 'slowly'. In Ghan Eng an adjective may be reduplicated to form a noun, as in *red-red* for 'fried plantains and bean stew' (Huber and Dako 2004:864). In Ind Eng, Kachru notes examples like *different-different things* and *one-one piece*. The semantics here is distributive, with a stylistic nuance of emphasis. Another type of reduplication applies to participles in Ind Eng, with the reduplicated participle standing for a whole clause, with the semantics [+ reason] and [+ excessive]. Thus *Walking-walking we got tired* 'We got tired on account of walking too much.' As outlined in Chapter 2, Mesthrie notes a constraint in IndSAf Eng for reduplicated adjectives, which do not occur with singular count nouns (apart from the distributive *one-one*). Thus *I bought big-big apples*, but not **I bought one big-big apple*. This contrasts with the L1 English 'comma intonation' associated with forms like *It's been a long, long day*. The constraint does not apply in Sgp Eng, as is clear from Wong's (2004) careful description of reduplication of nominal modifiers (chiefly adjectives and numerals). His examples frequently show the collocation of reduplicated adjectives with the sg. noun *one*, as in *the quiet quiet one* ('the very quiet person'), as well as with plurals *funny funny things* ('things that are really funny'). Wong notes that in many of the examples the modifiers relate to visually striking or identifiable properties that speaker and addressee share as common knowledge. In other words there is a pragmatic (shared knowledge, salience) as well as semantic dimension (intensity, plurality, etc.) to this feature.

Kachru (1983a:202) cites another type of reduplication in Ind Eng, also known as the echo word construction, in which a lexical item (most commonly a noun) is repeated, with the first syllable changed. Thus *acting-vacting* denotes 'acting and suchlike' (e.g. acting, stage dancing and singing); *petrol-vetrol* denotes 'petrol and other fuels'. Echo-word reduplication is a common feature which cuts across the language families of India (see Emeneau 1956). Its absorption into Ind Eng shows the process of indigenisation (i.e. making English structurally more like an indigenous language).

Hybridisation is in fact a general theme in New English lexical studies. Many scholars have pointed to the frequency of loan blends. These involve a combination of morphemes from English and a local language: *goonda-tax* 'tax charged by criminals, extortion' (Ind Eng); *jollof-rice* 'West African risotto' (Ghan Eng; Huber and Dako 2004:864).

Sometimes the combination is redundant in the sense that the two morphemes mean the same thing or have a hyponymous relation in that the (local) first term is a subset of the second: *challan-ticket* 'travel ticket' (*challan* = 'ticket') in Pak Eng (Mahboob 2004:1055); *nobat drums* in Mal Eng (*nobat* = 'type of drum' – Baskaran 2004:1082); *juju music* 'a type of dance music' in Nig Eng (Bamgbose 1992a:156). Scotton (1976) calls this a strategy of neutrality: forms from two languages are juxtaposed as a way of accommodating both languages (and cultures), rather than favouring one of them (see further Appel and Muysken 1987:127–33).

The majority of hybrid forms exemplified in New English studies are compounds. Compounding as a process involving English roots is noted as particularly frequent. Kachru described as 'rank-reduction' a process of turning NPs made of NP + PP in Std Eng into a compound noun in Ind Eng. That is, the general process reduces phrases to single words. Nihalani, Tongue and Hosali (2004) give examples from Ind Eng like *beer bottle* 'a bottle of beer' (not necessarily the 'empties') and *age-barred* 'barred by age'. Baumgardner (1993:47) gives similar examples from Pak Eng: *perfume bottle* 'bottle of perfume'; *matchbox* 'a box of matches'; *to headcarry* 'to carry on the head'; whilst *to airdash* 'depart quickly by air' has no exact or regular Std Eng equivalent lexeme. Mesthrie (1992a:109) gives examples from IndSAf Eng like *a cold-touch* 'a touch of cold', *top house* 'house at the top'. BlSAf Eng has the form *stop-nonsense* referring to a high wall to keep out noise from the neighbours (shortened from *stop-nonsense wall* 'a wall to stop nonsense').

Other lexico-grammatical neologisms noted by researchers include clipping of English words that would be unfamiliar outside a specific territory. Thus, *to barb* 'to cut one's hair' (Nig Eng; Bamgbose 1992a:156); *a colo* 'old, old-fashioned, from the colonial period' (Ghan Eng; Huber and Dako 2004:864).

For a comprehensive and lively account of the vocabulary of World Englishes, the reader is referred to Gramley (2001).

4.2 PHONETICS AND PHONOLOGY

This aspect of New Englishes has been less researched than syntax, morphology and vocabulary. For this reason our geographical coverage will be slightly more limited than that of Chapters 2 and 3. Our synopsis will provide a general overview of the main phonological and phonetic characteristics of New Englishes in Africa and South and South-East Asia (henceforth *Africa–Asia*). The treatment is not exhaustive; it is meant to give an indication of the range of phonetic variation in varieties for which such comparative information is available. This section draws upon individual descriptions of these varieties in *A Handbook of Varieties of English* (Vol. I, Schneider *et al.* 2004), and the synopsis provided in that handbook for Africa and South and South-East Asia by Mesthrie (2004:1099–110). The main sources from the handbook for the generalisations in this section are Finn (CFl Eng); Mesthrie (IndSAf Eng), van Rooy (BlSAf Eng), Gut (Nig Eng), Huber (Ghan Eng), Simo Bobda (Cameroons (CAM) Eng), Schmied (EAf Eng), Gargesh (Ind Eng), Mahboob and Ahmar (Pak Eng), Wee (Sgp Eng), Tayao (Phl Eng) and Baskaran (Mal Eng).

The focus will inevitably fall on those characteristics that differ from varieties that are more or less accepted as a norm in international English: RP and 'general American' (however hard the latter may be to define). These varieties are chosen as a convenient means of comparison, as well as the fact that they do have some prestige in the former colonies, especially for newsreading style (rather than for colloquial speech, where they might be deemed inappropriate). RP is the model promulgated by the British in all territories covered in this section, except for the Philippines, which after Spanish domination came under the sway of the USA and *ergo* US Eng. The features identified in this section are unlikely to be used by all L2 speakers in a given territory at all times. Rather, the principles of variationist sociolinguistics apply: there is a degree of intra-speaker and stylistic variation. In particular the features cited are mainly found in mesolectal and basilectal speech; acrolectal speakers usually have accents that are somewhat closer to prestige TL norms.

4.2.1 Vowels

In describing the vowels across a range of New English varieties, the most convenient method is that which utilises Wells' (1982) lexical sets. Wells devised a system which made it possible to compare sounds across English dialects without describing them as a deviation from a particular British (or American) standard; rather the vowels of English are labelled by a key monosyllabic word in which they occur in a wide number of varieties. Wells thus speaks of the KIT vowel rather than the vowel /ɪ/. The KIT class comprises all words that have the same vowel as the word *kit* in a particular variety: e.g. the vowels in *bit, sit, big, trip*, and the first vowel in *bishop, rhythm, build*, etc., in many varieties of English. The qualification 'many varieties of English' is necessary since not all varieties of English are identical in the exact details of their lexical sets. Thus, whilst there is broad agreement of the affiliations

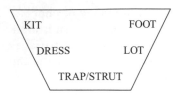

Figure 4.1 Five-vowel system: Type 1

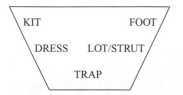

Figure 4.2 Five-vowel system: Type 2

of the BATH set in RP and US English (with RP having [ɑː] and US English having [æː]), *vase* belongs to this set in RP but not in US English, where it is often pronounced [veɪz], and hence belongs to the lexical set FACE.

(a) **The short monophthongs:**   New Englishes in Africa–Asia either retain the six-vowel system for short monophthongs or transform it into a five-vowel system. The latter is exemplified by almost all African L2 varieties (except educated varieties of Nig Eng). A six-vowel system for short vowels is found among CFl Eng, IndSAf Eng, the Asian varieties (Ind Eng, Pak Eng, Sgp Eng and Mal Eng; Phl Eng mesolect) and (with several structural changes) in southern Nig Eng. The five-vowel short monophthong system is in fact the core vowel system in its entirety for African varieties (except Nig Eng), since (a) schwa is marginal in these varieties and (b) length distinction between vowels is not a general feature. There are two subtypes of the five-vowel system for short vowels, depending on particular mergers:

Type 1, with merger of TRAP and STRUT is found in EAf Eng, Ghan Eng and some varieties of BlSAf Eng. Type 2 showing merger of LOT and STRUT is found in Cam Eng and southern Nig Eng.

In CFl Eng (as in White SAf Eng) there is a chain shift amongst the front vowels, with each vowel moving one step higher compared to RP, and /ɪ/ becoming centralised (as [ï]). We now turn to the specific characteristics of each lexical set in Africa–Asia varieties. In Sgp Eng the DRESS and TRAP classes appear to have merged (to [ɛ]) (Brown

1988:134). Wee (2004:1024) proposes that there may well be a crossover effect in terms of vowel height, with [ɛ] for TRAP and [æ] for DRESS. Further research is needed to confirm this crossover of a whole class rather than of individual and isolated words as sometimes happens in other varieties.

KIT

In CFl Eng and IndSAf Eng, KIT is 'split' into a subclass with [ɪ] (in velar and glottal contexts) and a subclass with a centralised vowel [ï] (in all other contexts). This rule is derived from a general rule of White SAf Eng. KIT may variably be realised as [ɪ] in CFl Eng, and all L2 African Englishes and in the South-East Asian varieties (Sgp Eng, Mal Eng, Phl Eng). In all African and South-East Asian New Englishes, the KIT vowel may also be lengthened in certain contexts (as with all potential long–short pairs, since length is non-contrastive).

DRESS

[e] is the main variant in CFl Eng, IndSAf Eng, EAf Eng, Cam Eng, Ind Eng and Pak Eng. [ɛ] is the main variant in BlSAf Eng, Ghan Eng and Phl Eng. In southern Nig Eng there is free variation between [e] and [ɛ]. [æ] occurs in Sgp Eng and Mal Eng; [a] is the usual variant in northern Nig Eng.

TRAP

A raised variant [ɛ̝] occurs in CFl Eng, BlSAf Eng, Sgp Eng. The usual variant is [æ] in Ind Eng, Pak Eng and Mal Eng. [a] is the usual realisation in Nig Eng, Ghan Eng and Cam Eng. [ɑ] is reported in Phl Eng. In Sgp Eng TRAP and DRESS have merged or may well even cross over, as discussed above.

LOT

[ɒ] is a major variant in CFl Eng, IndSAf Eng and southern Nig Eng. [ɔ] is found in BlSAf Eng, Ghan Eng, Cam Eng, Ind Eng, Sgp Eng and Mal Eng. [ɔː] is reported as a major variant in Ind Eng, Pak Eng and IndSAf Eng. [a] is the usual realisation in northern Nig Eng; [ɑ] in Phl Eng.

STRUT

[ɔ] occurs in Cam Eng, and southern Nig Eng. [ʌ] occurs in IndSAf Eng, Ind Eng, Pak Eng and Phl Eng. [a] occurs in BlSAf Eng, CFl Eng, EAfr Eng and Ghan Eng. [ɑ] is the usual variant in northern Nig Eng, Sgp Eng and Mal Eng.

FOOT

A (slightly) rounded [ʊ] occurs in CFl Eng, IndSAf Eng, Nig Eng, Ind Eng, Pak Eng and as a variant in Ghan Eng. A short [u] is the usual realisation in BlSAf Eng, EAfr Eng, Ghan Eng, Cam Eng, Sgp Eng, Mal Eng, Phl Eng and as a variant in Pak Eng.

(b) The long monophthongs: In most New Englishes in Africa and South-East Asia vowel length is not distinctive. In the sets KIT – FLEECE; FOOT – GOOSE; LOT – THOUGHT the usual realisations are [i u ɔ]. There is some variation within these sets (described below), and even more variation in BATH and NURSE.

FLEECE
[iː] occurs in CFE, IndSAf Eng, northern Nig Eng, Ind Eng, Pak Eng and occasionally in Ghan Eng and Mal Eng. [i] is reported in BlSAf Eng, EAfr Eng, southern Nig Eng, Ghan Eng, Cam Eng, Sgp Eng and Mal Eng. [ɪ] is reported as a lesser variant in Ind Eng. In Phl Eng there is no distinction between KIT and FLEECE: instead, under the influence of Philippine languages, there appears to be free variation, with a tendency towards [iː] rather than [i] or [ɪ].

GOOSE
There is symmetry with the FLEECE vowel in all varieties. Thus [uː] occurs in all the varieties that use [iː]; and [u] in all the varieties that use [i]. The noticeably centralised and unrounded equivalent [ʉː] that occurs in L1 Englishes of the USA, UK and South Africa is not generally reported for New Englishes. In Phl Eng there appears to be free variation between [uː] and [u] or [ʊ], with a tendency towards [uː].

THOUGHT
[ɔː] occurs in IndSAf Eng, Pak Eng and as lesser alternatives in Ghan Eng and Ind Eng. [oː] is used in CFl Eng and northern Nig Eng. Unlengthened [ɔ] or [o] occurs in BlSAf Eng, EAf Eng, southern Nig Eng, Ghan Eng, Cam Eng, Ind Eng, Sgp Eng, Mal Eng and Phl Eng.

NURSE
There is immense variation in the realisation of the NURSE vowel:

  [ɜː] in the non-rhotic varieties, CFl Eng, IndSAf Eng and in the rhotic Ind Eng, and as an occasional variant in Ghan Eng;
  [aː] in northern Nig Eng and as a lesser alternative in Ind Eng;
  [ɛ] in BlSAf Eng, southern Nig Eng, Ghan Eng, in the rhotic Phl Eng; and as a lesser alternative in Cam Eng;
  [a] in EAfr Eng and as a lesser alternative in Nig Eng;
  [ʌ] in Pak Eng (rhotic) and as a lesser alternative in Ind Eng;
  [ɔ] in Cam Eng;
  [ə] in Sgp Eng, Mal Eng and as a lesser alternative in Ind Eng;

BATH
The usual values are as follows:

[ɑː] in IndSAf Eng, Ind Eng, Pak Eng, and as an alternative in CFl
Eng;
[a] in EAfr Eng, southern Nig Eng, Ghan Eng and Cam Eng;
[ɑ] in Sgp Eng, Mal Eng, Phl Eng and as an alternative in CFl Eng;
[ä] in BlSAf Eng;
[aː] in northern Nig Eng and as a lesser alternative in Ghan Eng;
[ɔː] or [ɒ] as the main variant in CFl Eng.

(c) **Diphthongs:** FACE

[eɪ] occurs in IndSAf Eng, Pak Eng and as a lesser alternative in
BlSAf Eng, Ghan Eng and Mal Eng;
[ɛɪ] or slightly lower or backed equivalents of the nucleus occur in
CFl Eng and BlSAf Eng;
[e] occurs in EAfr Eng, Nig Eng, Ghan Eng, Cam Eng, Sgp Eng, Mal
Eng and Phl Eng;
[eː] occurs in Ind Eng and Pak Eng;
[eⁱ] occurs as a lesser variant in Ghan Eng.

PRICE

[aɪ] occurs in IndSAf Eng, Nig Eng, Ind Eng and Pak Eng;
[ɑɪ] occurs in EAfr Eng and Phl Eng;
[ʌɪ] occurs in BlSAf Eng;
[ai] occurs in Ghan Eng, Cam Eng, Sgp Eng, Mal Eng and as an
alternative form in Nig Eng and CFl Eng;
[ɐi] occurs in CFl Eng;
[a] occurs as a lesser alternative in Ghan Eng;

MOUTH
[aʊ] occurs in CFl Eng (before voiced segments), EAf Eng, Nig Eng, Ghan
Eng, Cam Eng, Ind Eng and Pak Eng. Nuclei with [ä] or [ɑ] are reported
in IndSAf Eng and Phl Eng. The glide element [u], rather than [ʊ] is
reported in Sgp Eng and Mal Eng. [aʊ] in CFl Eng (before voiceless
segments); [ɔʊ] in BlSAf Eng.
 Monophthongal qualities are also reported: [o] as an alternative in
BlSAf Eng; and [a] as a lesser alternative in Ghan Eng.

CHOICE

[ɔɪ] occurs in CFl Eng, IndSAf Eng, BlSAf Eng, Nig Eng, Ind Eng and
Pak Eng.

[ɔi] occurs in Ghan Eng, Cam Eng, Ind Eng, Sgp Eng and Mal Eng;
[oɪ] occurs in EAfr Eng and Phl Eng;

GOAT

[o] occurs in EAf Eng, southern Nig Eng, Ghan Eng, Cam Eng, Sgp
Eng, Mal Eng and Phl Eng;
[ɔ] is reported for BlSAf Eng;
[oː] occurs in northern Nig Eng, Ind Eng, Pak Eng and as a lesser
alternative in Mal Eng;
[ou] occurs in IndSAf Eng and as a lesser alternative in Ghan Eng;
[ɔu] occurs in BlSAf Eng;
[əu] is reported in Pak Eng;

Lowered and fronted nuclei also occur in [ɐu] or [ʌu] in CFl Eng.

SQUARE

[eː] occurs in CFl Eng, IndSAf Eng and Ind Eng;
[ɛː] occurs as a variant in Ind Eng;
[ɛ] occurs in BlSAf Eng, Ghan Eng, Cam Eng and as a lesser alternative in Mal Eng;
[æ] occurs in Sgp Eng and Mal Eng;
[e] is reported for Phl Eng;
[ea] or [ɛa] occur in Ghan Eng and Nig Eng;
[ia] occurs in southern Nig Eng and [eə] or [əɪ] in Pak Eng.

NEAR
The diphthongal realisations are as follows:

[ɪə] in Ind Eng and Pak Eng;
[iə] in Sgp Eng and Mal Eng;
[iɛ] in Ghan Eng and Cam Eng, and as [ijɛ] in IndSAf Eng;
[iɐ] in CFl Eng;
[ɪa] in EAfr Eng;
[ia] as a lesser alternative in Ghan Eng.

Monophthongal [e] is reported in BlSAf Eng, and, as a lesser alternative,
[iː] in Mal Eng.

CURE
There is a great array of variation here, and the lexical set has to
be studied in greater depth to ascertain whether all words associated
with this set in RP, say, are treated uniformly. It would be safer to treat
the following summary as referring to the word *cure*; rather than the
whole set for CURE. Among the diphthongal realisations (which are
usually preceded by [j] are the following:

[ʊə] in Pak Eng;
[əʊ] in CFl Eng;
[ʊa] in EAfr Eng;
[ua] in Nig Eng;
[uɛ] or [uɔ] in Ghan Eng.

Monophthongal values (preceded by [j]) are reported in the following:

[ɔː] in IndSAf Eng;
[o] in BlSAf Eng;
[ɔ] in Cam Eng, Sgp Eng, Mal Eng and as a lesser alternative in Ghan Eng;
[u] in Phl Eng (with postvocalic /r/).

(d) Unstressed vowels:

HAPP*Y*
The variants are as follows:

[iː] in IndSAf Eng, and as lesser alternatives in CFl Eng and Ind Eng;
[i·] in CFl Eng;
[i] in Ghan Eng, Cam Eng, Sgp Eng and Mal Eng;
[ɪ] in BlSAf Eng, EAfr Eng, Ind Eng, Pak Eng, Phl Eng and as a lesser alternative in Ghan Eng;
[iɪ] in Nig Eng.

LETT*ER*
The variants are as follows:

[ə] in white SAf Eng, CFl Eng, Ind Eng (plus postvocalic /r/), Sgp Eng and Mal Eng;
[ɛː] in IndSAf Eng;
[ɛ] in Phl Eng (with postvocalic /r/);
[a] in EAfr Eng, Ghan Eng and Cam Eng;
[äɪ] in BlSAf Eng;
[ʌ] in Pak Eng.

COMM*A*
The variants are as follows:

[ə] in CFl Eng, Sgp Eng and Mal Eng;
[ɐ] as a variant in CFl Eng;
[a] in Nig Eng, Ghan Eng, Cam Eng and Ind Eng;
[ɑ] in IndSAf Eng and Phl Eng;
[ä] in BlSAf Eng;
[ʌ] in Pak Eng and as a lesser alternative in Mal Eng.

HORS*ES*
The variants are as follows:

> [ə] in IndSAf Eng, Ind Eng, Sgp Eng, Mal Eng and as a lesser alter-
> native in CFl Eng;
> [ɐ] in CFl Eng;
> [iˑ] in BlSAf Eng;

[ɨ] as an alternative in Ind Eng;

> [ɪ] in Pak Eng;
> [ɛ] in Phl Eng.

4.2.2 Consonants

The lexical set mnemonic is not necessary for description of consonants. Instead we use the convention of capital letters standing for
particular consonants (except for problematic cases like TH which will
be designated by the usual phonetic symbols /θ/ and /ð/):

(a) **Stops:** P, T, K may be unaspirated in CFl Eng and IndSAf Eng (vari-
ably) and very commonly in Ind Eng, Pak Eng, Sgp Eng and Phl Eng.
No such deaspiration is reported in the African varieties researched.
T, D are retroflexed in Ind Eng and Pak Eng, and occasionally in Ind-
SAf Eng. Glottalising of syllable-final T is reported for Ghan Eng. Final
stops have glottalised variants in Mal Eng. P is realised as [p], [f] or [Φ]
and B as [b] or [v] in northern Nig Eng. T is realised as [ts] in some
Ghan Eng varieties.

(b) **Fricatives:** The most striking feature among fricatives is that *all*
New Englishes varieties treat /θ/ and /ð/ as something other than an
interdental fricative. /θ ð/ are realised similarly as a pair as follows:

> Dental stops [t̪ d̪] in CFl Eng (variably) and regularly in IndSAf
> Eng, Pak Eng;
> An aspirated dental stop [t̪ʰ] occurs widely in Ind Eng, but its
> voiced counterpart [d̪] is not usually aspirated;
> Alveolar stops [t d] in EAf Eng, Ghan Eng, Sgp Eng, Mal Eng, Phl
> Eng;
> Variably as [t t̪] for /θ/ and [d d̪] for /ð/ in BlSAf Eng and Ghan Eng;
> Affricate realisations [tθ] and [dð] are reported as lesser variants
> in Ghan Eng.

/θ/ is realised as [f] word-finally in some words in EAf Eng, Ghan Eng
and Sgp Eng.

In EAfr Eng /θ/ and /ð/ may be realised as [t s f] and [d z v] respectively. Other changes to fricatives are less widespread:

Velar fricatives [x] and [ɣ] occur in CFl Eng (as in White SAf Eng), mainly in borrowings, place names, proper names, etc.

H may be voiced in CFl Eng, BlSAf Eng, IndSAf Eng, Ind Eng, Pak Eng; it may also be murmured in the last three varieties. H may also be dropped in IndSAf Eng, Ind Eng and Mal Eng, especially by Tamil speakers in these areas. In Ind Eng it may be dropped in initial position with tonal adjustments, amongst Panjabi speakers. H may be substituted by [j] in CFl Eng or by [j] or [w] amongst Tamil speakers of IndSAf Eng, Ind Eng and Mal Eng. It may be dropped before [j] in Cam Eng (e.g. in *human*). Hypercorrection may also occur in those varieties that drop H, with sporadic forms like *hout* for 'out'.

F occurs as an approximant in CFl Eng, IndSAf Eng and Ind Eng. In northern Nig Eng, F is realised as [f], [p] or [Φ]; for many speakers of Ind Eng as [pʰ]; and in basilectal Phl Eng as [p].

V has the following realisations:

an approximant [ʋ] in IndSAf Eng and Ind Eng;
[v] or [f] in northern Nig Eng;
[bh] amongst Bengali speakers of Ind Eng;
[b] in basilectal Phl Eng;
[v] or [w] in Ind Eng and amongst Tamil speakers of Mal Eng.

/ʃ ʒ/ have the following realisations:

[s z] variably in CFl Eng, BlSAf Eng, EAf Eng and Ind Eng;
[tɕ dɕ] in Ghan Eng.

In addition /ʃ/ may occur as [z] occasionally in CFl Eng, Cam Eng and (in final position) in Mal Eng. It may occur as [s] occasionally in CFl Eng and Ghan Eng.

Z occurs as [dʒ] occasionally in Ind Eng and amongst Malay and Chinese speakers of Mal Eng.

(c) **Affricates:** /tʃ dʒ/ have the following realisations:

[s z] in EAf Eng;
[tɕ dɕ] in Ghan Eng;
[ts ds] in Phl Eng;

In addition /tʃ/ is realised as [ʃ] in BlSAf Eng, EAf Eng and occasionally in Cam Eng. /dʒ/ is realised as [ʒ] in CFl Eng, BlSAf Eng, EAf Eng and among Yoruba speakers of Nig Eng.

(d) Nasals: N is retroflexed before [t] and [ɖ] in IndSAf Eng, Ind Eng
and Pak Eng. Epenthetic [n] occurs before consonants in EAf Eng. Vowels are nasalised before final nasals, with subsequent loss of the nasal
consonant in CFl Eng and Ghan Eng. The progressive suffix -*ing* is
realised as [ŋ] in Ghan Eng.

(e) Liquids: The rhotic varieties in Africa–Asia are Ind Eng, Pak Eng
and Phl Eng. There is [r ~ l] alternation in EAf Eng, Ghan Eng and some
SAf varieties; the details often depend on speakers' home languages. R
is regularly realised as [l] amongst Chinese speakers of Mal Eng. Linking
[r] is absent in Ghan Eng and Cam Eng, and is rare to non-existent in
varieties of SAf Eng. L-vocalisation is reported in Ghan Eng and is in
fact common in other varieties of English in Africa. Dark [ɫ] is very
common in CFl Eng; whereas light [l] prevails in Ind Eng and amongst
older speakers of IndSAf Eng.

(f) Glides and approximants: [h] occurs in place of [j] or [w] in CFl
Eng (and other varieties of Afrikaans-influenced Eng in South Africa).
W is replaced by [hw] in *wh*-words in Ghan Eng. Clusters of /t/ plus /j/
and /d/ plus /j/ occur as [tʃ dʒ] occasionally in IndSAf Eng and other
varieties of South African Eng: thus *Chusday* for 'Tuesday'. There is
dropping of /j/ (yod-dropping) in Nig Eng, Ghan Eng and Cam Eng. W
and V occur interchangeably in Ind Eng (occasionally) and rarely in
IndSAf Eng.

4.2.3 Common phonological processes ▬▬▬▬▬▬▬▬▬▬

Two processes are very commonly reported. Final devoicing of obstru-
ents occurs in CFl Eng, BlSAf Eng, Nig Eng, Ghan Eng, Cam Eng, Sgp
Eng and Mal Eng. Consonant-cluster reduction is reported to varying
degrees in CFl Eng, BlSAf Eng, Ghan Eng, Ind Eng, Pak Eng, Sgp Eng,
Mal Eng and Phl Eng. Clusters can, of course, be broken up in several
ways. One way is to drop one of the consonants in the cluster. In Cam
Eng (Simo Bobda 2004:895) plosives like /d, p, k/ are prone to deletion
if they are the final consonant in a cluster; as in *past, missed, cold, end,
grasp, jump, task, dust*, which may all occur without the final plosive.
Such deletion is more likely if the next word begins with a consonant.
Another way to break up clusters is via vowel insertion (or epenthe-
sis). Tayao (2004:1055) gives examples from basilectal Phl Eng: [ku-lut]
for *cloth*, [di-ris] for *dress* and [ta-rap] for *trap*. Some varieties break up
initial clusters with *s* + consonant, via insertion of a vowel in initial
position. Basilectal Phl Eng has [is-tat] for *start*, [is-ta-rat] for *strut* and

[is-kuwir] for *square*. Similarly, Ind Eng has variants like [ispi:tʃ] for *speech* and [isku:l] for *school*.

4.2.4 Stress, tone and intonation

Assuming a continuum between syllable timing and stress timing, the number of New English varieties which exhibit tendencies towards syllable timing is impressive: IndSAf Eng, BlSAf Eng, EAf Eng, Nig Eng, Ghan Eng, Ind Eng, Pak Eng, Sgp Eng, Mal Eng and Phl Eng. For these varieties vowel reduction is not as common as in RP and in some of them [ə] is rare, or more a feature of fast and connected speech, rather than of citation forms. On the other hand some of these varieties are reported to avoid syllabic consonants, in favour of schwa plus consonant: Ind Eng, Sgp Eng, Mal Eng and Phl Eng. All varieties that were cited in connection with syllable timing also display stress shifts in individual words or sets of words, in relation to RP norms. These are often shifts to the right (e.g. *real 'ise* rather than RP *'realise*); though some words in some varieties exhibit shifts to the left (e.g. from penultimate to antepenultimate syllables as in Cam Eng *a 'dolescence*, rather than RP *ado 'lescence*). Most of these varieties do not use stress to differentiate between pairs like *'absent* (adj.) versus *ab 'sent* (verb).

As far as intonation is concerned most varieties report a smaller range of intonational contours compared to RP. Whilst this area is one that needs closer attention, claims for the ff varieties will illustrate this general claim:

> CFl Eng: great use of rising intonation in statements (Finn 2004:978);
>
> BlSAf Eng: tone and information units are shorter than in RP (van Rooy 2004:951);
>
> Nig Eng: sentence stress is rarely used for contrast. Given information is rarely de-accented (Gut 2004: 825–6);
>
> Mal Eng: less change of intonation (or pitch direction) occurs in sentences compared to RP (Baskaran 2004:1044).

Some African varieties like Nig Eng and Ghan Eng make occasional use of lexical and grammatical tone, and report an interaction between stress and tone: Nig Eng, Ghan Eng.

It is clear from this synopsis that the L2 varieties of English in Africa and Asia share a large number of phonological similarities. Particularly striking are the use of a five-vowel system, plus diphthongs in many varieties; the tendency towards syllable timing; and the non-fricative realisations of /θ/ and /ð/. In the interests of fidelity to the descriptions in *A Handbook of Varieties of English* (Schneider *et al.*, 2004), minute differences between vowels were retained in this summary, rather than attempting to 'normalise' some transcriptions (e.g. [a] versus [ä] versus [ɐ]), in the hope of uncovering further broad phonological similarities. This synopsis must therefore be taken as a starting, rather than end, point of the study of the systemic phonological similarities, as well as of the phonetic differences within those overall similarities amongst New Englishes.

4.3 CONCLUSION

Our focus in this chapter has continued to be mostly at a descriptive level in identifying recurring features of New English vocabulary and phonetics. This focus is a prelude to understanding significant aspects of variation, since vocabulary is a close reflection of the cultural context while phonetics and phonology are closely tied to issues of identity. New Englishes thus show indigenisation, as identified in Chapter 1.

STUDY QUESTIONS

1. Differentiate between 'borrowing' and 'retention' in the sense maintained in this chapter.
2. Differentiate between 'retention and 'archaism' as used in this chapter.
3. Define the term 'heteronym' and give some examples other than those in this chapter.
4. Review the treatment of vowel length in the different New English varieties.
5. Review the treatment of /θ/ and /ð/ in the different New English varieties.

Further reading

All works mentioned here are fully referenced in the bibliography.

For lexis a highly engaging book is Gramley, *The Vocabulary of World English* (2001); for phonology see *A Handbook of Varieties of English*, Vol. I, ed. Schneider *et al.* (2004).

5 Pragmatics and discourse

5.1 INTRODUCTION

Thus far we have concentrated on the main structural differences between New Englishes and metropolitan varieties. But varieties of English also differ considerably from each other in terms of the functions to which linguistic structure may be put. An innovative structure in a particular New English may serve a new function or add a certain nuance not generally found in other varieties. Or what appears to be the same structure as in, say, Standard English, may serve a new function. In this chapter we first describe differences at the sentence level, before proceeding to speech acts and genres found widely in New Englishes. Such linguistic diversity generally reflects differences in social arrangements, cultural practices and historical processes to which language use is closely tied. Thus, in Singapore one notices a McDonald's billboard advertising their new sandwich made with rice buns: *Have you eaten rice today?* This play on the common Chinese greeting *Have you eaten already?* is lost on those English speakers who are not aware of the local cultural practices of Singapore. Similarly, in India, where English is one of two 'official languages', it is not uncommon to read a front-page headline such as *Terror Tandava in Varanasi* in a major English newspaper (*Times of India*, 8 March 2006). English speakers not familiar with historical-cultural literacies of India will find the use of *Tandava* opaque and will need local help for purposes of interpreting it appropriately in context ('the dance of destruction performed by Lord Shiva'). To the typical reader of the newspaper, however, there are no interpretative problems with such local headlines. The interpretation of such localisms, in all varieties of English, demands pragmatic – local, contextual – knowledge. The use of such localisms sometimes becomes necessary, especially in post-colonial contexts, where a global medium like English is widely used to present the local cultural ethos.

It is not surprising, therefore, that this practice of embedding the local in the global sometimes receives negative evaluation by speakers of metropolitan or 'dominion' varieties, as discussed in Joseph (2005). She reports the reactions of two literary critics in Canada to a collection of short stories, *Tales from Firozsha Baag* (1987), written by the Indian creative writer Rohinton Mistry. The problem these literary scholars have with Mistry's work is best summarised by one of them, Michael Darling (1988:284), a professor of English and a writer of academic works: '[T]he Indian words are often strung together in what seems like an unnecessary striving for local colour...' Joseph argues that the problem is not with the text, but with the inability of first language readers to 'read' native sensibilities of second-language writers, where the medium often serves as the message. As academics like B. B. Kachru (1983c) have long emphasised, the pragmatic functions of New English texts, whether written or spoken, can be successfully understood if their uses are related to local meanings, local thought patterns and local sociocultural practices.

The main goal of this chapter is to demonstrate how New Englishes have altered the syntactic and discourse forms of metropolitan varieties to recreate, maintain, or represent more faithfully local cultural practices and culturally embedded meanings. We begin by exploring the different syntactic ways in which certain pragmatic functions of politeness are represented in New Englishes. This will be followed by a discussion of the use of certain particles that perform discourse-pragmatic functions. We will then discuss how new Englishes realise various speech acts, showing local cultural influence. Following this we identify different structuring patterns of English discourse across cultures. Finally, we present data to discuss a common linguistic strategy – code-switching – to index certain pragmatic meanings and functions.

5.2 THE PRAGMATICS OF SYNTACTIC FORMS

5.2.1 Tag questions

Tags have been traditionally analysed as utterance-final discourse markers (Biber *et al.* 1999). In Std Eng, tag questions are formed by a rule which inserts a pronominal copy of the subject after an appropriate modal auxiliary. A typical example is given in (1) below.

1. John said he'll work today, didn't he?

In addition to the canonical tags as in (1) above, there are other forms, grouped together as 'invariant tags' such as *isn't that so?* and *don't you think?* (see Quirk *et al.* 1985; Algeo 1988). Tags have been shown to express certain attitudes of the speaker towards what is being said in the main clause. Functionally, English tag questions generally behave like epistemic adverbials, such as *probably*, *presumably*, etc., as shown in (2) below.

2a. It's still dark outside, isn't it?
2b. It's probably dark outside.

Algeo (1988) identifies five pragmatic functions of tag questions in English: the informational tag (with rising pitch), used to make a genuine request for information; the confirmatory (or facilitative tag, with falling pitch), used to invite agreement from the hearer; the punctuation tag used for emphasis; the peremptory tag, used to end a discussion; and, the aggressive tag (with low tone) that is openly hostile, lacking consideration or good will. The first two tags index politeness, whereas the last three tags signal impoliteness. Tags are thus used to exert both authority and power, especially in asymmetrical discourses (Hudson 1975), as well as to appeal to solidarity (Winefield, Chandler and Bassett 1989).

There is variation in the use of tag questions across Englishes. In Ind Eng, for example, there are two syntactic variants, one that exhibits the syntax of canonical tags as in (1) above, and the other that does not. The latter, shown in (3) below, has been variously described as an undifferentiated tag question: one of the linguistic exponents of Ind Eng, especially in informal contexts (Bhatt 1995; see also Kachru 1983a; Trudgill and Hannah 1985). The meaning of the undifferentiated tag is not the one appended to the meaning of the main proposition; it signals important social meaning.

3a. You are going home soon, isn't it?
3b. You have taken my book, isn't it?

These undifferentiated tags play an important pragmatic role in the Ind Eng speech community, exhibiting how linguistic form is constrained by cultural constraints of politeness. These tags are linguistic devices governed by the politeness principle of non-imposition: they serve positive politeness functions (as outlined by Brown and Levinson 1987), signalling deference and acquiescence (Bhatt 1995). Thus, there is a contrast between examples (a), from informal Ind Eng, and (b), from more formal Ind Eng, in (4) and (5).

	Unassertive/Mitigated: (informal)		Assertive/Intensified: (Standard)
4a.	You said you'll do the job, *isn't it?*	4b.	You said you'll do the job, didn't you?
5a.	They said they will be here, *isn't it?*	5b.	They said they will be here, didn't they?

In contrast to the (b) examples above, Ind Eng speakers find the (a) examples non-impositional and mitigating (Bhatt 1995), placing them high on the scale of politeness. This intuition is more clearly established when an adverb of intensification/assertion is used in conjunction with the undifferentiated tag; the result is, predictably, unacceptable to the speakers of Ind Eng.

4a′. *Of course you said you'll do the job, isn't it?
5a′. *Of course they said they'll be here, isn't it?

On the other hand, it is possible to collocate *of course* with the (b) sentences above. In a culture where verbal behaviour is severely constrained, to a large extent, by politeness regulations, where non-imposition is the essence of polite behaviour, it is not surprising that speakers of Ind Eng use undifferentiated tags to sound less demanding in the requests that they make. Such tags have the added advantage of avoiding pronoun forms for the addressee, which would require other deference strategies.

As noted in Chapter 2, undifferentiated tags are common in New Englishes. In Hong Kong English they are often used when seeking confirmation and involvement (see Cheng and Warren 2001), in mainly positive politeness functions. Similarly, in colloquial Sgp Eng, tags do not vary as they do in standard varieties. Speakers of colloquial Sgp Eng use either the tag *isn't it* or *is it* (Pakir 1994; Alsagoff and Lick 1998b) mainly to signal solidarity. Pakir (1994) discusses the use of tag questions such as *You want go Singapore Swing, is it? Say so lah.* She asked her undergraduate students whether such an utterance was acceptable in their spoken English. The answer was a resounding *yes*, since the alternative standard form *You want to go to Singapore Swing, don't you?* 'would have prompted disbelief, concern or even distancing in the circle of friends' (Pakir 1994:178).

In most of the varieties of English that make productive use of undifferentiated tags, it has been shown that the form is often a reflex of language transfer from the native languages with which these Englishes come into contact (Kachru 1986). In most cases, the tags in local native languages are of the form *is not*, and these are then lexicalised in local varieties of English as *is it* or *isn't it*. Bamiro (1995) argues that undifferentiated tags in West African English (*isn't it, not, no*) are a transfer from West African languages such as Yoruba (cf. also Bokamba 1992). A more direct transfer can be found in the tags used by English speakers in Mongolia (Cohen 2005), who form affirmative or confirmation tags by inserting (code-mixing) their native language form (Mongolian *baixgui yy*: 'isn't it/you know') in an otherwise English sentence, as shown in (6) below.

6. Then I told the driver that we were out of gas, *baixgui yy*, and if we didn't stop soon the car will die.

5.2.2 Auxiliaries

Undifferentiated tags are not the only instances of New English linguistic forms exhibiting a different 'grammar of culture' (to use Bright's term of 1968) from Std Eng. Auxiliaries may serve new or additional pragmatic functions. Ind Eng uses the modal auxiliary *may* to express positive politeness. In the examples below (from Trudgill and Hannah 1985:109) *may* is used in informal Ind Eng to express obligation politely (7 and 9), which contrasts systematically with Std Ind or British Eng usage (8 and 10):

7. This furniture *may* be removed tomorrow.
8. This furniture is to be removed tomorrow.
9. These mistakes *may* please be corrected.
10. These mistakes should be corrected.

Likewise, a polite softener *may* replaces *could* amongst some BlSAf Eng speakers:

11. May you please give me a lift to town. ('Could you please...')

Similarly, Sgp Eng uses *would* as a polite form, a tentativeness marker, and as a marker of irrealis aspect (Alsagoff and Lick 1998b). The use of *would* in (12) in subordinate contexts indicates the irrealis aspect to indicate tentativeness in contrast to the use of *will* in the main clause expressing what is within the control of the speaker.

12. I will help you, but I am not sure if my brother would.

The negative form *wouldn't* serves similar functions in IndSAf Eng:

13. Q. When is the election taking place?
    A: I wouldn't know. (polite form for 'I don't know/ I couldn't tell you')

5.3 THE PRAGMATICS OF DISCOURSE PARTICLES

This section discusses the pragmatic functions of discourse particles that characterise innovations found mainly in New Englishes. Generally in English, discourse particles such as *so*, *of course*, *actually*, *anyway*, *after all*, *by and large*, etc., signal to hearers what they need to attend to, and how to interpret messages. These expressions thus serve a meta-pragmatic function: to guide the interpretation process (see Schiffrin 1987; Blakemore 2002). These particles have been analysed as lexical adjuncts, peripheral to the clausal syntax in which they appear; their meaning is generally inferred from the context of its use. Although they are non-truth conditional, they do seem to contribute to some aspects of the illocutionary force of the utterance, indexing speaker attitude or stance. These discourse particles share more or less the same distributional properties across different varieties of English. However, there is some evidence of their relatively restricted use in New Englishes (cf. de Klerk 2004 on BlSAf Eng). Furthermore, some discourse/pragmatic particles are variety-specific. The particles *la* and *what* typically appear in colloquial Sgp Eng, whereas clause- or phrase-final *only* is a quintessentially Ind Eng innovation. We next discuss the various pragmatic functions that these particles serve in their respective varieties of English.

5.3.1 *La* and *what* in Singaporean English ▰▰▰▰▰▰▰▰▰▰▰

The particles *la* and *what* are the most common discourse-pragmatic particles used mainly in colloq Sgp Eng, also known as *Singlish* (cf. Richards and Tay 1977; Gupta 1992; Wong 2004). *La* has been shown to occur with a range of interactional acts such as requests, invitations, promises, suggestions, etc., as long as the interlocutors share an element of solidarity. These particles are absent where there is a power asymmetry among the participants, and are also absent in most formal contexts of speech and writing. Richards and Tay (1977), for instance, discuss the case of two shop assistants who used Singlish without any occurrences of *la* as they spoke to each other while serving a customer. After the customer left, the *la* particle reappeared in their conversation, as in (14):

14. Why you wear your hair like that la?   Better you lift a bit at the back la.

The particle *la* carries a wide range of functions. Gupta (1992), for example, analysed the use of this particle in terms of a system of marking degrees of assertion, which results in different functions when the same particle is used in different sentence types. *La*, according to her, expresses speakers' positive commitments to what they are saying. Other scholars have shown this particle to appear either with different tonal-intonational patterns (Loke and Low 1988) – correlating with different communicative functions – or, as Kwan-Terry (1992) argues, with different lexical tones associated with different attitudinal or modal values.

Wong (2004) discusses three variants of *la* that contrast in terms of three pitch heights of low (la_3), mid-rising (la_2) and high-falling (la_4). The most extensively used *la* particle is the one that is pronounced with a low tone (la_3), the impositional *la*. This particle contributes an attitude of 'gentle persuasion' to the utterance, allowing the speaker to impose her/his views on the addressee or alter the latter's way of thinking, thus turning an ordinary utterance into a directive. This is most clearly seen in the mother–daughter interaction in (15) below, discussed in Wong (2004), where the mother tries to persuade her reluctant daughter that it is acceptable for her to read her daughter's diary.

15. Daughter: Mum, it's private. How can I let you read it?
     Mother: Can la. I'm your own mother.

The mid-rising tone of la_2 is similarly persuasive, but lower on the scale of assertiveness than la_3. Although used in the context of persuasion, la_2, the persuasive *la*, is used more to convince the addressee of something. It is in the persuasive context that a note of irritation or impatience is detected with the use of this particle (Kwan-Terry 1992). The data in (16)–(19) show this use of *la*, in which the speaker thinks that the addressee is reluctant to accept what the speaker thinks (Wong 2004).

16. Try this la. It's nice.
17. You tell him la; he'll listen to you la.
18. No need to count la. There are 365 la.
19. I cannot do it la. I really cannot.

Although both persuasive la_2 and impositional la_3 are particles that are persuasive in nature, the difference between them is that the persuasive la_2 seems less effectual than the impositional la_3 as a persuasive tool. The impositional la_3 seems much more overbearing, enabling the speaker to sound authoritative, dismissive, final or unamenable, and can thus appear with swear words, declaratives and imperatives (Wong 2004: 772–3).

The third *la* particle, pronounced with a high falling tone, *la₄*, the propositional particle, is lowest on the assertiveness scale, and is used by speakers to give advice or to present an idea (Gupta 1992; Wong 2004). This particle has been shown to carry a sense of conveying obviousness (Pakir 1992). The pragmatic use of this particle, of conveying obviousness, is exemplified in the following exchange (from Wong 2004):

> 20. A: Maybe he goes to the park when he is free?
>   B: He's got kidney problem and carries a bag around.
>   A: So he cannot go anywhere la.

The paraphrase of the last two turns in Std Eng could thus be (Wong 2004):

> 21. B: He's got kidney problems and carries a bag around.
>   A: That means he can't go anywhere!

5.3.2 *What* in Singaporean English

The other commonly used particle in colloquial Sgp Eng that has also been extensive studied is *what* (also spelt *wut*) (Platt 1987; Gupta 1992; Wong 1994). It appears to be characterised by a low-falling tone (Platt 1987), carries a meaning of objection (Kwan-Terry 1992) and is used in maximally assertive contexts in utterances that can usually be described as rejoinders (Gupta 1992). In (22) below, *wut* is used twice by speaker B to negate two assumptions made by speaker A. The Std Eng paraphrase in (23) of the data in (22) shows this most clearly (Wong 2004: 776):

> 22. A: How come you borrow my shirt now got hole one?!
>   B: Borrow that time already like that, wut!
>   A: Then why you never say first?
>   B: You never ask, wut!

> 23. A: Why is there a hole in my shirt after you borrowed it?
>   B: It was like that when I borrowed it from you.
>   A: Then why didn't you say so?
>   B: You didn't ask.

In example (22) above, and those below in (24)–(25) (Kwan-Terry 1978:25), the function of *what* clearly appears to be linked to invalidating an implication, or an assumption, in a prior utterance.

> 24. A: Why didn't you come in?
>   B: You told me to wait here, what

> 25. A: Our professor often complains of our being late for his classes.
>   B: But he is often late himself, what.

In sum, the pragmatics of discourse particles in colloq Sgp Eng can be understood, as Gupta (1992) argues, in terms of a cline of assertiveness: *what* appearing on top of that cline as most assertive (challenging and contradicting), whereas the propositional *la* at the bottom of that cline as least assertive (giving advice).

5.3.3 *Only* in Indian English

In Ind Eng, phrase- or clause-final *only* is used to mark focus. Focus, in traditional descriptions, is the non-presupposed information, while the rest of the sentence is presupposed, i.e. information that is shared by the speaker and the listener (Chomsky 1971, 1976; Jackendoff 1972). Focusing strategies in standard varieties of English involve the nuclear stress rule, i.e. the constituents that contain the main stress of the sentence are part of the focus set, generally signalling new information. However, in Ind Eng, there is no nuclear stress rule. Thus, in order to highlight neutral focus (the focus that is identified by an interrogative context) and contrastive focus, Ind Eng uses the pragmatic particle *only*, immediately following the constituent that needs to be emphasised/focused, as shown in (26) below.

> 26. A: When does he work?
>   B: He works on Thursdays and Fridays only.

The interpretation is similar to Std Eng clefted constructions such as *It is only on Thursdays and Fridays that he works* (and not to the ordinary declarative *He only works on Thursdays and Fridays*). The focus in (26) is the part of the sentence that substitutes for the *wh*-phrase (*when*) in the context question. This focus presents a contrastive (exhaustive, exclusive) reading of the prepositional phrase, associated with *only*, which is the new information. However, there are instances when old information needs to be focused. In Std Eng, this can be done by focus-shifting, by stressing the focused constituent (making it prosodically prominent), as shown in (27) below:

> 27. A: What did John give to Mary?
>   B: John gave MARY a book.

The data in (27) demonstrate the relation between focus and prosody in standard varieties of English. In the absence of the use of prosodic marking for focus, Ind Eng, especially in informal contexts, focuses old information by using the pragmatic particle *only* which appears immediately to the right of the presentationally (non-contrastively) focused constituent, carrying a specific semantic/pragmatic function. In (28)–(30) below, the particle *only* immediately following the subject phrase carries a specific semantic reading of 'least likely', and performs the pragmatic function of indexical assertion, as argued in Kidwai (1997), drawing the attention of the hearer to a particular part of the speaker's utterance. In (31), the particle *only* appears after the object phrase, again marking presentational focus: *only* (a) expresses the unexpectedness, the 'least likely' component of the meaning, and (b) makes salient part of A's utterance.

28. A: What did her mother do?

29. A: Why didn't you ask your teacher to show you how to write an essay?
     B: *She only* told us to write like this.

30. A: What are these politicians doing about it?
     B: *These buggers only* are responsible for this mess.
        [*buggers* refers to local Indian politicians]

31. A: Why are these women dressed like that?
     B: These women wear everyday *expensive clothes only*.

It is perhaps worth pointing out that none of the data above in (28)–(31) carry contrastive focus reading, as in (26), which suggests that the use of *only* with old information in these data carries nonquantificational (referred to here as 'presentational') focus. This is an important innovation which is widespread in all varieties of Ind Eng (Sridhar 1992, 1996; Bhatt 1995; Kidwai 1997) and asserts the presuppositional structure of an utterance (Bhatt 2000).

5.4 SPEECH ACTS IN NEW ENGLISHES

Several researchers have provided evidence of cross-cultural differences in the way the same speech act is realised in different languages (Cohen and Olshtain 1981; Blum-Kulka, House and Kasper 1989), and there have recently been studies that have shown how speakers-writers of institutionalised varieties of English choose different, culture-specific strategies to perform acts such as offering gratitude, leave-taking, requests, apologies, etc. (K. Sridhar 1991; D'souza 1991; Y. Kachru 1991). The culture-specific use of items such as the palliative *just* or *a little* in Ind Eng performs politeness functions, mitigation in requests, for instance. These items are used to situate the epistemological viewpoints of the speaker-writer, calling into consideration the beliefs, preconceptions and values that the speaker-writer shares with the addressees within a sociocultural context.

Patterns of expressing politeness, apologies, compliments and face-saving devices are often carried over from L1 practices to New English. Where these are different from habitual Inner Circle patterns, there is some potential for misunderstanding. People putting on their best cultural manners might be misjudged as being insincere or fawning. The opposite is also possible, when unmarked requests like *Will you give me water?* (from Ind Eng, Sridhar 1996:150) might appear to be rude according to Inner Circle expectations. Sridhar notes that such expressions do not carry overtones of being brusque or rude in Ind Eng. Mesthrie (1999b) discusses two examples of the experiences of African and Asian students in the United States, concerning linguistic manners at table. More than one African graduate student has gone hungry at his (or her) first Thanksgiving or other hosted dinner, because of responding to the host's offer of a second helping with an automatic *No thanks*. Back home this would have been recognised as a politeness strategy, with no truth-conditional semantics. There it would have been impolite to accept a meal or a second helping from a host outside one's home the first two or three times of being asked. One allows oneself to be eventually persuaded, often with the mitigative 'just a little bit', before taking or allowing oneself to be served a usually large helping. In the United States students found to their dismay that their *No thanks* was taken literally, with no second offer ever materialising.

Japanese students face the opposite dilemma, since in their cultural grammar, it would be rude to refuse an offer of food. One student reported that on her first flight on a United States airline, she drank six glasses of orange juice, before the plane had barely left Tokyo. She was not particularly thirsty! The American stewardess had assumed that it was within the passenger's rights to refuse the offer, whereas, once asked, the passenger felt obliged to accept.

In (32) below, an excerpt from an email-text (used with the writer's permission) to one of the authors requesting advice on a specific issue, a number of strategies to mitigate the potentially face-threatening act of request can be seen. The structure of this email-letter follows a rather standard pattern in non-native varieties of English (see Kirkpatrick and Zhichang 2002): The salutations initiate the discourse, followed by what Scollon and Scollon (1991) have called 'facework', followed by the reasons and justifications for the 'request', and finally the actual request. From the perspective of pragmatics of language use in Ind Eng, especially the linguistic devices used for performing various speech acts, several points are noteworthy here. First, one notices the transfer of discoursal and rhetorical norms of the first language, Kashmiri, in the use of the 'greeting', *handfolded Namaskar*, and conveys 'blessings' from others using the culturally appropriate Kashmiri form, *AAHI*. The capitalization of *AAHI* is presumably a textual cue to the reader of its special status, a Kashmiri word code-mixed for the special purpose of conveying 'blessing' at once establishing solidarity in an English text. Second, the use of the form *Respected Sir* in the salutation section letter opening presents an asymmetric relationship between the writer and the intended reader. This strategy is often used in local cultural contexts to minimise the threat to face and to express polite behaviour, as noticed elsewhere in Nig Eng by Bamgbose (1992). Furthermore, the 'no-naming' strategy is part of a structured system of 'expressing respect' in the South Asian context (see Jain 1973; D'souza 1991). Third, the actual 'request' is made after considerable facework is done, and reasons and justification for the request are presented. Finally, the palliative forms, *a little* and *just*, are used precisely when a 'request' is mentioned in a bid to minimise the illocutionary force of the speech act. (Parts of the text are deleted to protect the identity of the people mentioned in the email.)

32. *Respected Sir,*
    Handfolded Namaskar!
    Hope this e-mail of mine will find you in a good mood and sound health. We met in Delhi at the Press Club of India some time back and I hope you will recollect that meeting with Kashmiri writers and scholars.
        To me as a student of literature interacting with you was a fascinating and memorable experience. I am sure you also must have enjoyed that interaction. I believe you must have concluded your research by now and must be preparing to compile the findings.
        I and all other writers whom you met send you *AAHI* and wish you good luck.
        Sir, I have a *little* request. I am to speak at a seminar at Delhi on Wednesday next and my topic is '[xxxxxxx.]' In my paper I am certainly to argue against certain points raised by Sh. X, in favour of his claim that 'xxxx.' I do not agree with him.
        Sir my request to you is *just* to kindly let me know, if you may, whether you also think and believe as Dr. X believes or you have a contrary view after touring the 'Language region'.
        Sir, you as a professional Linguist have very deep understanding of the subject and your opinion is certainly more considered, valid and authentic and it is definitely going to add a new dimension and authenticity to this subject of great importance.
        Sir, This is a scholarly urge which I hope you will respond to in a positive manner.
    With very warm regards.
    [XYZ]

D'souza (1991:311–12) presents evidence to show how the syntax and the sentiments which contribute to the illocutionary force of 'request' in (33) are 'very Indian'. In (33), the speaker uses a mix of colloquial and formal speech simultaneously to make a direct request and give an indirect 'compliment' to his visitor. Note also the use of transfer of the local idiom 'creating earthquakes', to express raucous, rowdy behaviour. Compliments, generally, and 'thanking', in the Indian context, are rare and are used to index formality and distance.

33. 'Poltoo, kindly stop this nonsense straightaway! We're having a brilliant and cultural lady guest and you're creating earthquakes.'

In expressing 'gratitude', a very ornate, high, deferential style is characteristically preferred, as Y. Kachru (2001:348) argues, to express cultural identity within set hierarchies. Y. Kachru discusses an example of an 'Inner circle speaker of English' who upon converting to Hinduism and later becoming Acyutananda Swami expresses his gratitude to his spiritual teacher in the traditionally expected prose (34):

34. I offer my prostrate obeisance first unto all the devotees that have surrendered unto his divine lotus feet and next unto the devotees who will in the future take shelter of his lotus feet, and then I offer my humble obeisances unto his lotus feet again and again. May he bless this first translation attempt so that it may be accepted by the Lord Sri Krsna, and may he engage me in the service of the six Goswamis of Vrindanava, Lord Caitanya, and Radharani.

Finally, in (35) below, we see an example of speech acts of 'greetings' and 'blessings' as part of the overall speech act of 'leave-taking' in Ind Eng (Y. Kachru 1991:301). In the excerpt below, the greeting functions, are taken directly from Panjabi, as a presequence for blessing, and the two together are interpreted as leave-taking in the context of the interaction.

35. ... She bent her head to receive her mother-in-law's blessing. '*Sat Sri Akal.*' '*Sat Sri Akal,*' replied Sabhrai lightly touching Champak's shoulder. '*Sat Sri Akal,*' said Sher Singh. 'Live in plenty, Live a long age,' replied Sabhrai taking her son's hand and kissing it. 'Sleep Well.'

The excerpt in (35), taken from Khushwant Singh's novel *I Shall Not Hear the Nightingale*, uses ritualised greeting common among Sikhs for both meeting and parting. The routine response from elders to this greeting is a blessing. Given this context, Y. Kachru (1991) argues that the interpretation of the difference in mother's response in the two action chains (with daughter-in-law and with son) therefore does not follow from ordinary conversational implicature. Rather, it has to be calibrated along the dimensions of domain (family), setting (home), mutual relationship participants (mother/son/daughter-in-law), occasion (leave-taking for the night) and linguistic context (the two action chains).

In sum, the use of speech acts in New Englishes requires an understanding of the form–function relations inherent in the speech acts, an understanding of the sociocultural practices of the speech community that invest individual acts with different values, and an understanding of the multiple norms underlying the styles and strategies of bilingual users.

5.5 DISCOURSE ACROSS CULTURES

One generalisation that has emerged from studies of English discourse across cultures is that there is a strong relationship between the forms that English manifests and its speakers' perceptions of reality and the nature of their cultural institutions (Gumperz 1982; Y. Kachru 1983). In the WE context Y. Kachru (1983) observes that it is the cultural context and not the English language which constrains the ways of encoding interactions and leads to different discourse patterns. The interactional exchange, (36) below (from Scollon and Scollon 2000:122), between a Chinese businessman and an American businessman with the same business interests, exemplifies the role played by the context of culture – here the address system (Ervin-Tripp 1968) – in different interpretations of that exchange.

36.	Mr Richardson:	By the way, I'm Andrew Richardson. My friends call me Andy. This is my business card.
	Mr Chu:	I am David Chu. Pleased to meet you, Mr Richardson. This is my card.
	Mr Richardson:	No, no. Call me Andy. I think we'll be doing a lot of business together.
	Mr Chu:	Yes, I hope so.
	Mr Richardson (reading Mr Chu's card):	'Chu, Hon-fai.' Hon-fai, I'll give you a call tomorrow as soon as I get settled at my hotel.
	Mr Chu (Smiling):	Yes. I'll expect your call.

Scollon and Scollon note that the two men left the exchange with very different impressions of the situation: Mr Richardson was pleased that he got off to a good start, whereas Mr Chu was uncomfortable and feels that he will have difficulty working with Mr Richardson. The difference in the readings of the two situations by the two men resides in the respective cultural context that each uses in interpreting the exchange. Coming from a cultural system of symmetric solidarity, in which establishing egalitarian relationships is the communicative norm, Mr Richardson uses the given name, Hon-fai, as an involvement strategy of politeness in a bid to establish solidarity. What Mr Richardson does not know is that the Chinese have a complex structure of names, which depends on situations and relationships; in the system of symmetrical deference in initial business relationships, the given name is never used, especially by a stranger. Mr Chu thus feels quite uncomfortable. He instead prefers to use independence strategies of politeness, realised as the address form of Title-Family Name. The difference in meaning in the above exchange, Scollon and Scollon argue, results from differences in cultural resources used for linguistic interpretation.

The influence of native sensibilities on discourse patterns is also observed in other forms of second-language writing: academic, expository and persuasive. Eades (1991) and Harkins (2000) have discussed in detail the transfer of pragmatic norms from Aboriginal Australian languages into Australian Aboriginal English, thereby indexing an Aboriginal identity for its use as a lingua franca across the linguistically diverse Aboriginal communities. Y. Kachru, in a series of articles analysing expository writing in second languages, demonstrates the different stylistic and discoursal conventions that writers, working within new linguistic and cultural paradigms, use in new varieties of English, giving rise to multinorms of styles and strategies. She argues (1996:130) that the writing conventions in ESL contexts do not follow the monolithic structure of expository writing in English (described in, e.g., Smalley and Hank 1982), i.e. an introduction, which consists of thesis statement, claims and background information, followed by the body, which consists of an elaboration of the initial thesis statement or supporting evidence of the claim, followed by a conclusion. In her data (Kachru 1996:133) on essays written in English by college students in India, there were twice as many essays that show a non-linear structure (see 37 below) that is characteristic of native Indic languages as those that feature the American English norm of straight linear structure (see 38 below). Although there were some essays that show mixed properties, both linear and non-linear, the structure of the majority of essays supports the hypothesis that texts produced by bilinguals in a second language will show effects of the linguistic and rhetorical conventions of the first language environment (Y. Kachru 1996:130).

37. Non-linear structure
    Paragraph 1   introduction/background
    Paragraph 2   problem/elaboration
    Paragraph 3   introduction/comment
    Paragraph 4   elaboration/solution/further elaboration
    Paragraph 5   solution/conclusion/comment

38. Linear structure
    Paragraph 1   introduction/background
    Paragraph 2   problem
    Paragraph 3   comment (clue to writer's stance)
    Paragraph 4   elaboration of problem
    Paragraph 5   further elaboration/comment
    Paragraph 6   further elaboration
    Paragraph 7   solution

Expository writing in Ind Eng thus is unique in that it (a) allows for an affective style, (b) lacks a straight linear progression of thought, (c) involves a high level of tolerance for structural diversity and digressions (which are also tolerated in academic English discourses in Germany, cf. Clyne 1987) and (d) shows transfer of pragmatic-discoursal norms from local languages (Y. Kachru 1987). Others have corroborated Y. Kachru's view. Saville-Troike (2003) analyses contrastive patterns of communication in 200 statements of purpose, written in English by students from all over the world applying for admission to graduate programmes in the United States. These statements show how individuals present their 'face', as a negotiated public image in a communicative event that lacks face-to-face interaction. One of the salient contrasts they find in the patterns of communication is in the strategies for politeness that applicants choose to adopt between themselves and whoever they perceive their addressee to be. By and large, the results show that Asian writers choose deferential strategies of (negative) politeness compared to others who choose strategies of positive politeness. Asians, for example, choose deferential strategies such as 'your respected university', be part of 'your distinguished graduate program', and studying with 'your outstanding faculty' in declaring their reasons for application. Non-Asian students, on the other hand, use non-deferential strategies such as: 'Given my background, experience, and interest, I do believe myself to be the ideal candidate'; 'The reasonable prices and good atmosphere in [state] encouraged me to apply at your University.' Saville-Troike (2003:182) concludes that writers of the statement of purpose use a variety of strategies: they 'are influenced not only by the conventions of their native language and culture, but also by the knowledge they have of the addressees' language and culture, by their knowledge of the resources of the lingua franca for this situation (English), and by the expectation and attitudes they hold and develop in the process of constructing a "face"'. These conclusions also hold for the structure of argumentative texts written by non-native writers of English. Y. Kachru (1997) and Choi (1988) present data from Indian and Korean argumentative writings in English, respectively, that do not conform to the standard text structure – problem–solution analysis – proposed by Tirkkonen-Condit (1985) and Teo (1995): argumentative texts show evidence of multiplicity of forms and diversity of rhetorical methods that bilinguals use as a model underlying 'an *interrhetoric* of transferred, transmogrified, and partially adopted pragmatic strategies for self-presentation and management of "face" in interaction' (Saville-Troike 2003:182).

5.6 DISCOURSE CONTEXT IN NEW ENGLISH LITERATURE

The topic of New English literature is a vast one that would take us away from our immediate goals of characterising 'ordinary' language use. We limit ourselves to some broad characteristics of language and discourse in literature emanating from New English territories. In former times much literature from the colonies strived to mirror metropolitan themes and styles. However, their new cultural contexts also impacted on the production of literary discourse, representing different ways of saying and meaning. In this section we draw on literary illustrations of these processes from Africa and Asia. As we noted in section 2.1, literary texts do not always exemplify the exact structural patterns of New English speech. Rather they are authorial representations of such speech, which may vary in accuracy and degree of literary licence taken. Moreover, some authors do not intend to represent English but the indigenous language(s) of a territory via the medium of English.

The most celebrated example of the production of difference in English discourse is discussed by the creative writer Chinua Achebe (1965:29), using the following passage from *Arrow of God* as an illustration where the chief priest is telling one of his sons why it is necessary to send him to church:

39. I want one of my sons to join these people and be my eyes there. If there is
    nothing in it you will come back. But if there is something then you will
    bring back my share. The world is like a Mask, dancing. If you want to see
    it well, you do not stand in one place. My spirit tells me that those who do
    not befriend the white man today will be saying 'had we known' tomorrow.

Achebe then speculates, 'supposing I had put it another way. Like this
for instance':

40. I am sending you as my representative among those people – just to be on
    the safe side in case the new religion develops. One has to move with the
    times or one is left behind. I have a hunch that those who fail to come to
    terms with the white man may well regret the lack of foresight.

The first passage expresses the local rural sensibilities by the use of
local proverbs and other culture-bound speech patterns, expressing
a local Nigerian discoursal identity. Achebe concludes that though
the material is the same, 'the form of the one [listed here as (39)] is
in character, and the other [(40)] is not'. B. Kachru (1986) notes that
the production of difference in English discourse across cultures has
more to do with the use of native similes and metaphors, the transfer
of rhetorical devices, the translation ('transcreation') of proverbs and
idioms, the use of culturally dependent speech styles and the use of
syntactic devices.

While in Achebe's example above we notice the transfer of discourse
and rhetorical norms of Igbo into literary English, in example (41)
below, from Raja Rao's *Kanthapura* (1938:10), we observe a slightly different acculturation of text: a narrative loaded with historical and
cultural presuppositions that are different from the traditional historical and cultural milieu of English literature (B. Kachru 1987). The
references to local cultural-historical practices juxtaposed with local
contemporary political events of the time results in a text with a highly
culture-specific meaning system.

41. 'Today,' he says, 'it will be the story of Siva and Parvati.' And Parvati in
    penance becomes the country and Siva becomes heaven knows what! 'Siva
    is the three-eyed,' he says, 'and Swaraj too is three-eyed: Self-purification,
    Hindu-Moslem unity, Khaddar.'
        [Glosses: *swaraj* 'self rule, self sufficiency, independence'; *khaddar*
    'hand-woven cotton cloth – a symbol of *swaraj*]

The other strategic difference in organisational design of literary
texts in New Englishes lies in the linguistic transfer from mother-
tongue patterns. One finds in Raja Rao's *Kanthapura* (1938:137) large-
scale syntactic transfer from Kannada narrative style, marked with

'endless coordination', into Rao's English prose (see Sridhar 1982: 297), as evidenced in (42) below:

> 42. Then the police inspector saunters up to the Skefflington gate, and he opens it and one coolie and two coolies and three coolies come out, their faces dark as mops and their blue skin black under the clouded heavens, and perspiration flows down their bodies and their eyes seem fixed to the earth – one coolie and two coolies and three coolies and four and five come out, their eyes fixed to the earth, their stomachs black and clammy and bulging, and they march toward the toddy booth; and then suddenly more coolies come out, more and more and more like clogged bullocks …

Likewise, the Nigerian author Gabriel Okara uses local Ijaw syntactic patterns such as Subject-Object-Verb word order in his use of English in *The Voice*. The following excerpt from his work (1964:13) presents this clear case of syntactic transfer as part of his creativity, embedding African cultural practices, folklore and imagery in an attempt to bridge the cultural gap between the foreign and the local. The result is a Western language transmitting non-Western thought processes.

> 43. It was the day's ending and Okolo by a window stood. Okolo stood looking at the sun behind the tree tops falling. The river was flowing, reflecting the finishing sun, like a dying away memory. It was like an idol's face, no one knowing what is behind. Okolo at palm trees looked. They were like women with their hair hanging down, dancing, possessed.

In sum, literary creativity in English discourse across cultures takes different structural-textual forms, as the above examples illustrate, because literary texts as discourse reflect the underlying thought patterns, social norms, cultural practices, attitudes and values of the people writing, as well as represented in, the texts. The connection between text and context not only results in cultural authenticity, but also enables a new way of meaning making, of representation that is different from traditional canons; consequently, English is ritually de-Anglicised. Creative writers, in experimenting with the English language, draw on their native sensibilities and inherited forms of culturally sanctioned discourse patterns. This is not always appreciated by outside readers and critics, as noted at the beginning of this chapter.

5.7   STYLE SHIFTING AND CODE-SWITCHING

In multilingual settings, alternation between codes – dialects or languages – is the norm rather than the exception. The new alchemy of English in multilingual contexts is also characterised by extensive switching and mixing with local dialects and/or languages, serving several pragmatic functions such as new articulations of identity, values, power and solidarity. In their seminal paper, Blom and Gumperz (1972) identified two different types of code-switching in a small town called Hemnesberget in Norway: situational switching and metaphorical switching. Situational code-switching involves change in social setting, as for instance when teachers deliver formal lectures in the standard dialect (Bokmål) but switch to the local dialect (Ranamal) to encourage open discussion. Metaphorical code-switching, on the other hand, is triggered by changes in topic rather than situation. Blom and Gumperz observed that the interactions between clerks and residents in the community administration office involved the local dialect for greetings, but the standard dialect for business transactions. The switching serves both situational and metaphorical functions. At the situational level, it differentiates 'small talk' from 'business'. At the metaphorical level, it carries different discourse functions such as power vs solidarity, exclusion vs inclusion, intimacy vs distance, etc.

Code-switching in new Englishes also indexes several discourse functions. Mesthrie (1992a:219), for example, discusses a case of downshifting in the use of the mesolectal variety of IndSAf Eng by a young Indian attendant at airport security in South Africa to a passenger of the same ethnic background, in (44) below.

44. You haven' got anything to declare?

The unmarked choice in this context would normally be the formal acrolectal equivalent, 'Do you have anything to declare?' As the author notes, although the security guard and the passenger were strangers, the speaker was tacitly defusing the syntax of power in favour of mesolectal, ethnic solidarity, whilst still doing his duty.

Other instances of code-switching involve the use of local languages in English discourse to perform various functions. In (45) below (taken from *Times of India* news-brief, *www.timesofindia.com*, 12 Oct. 2001), we notice a strategic use of Hindi in English to create new semiotic opportunities for Ind Eng users.

45. There have been several analyses of this phenomenon. First, there is the 'religious angle' which is to do with Indian society. In India a man feels guilty when fantasizing about another man's wife, unlike in the west. The *saat pheras* around the *agni* serves as a *lakshman rekha*.
     [Glosses: *saat pheras* 'seven circles made by bride and groom at wedding'; *agni* 'sacred fire'; *lakshman rekha* 'protective circle for a wife']

The italicised phrases in (45) are clearly instances of code-switching, not borrowing, since they are not part of Ind Eng. The switch to Hindi in the bilingual mode of this news-feature presentation realises a significant pragmatic function: these words serve as vehicles of cultural memory; recalling the local-cultural practices of the past within the global medium of news reporting in English. The Hindi words in (45) are rooted in the most important historical narratives (Vedas) and the great Hindu epic (the *Ramayana*) of India, and a full appreciation of the text therefore demands knowledge of the Sanskrit Vedic traditions and cultural-historical literacy of the indigenous people. The switch to Hindi produces an immediate, authentic and particularised interpretation of meaning among the bilingual readership of the Ind Eng newspaper. Such strategic uses of local languages in English reflect a new socio-ideological consciousness, a new way to negotiate and navigate between a global identity and local sociohistorical practices.

The code-switching between English and Hindi in the register of newspapers also serves to foreground the contrast between cultures and ideologies; specifically, the appearance of Hindi enables a new representation of the indigenous social and cultural practices in a global idiom. The news report in (46) below appears to be supporting the Italian-born wife of the former Prime Minister of India, now the leader of the Congress Party, who was demonised by the then nationalist government of the Bharatiya Janata Party. The semantics of *layak bahu* (competent daughter-in-law) is socioculturally grounded, its explication offered in the relative clause that follows the noun *bahu*.

46. What's more we should respect her for being a *layak* Indian *bahu* who stayed on to do her duty by her husband's family, she reared her children and instilled in them the best Indian values, she took care of her mother-in-law and husband's legacy . . .

The data above show that it becomes communicatively economical to move from a 'modern' public voice (of English) to a distinctive 'ethnic voice'. In this new, hybrid code with modern and traditional associations, the matrix language is English, supplying the grammatical frame in the sense of Myers-Scotton (1993a), and the embedded language is Hindi, supplying only certain content morphemes. These content morphemes are used to express cultural meanings; the socio-pragmatic function of code-switching is the symbolic transformation of the medium into the message.

The bilingual code-switched mode serves several other functions as well: (i) it authentically expresses the sociohistorical experiences of the English bilingual population; (ii) it captures the cultural-semantics of the utterance; and (iii) it reflects the hybrid, bicultural nature of identity. Furthermore, the switching also highlights another important aspect: the use of Hindi as a rhetorical authentication of indigenous gendered practices. The text presents a 'foreigner' as entrenched in indigenous discursive practices (men-women roles), authenticating her as (one of) 'us', through the use of an indigenous language (Hindi).

For East Africa (and beyond) Myers-Scotton (1993b) has shown convincingly how code-switching in ordinary speech plays out a post-colonial identity. Whereas English frequently indexes 'education', 'status', 'Westernisation', etc., local languages signal local and community orientations. Myers-Scotton (1993b) demonstrates how code-switching is frequently used to play these orientations strategically against each other. More specifically, a switch in code changes the prevailing rights and obligations associated with the interaction up to that point. A speaker may switch from Kiswahili (which indexes neutrality between ethnicities) to a more localised language like Luhya in emphasising kinship obligations. Or a speaker may switch from either of these to English to emphasise status or power and distance from the interlocutor.

5.7.1 Code-switching in creative performance

In this section we turn to contexts which exploit code-switching for aesthetic reasons, and which create new sociocultural spaces within specific WE societies. The use of Hindi in English texts to authenticate gendered practices in India appears in different possible variations. In (47), for instance, the switch to Hindi corresponds to local cultural etiquette: it recalls a particular ritual-cultural practice that cannot be translated into English without losing some of its cultural semantics.

47. The young women – always overdressed – will typically say, *'Mummyjee, aap rahne deejeye, Chai mein bana ke laungi, mujhe apne kartavyon ka ehsas hai.'* [= Mom, you leave it (do not worry). I will make (and bring) tea. I am aware of my (traditional) responsibilities.] (*Times of India*, 12 May 2002, p. 10)

The insertion of content morphemes from local languages into an English frame, or vice versa, is also used in other registers and genres. In increasingly many New English contexts, popular music, especially hip-hop and rap, uses English mixed with local languages to express agency and identity, in rather prestigious and lucrative music genres. (Some critics caution that these practices carry a great deal of gender bias.) In parts of East Africa, for instance in Tanzania and Malawi, hip-hop has become both a marker of identity and a vehicle of social commentary (Perullo and Fenn 2003). In these countries, Perullo and

Fenn (2003:37) argue, hip-hop 'is viewed as dynamic instances of both local and global culture... One significant component of rap musical practice in Malawi that illustrates the confluence of multiple influences and forces is language choice.' In these countries, the language choices for rap include not only English, Swahili or Chichewa, but also language-mixed varieties. Language mixing, as in the Tanzanian rap album, *Swahili Rap*, is part of the linguistic repertoire used in this genre: the lyrics are mostly in Swahili but the choruses are in English (Perullo and Fenn 2003:37). The local languages, Swahili and Chichewa, serve to present and emphasise local meanings, as we have frequently emphasised. Omoniyi (2006) gives an example of Nigerian hip-hop, as shown below in (48), from the lyrics of the Plantashun Boyz *In Life*, which is a mix of Standard English, Pidgin English and Yoruba. The use of local languages and pidgin has a specific pragmatic function: it is an act of linguistic resistance 'to wholesale assimilation by global hip-hop culture and to carve out an independent glocal identity' (Omoniyi 2006:198). 'Glocal' is the term used to describe a hybrid space, in which the global is adapted to the local (and perhaps vice versa).

48. Body
   Omoge show me right from wrong   [Baby]
   Jowo wa sinu aiye mi   [Please come into my life]
   Ko je kin da bi okurin   [Let me be like a man]
   We'll be loving one on one
   Till we see the morning sun

   (Pidgin Rap)
   Ah ah ah,
   Ah check am
   Baby anytime I see your face
   My heart go start to scatter
   After I check am na you be my desire
   I no dey tell you dis because I wan dey talk am
   I dey tell you dis based on say no say I day mean am
   And I mean am
   So mek you try to understand my point of view
   Day and night infact *I just dey think of you*
   Na you I want and na you I got to have

In many instances, the selective inclusion of local languages simply underscores the multilingual character of the society. In Singapore, for example, the use of different languages in English pop music, such as that of Dick Lee, reflects the intermingling of diverse cultures, and the broader cosmopolitan and global influences on Singapore's culture (Kong 1997). The data in (49) show that in a space of one verse, where the matrix language is English, content morphemes from French, Tamil and Malay are used essentially as terms of endearment, whereas Mandarin is used to express 'I love you'.

49. *Cherie je t'aime, cherie je t'adore*
     My darling I love you a lot more than you know
     Cherie je t'aime, cherie je t'adore
     My darling I love you a lot more than you know
     Oh Mustapha, Oh Mustapha
     Sayang, sayang na chew sher wo ai ni
     Will you, will you fall in love with me.

Rap in other contexts of New Englishes offers similar linguistic mechanisms to produce a sociolinguistic distinction. Japanese pop (J-Pop) and Korean pop (K-Pop) present other exemplars of the process. In J-Pop, Japanese rappers create a new musical 'dialect' by adding English words to Japanese to make compelling rhymes (Condry 2000), but more importantly, as Pennycook (2003) notes, the use of English enables a re-fashioning of (mixed) identity in the very act of (Japanese) performances in English. In Korea, as Lee (2005) argues, pop music provides a discursive space in which the singers assert their self-identity, create new meanings, challenge dominant representations of authority, resist mainstream norms and values, and reject older generations' conservatism. In (50) below, the use of English and Korean is presumably involved in the sociolinguistic process of production of difference, between what can be explicitly articulated and socially sanctioned (in Korean) and what must be tacitly assumed (in English) because it is not socially licensed.

50. *Milayuy kkwumul kkwuko issnun neykyekey*   [You are dreaming of a
                                                     future]
     wusumul cenhay cwukosiphun naciman   [I want to send you a
                                                     smile but]
     Destiny is shine or not?
     newa nan etilo hyanghaykako issnunci   [I wonder where you and
                                                     I are headed]
     Please hold me tight across the time.

5.8   CONCLUSION

In this chapter we presented innovations in linguistic forms of new Englishes that are made to serve different pragmatic functions. These innovations – in syntactic forms, discourse particles, speech acts and discourse structure – are involved in the social production of difference. They transform global English into local Englishes that reflect local cultural contexts of English language use, and blend with the linguistic norms of multilingual communities. In this regard the prominence of code-switching is unsurprising as is the rise of distinctly hybrid forms of literary production.

STUDY QUESTIONS

1. Discuss how the linguistic innovations in New Englishes perform different social functions from Std Eng.
2. Using data from New Englishes, discuss the ways in which discourse particles help in the interpretation of messages.
3. What are the different, culture-specific strategies that New Englishes speakers choose to perform acts such as offering gratitude, leave taking, requests and apologies. Give examples.
4. Discuss, giving examples, how the cultural context impacts upon the production of literary discourse in New Englishes.
5. What does mixing of local languages with English accomplish for users of New Englishes?

Further reading

All works mentioned here are fully referenced in the bibliography.

Foundational books on topics covered in this chapter include Brown and Yule *Discourse Analysis* (1983); Levinson *Pragmatics* (1983); Brown and Levinson *Politeness: Some Universals in Language Usage* (1987); Saville-Troike *The Ethnography of Communication* (2002); Smith's *Discourse Across Cultures* (1987); and Myers-Scotton *Social Motivations for Code-Switching: Evidence from Africa* (1993b).

6 Language contact and language acquisition issues in New English research

6.1 INTRODUCTION

This chapter is concerned with issues pertaining to the acquisition of New Englishes. Our first task is to locate New Englishes as a class within the wider field of language contact. In particular we examine the views of scholars who see considerable overlaps between New Englishes and other contact varieties like Creoles. This necessitates a closer look at the role and nature of the superstrate, at the role and nature of substrate languages and at the possibility of 'universals' of language contact. However, since – unlike most contact varieties – New Englishes are to a large extent the products of educational systems, they also warrant an examination in terms of findings in the field of Second Language Acquisition (SLA). Finally, since some New Englishes are showing signs of becoming first languages for some of their users, certain perspectives from the study of language shift are necessary. Most studies concerned with these issues have focused on the syntax of specific New Englishes. We begin with the field of SLA.

6.2 NEW ENGLISHES AND SECOND LANGUAGE ACQUISITION: A PARADIGM GAP?

Given that New Englishes arose mainly in situations of bilingualism stimulated by classroom education, it is a natural expectation that they should be characterised, especially at earlier stages of development, in terms of the processes of SLA. To date this is an under-researched area in New English studies. Sridhar and Sridhar (1986) referred to this lack of interface between SLA studies and New English as 'a paradigm gap'. Before analysing their arguments, it is necessary to give an overview of the main preoccupations of SLA research. The term 'interlanguage' dates to the 1960s when applied linguists at Edinburgh began studying the developing competence of speakers of a second language. The term (coined by Selinker 1972) was meant to capture the insight that a second language acquirer frequently used a system that was different from his or her L1 (native language) and from the dominant language. Such learner language was variable, along fairly systematic lines, and there were specific pathways along which interlanguages developed. For the most part the trajectories of L2 acquisition were not qualitatively different from L1 acquisition by children. We illustrate this in relation to the acquisition of negation in 6.2.1.

For the most part interlanguage studies focused on individual learners in an 'Anglo' environment (the UK or USA), where the target language (TL) of the metropolis was readily available. On the whole an interlanguage was not considered a new language (it was an individual's competence rather than a group phenomenon) and hence would hardly count as a contact language. The position is quite different for New English varieties outside the metropolis. There we see the interlanguage concept applying to aggregates of people who would use their interlanguages with each other in certain domains. In this process new structural, lexical and pragmatic norms stabilise. ESLs may at first blush not seem to have a great deal in common with Creoles, especially if we consider that they are mostly introduced via an educational system and are mutually intelligible with the superstrate. On the other hand, as most ESL countries are multiethnic and multilingual, basilectal varieties may arise amongst people who have insufficient access to the superstrate, but who need it for communication in inter-ethnic contacts fostered by colonialism. Such varieties have been claimed to have considerable overlaps with extended pidgins and creoles. EFLs have been characterised as 'performance varieties' (Kachru 1992), suggesting that they do not have a clear-cut status and norm, in contrast to ESLs which are 'institutionalised' in educational and bureaucratic contexts. In so far as they are not used for 'internal' communication and in so far as they are the outcomes of formal teaching, EFLs are different from pidgins. However, the remoteness of the TL outside the classroom may well make the English of some tour guides an interlanguage worthy of comparison with pidgins and pre-pidgins.

Sridhar and Sridhar's observation was that much of the Edinburgh-inspired research concentrated on individual learners in 'Anglo' environments, where the TL was dominant. The assumption was that these learners should be aiming to acquire native-like competence, not just in grammar and pronunciation, but in the range of speech acts, styles and register differentiation of TL speakers. SLA researchers in the metropolis seemed to have overlooked the fact that the goal of SLA is bilingualism. Sridhar and Sridhar lamented that the SLA research ignored a large body of speakers and a database which offered the opportunity of understanding the dynamics of acquisition in environments where the aim of learners of English was to become functionally bilingual, whilst still competent in a local language and participating in its cultural milieu. That is, the social and cultural dimension was noticeably absent in SLA theorising. Furthermore appeals to factors like 'instrumental' versus 'integrative motivation' were particularly contingent upon assumptions that the host community was *in situ*, and ready and willing to interact with interlanguage users. In New English territories motivations were rarely integrative, given the colour–class stratification and the demographic imbalance between settlers and indigenous people. Yet characterising motivations as merely instrumental did injustice to the lure of education, English literature and culture felt by many New English elites. Individuals with a non-integrational motivation like the 'non-Westernised' women in Bombay studied by Lukmani (1972) demonstrate that instrumental motivation can lead to successful functional bilingualism. Finally, the notion of fossilisation needed greater nuance before it could be accepted in New English studies. Selinker (1972) had characterised Indian English as an interlanguage relative to English which seems to fossilise the *that* complement or *V that* construction for all verbs that take sentential complements (as in I *wanted that he should go*). As a somewhat negative concept the notion of fossilisation paid scant respect to issues of identity and culture. Substrate influence may not be evidence of a failure to learn a TL construction, but of an acceptance of an item from a pool of variants on the grounds of harmony with L1 constructions.

Sridhar and Sridhar consider transfer as a process that has been underplayed in the SLA literature – not so much by its original proponents at Edinburgh, but under the later influence of US scholars like Dulay and Burt (1973). The latter argued that SLA followed the pathways of L1 acquisition, and that very little influence from home languages could be detected in their database of children from a variety of international backgrounds learning English in the USA. Sridhar and Sridhar's position (1986:9) is the opposite: 'anyone familiar with the formal and pragmatic characteristics of [New Englishes] cannot fail to be struck by the fact that many of these features can be related to features of the speakers' mother tongue in a fairly transparent fashion'. How does one reconcile these disagreements regarding transfer? A significant difference is that the children studied in the USA are on their way to dominance in English (language shift, subtractive bilingualism) whilst the New English cases cited by Sridhar and Sridhar are not (language maintenance, additive bilingualism). We return to issues pertaining to transfer in section 6.2.2.

Sridhar and Sridhar (1986:12) acknowledge that the paradigm gap is also partly due to New English studies remaining (in 1986) 'descriptive and atheoretical, rather than based on rigorous and systematic empirical research'. We would go further and argue that, with a few exceptions, there is insufficient attention to processes of acquisition in the New English literature. When this issue *is* considered there is an over-reliance on transfer as the major acquisitional strategy. Indeed, Quirk, Greenbaum and Svartvik (1972) refer to New Englishes as 'interference varieties', a characterisation accepted by Sridhar and Sridhar (1986:10) and by Kachru (1983b:1–2).[1] This suggests a major role for transfer, as the defining characteristic of specific New English varieties. However, there is no reason to take this for granted. There is every reason to begin with a hypothesis that as natural languages, New Englishes follow ordinary processes of acquisition, with transfer playing a special (but not exclusive or even a major) role. To do justice to the acquisition of New Englishes we would have to consider the following:

(a) Comparing natural SLA (of individuals) with L1 acquisition
(b) Comparing classroom acquisition (of individuals) with natural SLA
(c) Comparing (group) New English acquisition with natural SLA
(d) Comparing (group) New English acquisition with classroom SLA

These would involve a consideration of language acquisition theory and transfer as well as of common processes amongst New Englishes.

Lalleman (1996) identifies four approaches to SLA that follow from different theoretical perspectives: (a) process as central, (b) language theory as central, (c) society as central and (d) instruction as central. The first perspective is largely a psycholinguistic one, concerned with language learning as a cognitive process, leaving it open whether there is a special language-learning capacity as opposed to general problem-solving strategies. This approach is especially concerned with processes of SLA. The second approach is more firmly embedded in linguistic theory, arising from the Chomskyan enterprise, which sees language as not just specific to the human species, but as a special genetically specified capacity different from other cognitive abilities. The prevailing Chomskyan view still rests on the notion of a critical period around puberty after which the genetic language acquisition

---

[1] Sridhar and Sridhar (1986:10), however, prefer the term 'transfer' to 'interference'.

endowment is believed to fade. Some researchers working within the Chomskyan framework (e.g. Flynn 1989) have, however, been actively engaged in ascertaining whether the same principles operative in L1 acquisition are to be found in SLA. The third approach grounds SLA within the field of bilingualism and contact, and focuses on issues pertaining to motivation, identity, attitudes and status. The fourth approach has overt pedagogical goals, aiming to institute or improve educational materials that make for more effective SLA classrooms. In the following subsections we examine some of the main issues within these approaches that are relevant to the field of New Englishes. In particular we look closer at (a) routes of development; (b) transfer; (c) linguistic universals; (d) strategies of processing.

6.2.1 Routes of development

SLA studies have established that the acquisition of a second language is not the piecemeal, hit-or-miss affair that it may sometimes appear to be. Learners, in fact, go through stages in acquiring the rules of the TL. Learning a new language is not done by imitations of surface structures alone, but by making deductions (sometimes incorrect ones) about the rules that underlie the output. Many errors made by adult language learners are indications of the process of deduction or hypothesis formation. Errors may be – paradoxically – evidence of learning. Many SLA studies (especially Dulay and Burt 1973) draw significant parallels between second- and first-language acquisition. Like adults learning a second language, children learning their first language make deductions about the rules of the TL, and often make developmental errors like *See how clever I'm is?* (where the 'chunk' *I'm* functions as a pronoun, and the verb *is* is overgeneralised as the copular form in 'exposed' sentence-final position). Children appear to learn linguistic subsystems in stages that have little basis in the actual input they receive from adults and from their peers. Early SLA studies focused on the acquisition of subsets of grammar like questions (e.g. Ravem 1974) and negation (e.g. Bellugi 1967). A longitudinal study of a few select speakers suggested similarities (in an Anglo environment) between L1 and L2 'naturalistic' acquisition. We take as a brief example verb phrase negation. L1 English negation was studied by Bellugi (1967) who found that children go through three phases in acquiring the rule. Stage A involved external negation (*No want stand head*, followed by Stage B, with internal negation (*He not bite you*). Stage C involves the availability of modal auxiliaries for negative attraction (*I can't see it*). For SLA a convenient summary of learners of English from a variety of backgrounds (Japanese, Spanish, German, Norwegian) and types of acquisition (natural, instructed, a mix) is given by Ellis (1994:99–101). These are individual learners from the Expanding Circle, not group ESL learners. Ellis identifies four stages, the first three of which are essentially the same as Bellugi's, and adds a fourth which is essentially a slight advance on stage III, showing the further development of the auxiliaries with negation. Ellis emphasises that the transition from stage I to IV is a gradual one, with intermediate overlapping stages. There is a gradual loss of earlier rules in favour of later ones. Minor differences might occur according to a speaker's language background, e.g. Norwegian and German learners have an additional stage involving postverbal negation; Spanish speakers seem to spend longer on the external negation stage I.

Longitudinal studies have rarely been carried out in New English research (an exception is Gupta 1994), where the traditions of dialect study (one-off interviews) seem more appropriate. However, adopting or simulating a longitudinal approach can offer certain insights. One simulation is based on studying not just the most fluent or educated exemplars of the New English, but a cross-section of speakers who may have fossilised at different stages of acquisition, depending on their personal needs or circumstances. Deciding what stage of acquisition a learner is in is not straightforward. In child-language studies the MLU (mean length of utterance) serves as a measure to grade children into stages, against which their grammatical (or other) subsystems can be characterised, evaluated or compared. In Language Contact studies adult subjects are usually grouped loosely into categories like basilect-mesolect-acrolect (see section 2.1). Deciding which lect a speaker falls into is often done impressionistically; hence the terms – as Bickerton (1971:464) stresses – are used for convenience of reference, rather than in any rigorous sense. Implicit in the terminology is the claim that the lects vary immensely, but that they are linked by characteristic linguistic processes.

One study that has examined negation from a development perspective is Mesthrie (1992a) on IndSAf Eng. There are speakers who have fossilised at a very early stage showing both external negatives (*No talkating* = 'I can't talk English') and internal negatives with *no, not* or partially analysed *don't* (*I not working in the mill* = 'I wasn't working in the mill'). Another group shows no trace of stage I negation nor the use of *no* as negator. It has generally progressed into Ellis' stages II and IV, though there are some fossilisations (e.g. some speakers use a double modal to express negation in sentences like *I might won't go* = 'I might not go'; and *din* is unanalysed for tense, resulting in forms like *din wanted* = 'didn't want'). A third group has progressed well beyond

stages I and II (showing no traces of these) into III and IV. This group
retains some salient structures like *shouldn't* for 'never used to' and
wouldn't in the expression *I wouldn't know* = 'I don't really know' and
never as an unemphatic negator in apparent free variation with *didn't*
(though it may also have the emphatic semantics of the TL). Finally,
there is a group whose norms are essentially those of the TL, with
minor variations like the absence of *shall* and *shan't*, and a preference
for *'s not* rather than *isn't* (speakers thus favour forms like *She's not at
home* rather than *She isn't at home*). This group essentially shows dialect
differences, rather than differences in acquisition stages (fossilisation)
characteristic of the other groups.

What is to be gained from such a developmental perspective? Firstly,
it clarifies what can be considered features of a New English, as distinct from developmental forms. This is done by internal comparisons
rather than by the dictates of the TL. For IndSAf Eng *shouldn't* (= 'didn't
use to / never used to / used not to') is a consistent feature of all but
the most acrolectal speakers. On the other hand, the status of double-
tensed negatives like *din wanted* (from **didn't wanted*) is clearly a fossilised developmental form, limited in practice to basilectal speakers.
Secondly, a developmental perspective helps characterise transfer by
identifying the stage at which it occurs. For negation in IndSAf Eng
there appear to be no transfer effects, despite the fact that postverbal
negatives occur in three of the substrate languages (Tamil, Telugu and
Gujarati). Thirdly, this perspective suggests (assuming the simulation
is valid – that fossilised stages of different speakers mirror an internal
developmental path of learners, especially non-acrolectal/elite ones),
that New Englishes are not products of relexification, which is what
the transfer hypothesis in its strongest form would indicate. There is
a 'relexification hypothesis' for Creoles (e.g. Lefevbre 1986 for Haitian
Creole) but not to our knowledge for New Englishes, though the very
phrase 'interference varieties' implies such an assumption.

Mesthrie's (1992a) study involved a community which acquired
English initially within the classroom, but also via work contacts outside the classroom. On the whole, the classroom is not the main determinant of the characteristics of IndSAf Eng, since it has been involved
in language shift, which brings the TL into informal and domestic
domains. Indeed a comparison with the English of India makes this
clear. Kachru (1983a:39) cites characterisations of Indian English as
'bookish' even in informal usage and 'imbued with a moralistic tone',
on account of the formal contexts of language acquisition. By contrast,
IndSAf Eng is often hyper-colloquial in situations requiring some formalese. (This appears to apply to Sgp Eng too.) The question can be

raised whether there is a difference in the route and rate of acquisition if exposure is mainly via the classroom rather than in more naturalistic circumstances. There is little consensus about the effect of formal instruction on the SLA process (Stern 1983, Ellis 1994). It is often difficult to separate the effects of formal instruction from the role of the additional input it provides. Nevertheless, many researchers hold that education influences the tempo and proficiency level finally reached, but not the order – or the route – of SLA (Lalleman 1996:5; Ellis 1994).

6.2.2　The role of transfer

One major factor that clouds the issue of the rate of development is transfer from the L1. This phenomenon (formerly referred to as 'interference') was overstressed in the earlier literature, especially in the school of Contrastive Analysis of the 1950s and 1960s. Differences between L1 and TL were seen as the main difficulties to be overcome in SLA (see Ellis 1985:19–30). Under the influence of the Chomskyan revolution later scholars erred in the other direction, in underplaying the role of transfer. Ellis (1985:40) puts the middle view succinctly:

> The learner's L1 is an important determinant of SLA. It is not the only determinant, however, and may not be the most important... The L1 is a resource of knowledge which learners will use both consciously and subconsciously to help them sift the L2 data in the input and to perform as best as they can in the L2.

Transfer is still a much-debated explanation in SLA. Little attention was paid in the traditional literature on Contrastive Analysis to questions like when and how transfer was likely to occur and whether it was subject to any constraints. Likewise by appealing to negative and positive transfer, the impression was created that SLA was essentially a process of relexification of the L1. Where structures of the L1 and the TL matched there was positive transfer; where they did not negative transfer was likely. Positive transfer opens the door to the theory of relexification mentioned above. One problem with this approach is that it ignores the fact that interlanguages are developing systems, which go through stages of complexity. The approach also wrongly assumes that the TL is present in its entirety to the learner to perform a contrast with the L1.

Subsequent approaches (notably that of Siegel 2003) have addressed the issue of transfer in contact languages. Although his main focus is on the development of pidgins and Creoles, his perspective on transfer can be applied to the development of New Englishes. Siegel draws a distinction between L2 performance and acquisition. He suggests that structures showing the influence of an L1 do not immediately appear as part of the L2 grammar. Rather, they are first added to the pool of variants in the interlanguage used for communication. Transfer, it is hypothesised, occurs when speakers are under duress to communicate at a higher level than they are ready for in the L2. Sharwood-Smith (1986:15) lists two such situations: (a) 'overload' situations or 'moments of stress' when the existing L2 system cannot cope with immediate communicative demands and (b) through a desire to express messages of greater complexity than the developing control mechanisms can cope with.

Later the pool of variants is subjected to processes of selection. Some variants may stabilise as part of competence, depending on both linguistic and social factors. A feature of the L1 may be retained in the L2 because it fits in with certain L1 patterns (the 'transfer to somewhere' principle discussed below). Social factors may also contribute, if there is desire not to sound entirely like a native speaker of the TL. Non-native-like structures may be deployed 'resourcefully and strategically to accomplish social and interactional ends' (Firth and Wagner 1997:292) or even as a form of resistance to the full power of the TL (Rampton 2005).

Research on constraints on transfer is an important and on-going area of enquiry, which tries to ascertain why certain features of an L1 – but not others – end up being transferred. Some researchers have evoked the criterion of markedness, claiming that marked structures of an L1 are seldom, if ever, transferred. Hyltenstam (1984:41–3) made this claim in connection with research on the learning of Swedish by people of different language backgrounds.

(a) Initial stages of interlanguage of a given TL are qualitatively similar for learners with different native languages.
(b) Unmarked categories from the native language are substituted for corresponding marked categories in the TL.
(c) Marked structures are seldom transferred, at least in initial stages, and if they are transferred, they are much more easily eradicated from the interlanguage.
(d) Unmarked categories occur in the early phases of interlanguage development, even if there is no structural basis for them in either L1 or L2.

However, such claims remain hypotheses rather than proven. Work on markedness in linguistics itself is inconclusive. Some formulations of the concept within the study of typology and universals

(Greenberg 1966; Comrie 1989) offer clear cross-linguistic guidelines for some constructions (e.g. for relative-clause formation with particular noun phrase functions). Markedness in respect of negation (which Hyltenstam initially focused on) is a bit more fuzzy.

An important constraint known as the 'transfer to somewhere principle' was formulated by Andersen (1983):

> A grammatical form or structure will occur consistently and to a significant extent in the interlanguage as a result of transfer if and only if (1) natural acquisitional principles are consistent with the L1 structure or (2) there already exists within the L2 input the potential for (mis-)generalization from the input to produce the same form or structure. Furthermore, in such transfer preference is given in the resulting interlanguage to free, invariant, functionally simple morphemes which are congruent with the L1 and L2 (or there is congruence between the L1 and natural processes) and [to] morphemes [which] occur frequently in the L1 and/or the L2. (Andersen, 1983b:182)

Part 1 of the above formulation proposes that an L1 structure is transferred if (and only if) it is unmarked. Part (2) proposes that there must be the potential for misgeneralisation in some (actually *other*) part of the TL grammar. Andersen cites Zobl's (1980) example of object pronoun placement in the interlanguages of English learners of French and of French learners of English. The French TL equivalent of 'I see them' is *Je les vois*, with the pronoun placed before the verb, unlike the usual English TL order. Zobl observes that English learners produce an interlanguage French form like *Je vois les* ('I see them'), while French learners never produce an English form like *I him see*. How does one explain this differential effect of transfer? By Andersen's principle English learners have a model in other French sentences in which objects (actually non-pronominal objects) follow verbs, and so transfer of the English structure is seen as viable. On the other hand French learners do not have a model in the English input for objects (pronominal or full nouns) to precede verbs; hence transfer of the French pattern is blocked. In other words, transfer interacts with over-generalisations in a fairly complex way in SLA.

It is a common finding in the subfield of error analysis to find that more than one explanation holds for certain interlanguage forms. Many instances of suspected transfer turn out to be also overgeneralisations of TL structures; whilst many overgeneralisations of TL structures turn out to be motivated by L1 considerations. Andersen's principle (or constraint) holds that each act of transfer is also an instance of over-generalisation (but not vice versa). Before a L1 feature can be transferred 'it must have somewhere to transfer to' – i.e. there must be a morpheme (or string of morphemes) in the TL that can be used or reanalysed to serve as a basis for the over-generalisation. The last part of Andersen's formulation stresses that the morpheme (or string of morphemes) being transferred must be perceptually salient in the TL (as a word or words or at least a stressed syllable) and must have a function or meaning related to the corresponding L1 morpheme.

One recent proposal on transfer by Bao (2005) merits some discussion here, as it relates to the genesis and development of novel grammatical features in contact varieties of English. Like Andersen, he argues for the contributions of both the substrate and superstrate to the developing variety. The aspectual system of Sgp Eng shows considerable substrate influence from Chinese. For example, the use of *already* and *ever* as perfective forms (outlined in section 2.4.2) display striking similarities in distribution to that of the Chinese morphemes *le* and *guo*, respectively. From these distributional similarities, Bao concludes that *already* and *ever* in Sgp Eng are grammaticalised from Chinese to express the perfective aspect. However, there are other aspectual forms of Chinese like the 'stative imperfective' and the 'tentative' that do not transfer into English. Bao proposes that linguistic innovations arise from systemic restructuring that takes place under pressures of language contact. Specifically, he argues for systemic substrate transfer subject to 'lexical filtering'. That is, if one substrate grammatical feature is transferred, other features of the same type will be transferred as well, provided they can be linked to morphosyntactic devices from English that can be readily adapted.

It appears to us that those New Englishes that are L2 systems taught via the classroom may well uphold Andersen's principle. On the other hand, in other New Englishes involving several substrate populations and incipient or completed language shift, language acquisition is less targeted and more 'off-track' (as in creolisation), leading to the transfer of some features that are not motivated from the TL. Consider the following sentences cited in Chapters 2 and 3:

1. Can or not? (Sgp Eng)
2. Have you Finnegans Wake read? (Ir Eng)
3. Who-who came? (IndSAf Eng)

These are uncontroversially examples of transfer from the substrates cited in Chapter 2. Yet it is hard to think of a template from the TL for them. These appear to be transfer without overgeneralisation, hence violations of Andersen's principle.

For this reason we will be examining (in section 6.4) insights for New Englishes that the field of Creolistics can offer. Sankoff (1994) shows how Tok Pisin-speaking children who are more distant from the Austronesian substrate than their grandparents actually use more of the preverbal particle *-i* with serial verbs. Earlier generations bilingual in Tok Pisin and an Austronesian language did not use this pattern. Sankoff concludes that people shifting to Tok Pisin made greater use of this form. 'It may be that when people want to express complex ideas they have not previously needed to communicate in the new language, they find themselves drawing more deeply from the resources of their native languages.' That is, the point of shift throws up the most innovations, including those produced by transfer, whilst the next generation of children serve as filters for these innovations (Mesthrie 2003).

6.2.3 Universals of SLA: parameter setting and newer approaches

The interlanguage approach typically charted the development of individual constructions in the learner's L2 as evidenced by the performance of speakers. Where possible this was done developmentally, by studying the output of the same learner over a period of time. Accounting for learners' development proved to be a complex matter in so far as numerous factors other than purely linguistic ones were involved in L2 acquisition – namely a speaker's motivation, nature of contacts with TL speakers and so forth. Interlanguage theory proposes that L2s of learners develop from simple systems to more complex ones, on the basis of interaction with TL speakers, with the L1 playing some role in the process. Approaches based more firmly on Chomskyan linguistics adopt a slightly different view of language development. For the Chomskyan the data are necessarily incomplete and the input (for both child L1 learner and any L2 learner) is somewhat 'impoverished'. This is not a sociological observation but a 'scientific system' one. In this section we review some work in the 'principles and parameters' model of Chomsky, which was dominant until the mid-1990s when a newer 'minimalist' approach was adopted. We offer a brief overview of the latter. It will not be possible to go into minute details of the approaches here: rather a skeletal approach will be adopted, with a view to seeing how SLA (and ultimately New English studies) can benefit from these approaches.

(a) **Parameter setting:** Chomskyan linguistics of the 1980s and 1990s viewed first-language acquisition not so much as a process of acquiring specific grammatical rules, as a procedure whereby the child sets the parameters of the principles of Universal Grammar. Chomsky (1986) hypothesised that Universal Grammar consisted of various subsystems of principles, many of which are associated with parameters that are fixed by experience of relatively simple data. Parameters involve certain options associated with various principles of linguistic organisation. Once the values of the parameters are set, the whole system is fully operative. As Chomsky (1986:146) pointed out, a useful analogy is to conceive of language as an intricate system associated with a finite set of switches – each of which has a finite number of positions, possibly as low as two in some instances. Parameter setting is thus a persuasive model in characterising the particular rules of a language within the perspective of Universal Grammar. For SLA and New English research the consequence of this line of thinking is important: subsets of language rules (which might not be closely related on the surface) work together and are acquired as one process. We illustrate this with the so-called 'pro-drop parameter', proposed by Chomsky (1981). According to Hyams (1986) the following phenomena relevant to all languages can be studied as one set:

  (i)   absence of empty pronoun subjects
 (ii)   presence of lexical material in AUX (e.g. uninflected modal auxiliaries)
(iii)   presence of pleonastic subjects (i.e. dummy *it* and *there*)

Languages can be characterised as [−Pro-Drop], or [−PD] for short, if they exhibit all three characteristics. Thus English and German are [−PD]. English for example has the setting 'negative' for the parameter, since:

  (i)   Empty pronoun subjects are disallowed (*He is my brother* rather than **Is my brother*);
 (ii)   Verbs like *will* and *may* are part of the AUX component of English grammar;
(iii)   Dummy subjects are preferred in examples like *There's someone at the door, It's snowing*, rather than **Is someone at the door; *Is snowing*.

On the other hand, languages like Spanish and Italian are [+PD] since they favour zero pronoun subjects; do not use dummy elements equivalent to English dummy *it* and *there*; and do not have a group of uninflected modals (i.e. modals behave like full verbs rather than specifically AUX elements). Hyams (1986) studied the emergence of this parameter in children's L1 English and Italian. She posits that the initial setting is [+PD]. With continued exposure to the data of their mother tongue, children work out whether the setting stays the same or has to be reset as negative. Hyams hypothesises that dummy *it* and *there* act as triggers that suggest to the learner that L1 English is [−PD].

Experimental SLA studies (for example Flynn and Espinal 1985; Flynn 1989) have tended to support Hyam's findings. Furthermore, in examining the SLA patterns of Jorge, a twelve-year-old Spanish speaker who had moved from Columbia to the United States, Hilles (1987) found support for Hyam's hypothesis in a more natural SLA setting. In the beginning of the taped sessions (weeks 1 to 4) Jorge used few auxiliaries and few pronouns, evincing a [+PD] setting. By the end (week 40) he had become fluent, showing amongst other things a reversal of the parameter to [−PD]. Hilles suggests that the emergence of dummy *it* and *there* coincide with a time when his data show a shift from one setting to another (around week 12).

For New English studies there is great potential value in the parameter-setting model since it adopts a unified approach to different facets of interlanguage grammar. Acquisition is not presented as a piecemeal process. Learners must set (or reset) parameters on the basis of experience with the TL. The issue of markedness is relatively clear if we accept that there are default settings in Universal Grammar – e.g. 'positive' for the pro-drop parameter. These settings are evident in initial child L1 and adult L2 language. The issue of transfer within this model boils down to whether the initial setting for a particular parameter is influenced by the value assigned in the L1 or not. It is likely that learners start with the default setting for pro-drop (which may or may not coincide with that of the L1). The marked setting of an L1 parameter ('negative' for pro-drop as in German and English) is presumably not transferred when learning a new language.

Mesthrie (1992a:167–74) examined the data from IndSAf Eng with a view to testing Hyam's hypotheses. The data supported claims of parametric unity and the switching of the parameter value from [+PD] to [−PD]. Mesthrie's demonstration is based not on individual interlanguage development, but on group norms. In particular, a small group of pre-basilectal speakers (whose English is essentially that of an early fossilised interlanguage) show an unambiguous [+PD] norm. Pre-basilectal sentences like the following occurred in the database:

4. Φ was working in the hospital. ('he' understood).
5. What time Φ go back Durban? (= 'When will you go back to Durban')
6. Not mark Φ be. (= 'There mustn't be a mark')

By contrast, the basilectal speakers' data are variable with some evidence of a shift taking place in the direction of [−PD]. Pronoun absence is infrequent (7.5 per cent of the time); auxiliaries are in use commonly; and dummy pronouns are in use, though by no means mandatorily. Mesthrie (1992a:173–4) argues that the resetting of the parameter is not instantaneous; it happens gradually with an intermediate phase of fluctuation between plus and minus. Moreover, New Englishes are well known for the phenomenon of backsliding, where speakers retain earlier forms of their interlanguage as part of a stylistic repertoire. In informal and intimate styles – and sometimes under stress – speakers may backslide towards earlier norms of the interlanguage. In IndSAf Eng speakers who generally use dummy subjects may drop them in informal or intimate styles:

7. Get off by the bus stop. (= (in context) 'I'll get off at the bus stop').

Ritchie (1986) argued that the basilect of Sgp Eng and Mal Eng is typologically different from that of metropolitan English. We can think of this in terms of a parameter 'subject-prominent' versus 'topic-prominent' language. In subject-prominent languages like English the delineation of topics is irregular, whilst in topic-prominent languages like Japanese the presentation of topics is a regular and basic part of sentence formation. Example (11) is taken from Kuno (1978:77).

8. Zoo   wa   hana ga   nagai
    elephant TOPIC nose SUBJECT long

Here the topic is *zoo* 'elephant' and the comment 'nose is long'. Sentence (11) would usually turn out in a subject-prominent language as 'Elephants have long noses' in which elephant as subject controls verb agreement. In Japanese the sense is 'As for elephants, noses are long', with elephants not controlling verb agreement nor having a direct genitival relation with the noun noses.

   Ritchie (1986) attempts to link the formation of topics and a few related constructions to the substrate influence of Chinese, which is a topic-prominent language. In particular the dialect exhibits three of the four factors which Li and Thompson (1976) consider diagnostic of topic-prominent languages:

  (i) topic-comment structures in which the topic is not understood
       to have a grammatical function within the comment clause
 (ii) richness of the class of expressions that can serve as topics
(iii) zero pronouns that are understood to be co-referential with overt
       topics (e.g. Q: *Did she see you?* A: *Saw*)
 (iv) Lack of dummy subjects (*there, it*)

Ritchie argues that the last three are characteristics of Singapore English and that he had insufficient information about the first. Although the case for influence from Chinese is persuasive here, as for the previous example (on pro-drop), explanations concerning default 'universal' settings also come into play and would appear to reinforce rather than contradict the argument for substrate influence.

(b)   The minimalist approach: A problem for SLA studies is that the syntactic theory (Government and Binding) which gave prominence to studies of principles and parameters is currently followed with less enthusiasm now than a decade or so ago, giving way to a new conception labelled 'minimalism'. It is too soon to assess the use of this framework as a tool for SLA study. We present some pointers, however. Chomsky (1995:219n.) outlines a minimalist programme for syntax which reduces the computational component of the grammar to two central mechanisms:

> MERGE, a stepwise combinatorial process which forms structures from syntactic elements and which is a general characteristic of all language-like systems.

> MOVE F which allows for movement of features (F) depending on whether lexical entries are defined as strong or weak which typically corresponds to richness of morphology. MOVE 'reflects the peculiarities of human language'. (Chomsky 1995:378)

It is not clear whether this illuminates the SLA process. Klein and Perdue (1997:336–42) posit that the basic syntax of early interlanguage can be described by the MERGE process, while the general absence of morphology in early interlanguage accounts for the absence of MOVE F. Further interlanguage development is dependent on a process of 'feature strengthening' in which the learner has to intuit from the input which features are strong in the TL. In their comments on this position, Bierswisch (1997) and Meisel (1997) take the opposite view that early interlanguage does not reflect UG; rather it evidences general cognitive strategies of linearisation. The term 'basic variety' is becoming increasingly popular within this approach to early SLA. The basic variety is hypothesised to underlie SLA (Klein and Perdue 1997) and pidginisation (Siegel 2003). It is characterised by a small set of organisational principles based on pragmatic constraints which account for the structures of early SLA and pidgins. The basic variety has the following characteristics: (a) it uses uninflected verbs and their arguments as the basic structure; (b) there is no copula; (c) it uses adverbials to mark aspectual categories of time, duration or frequency; (d) it uses verbs as boundary markers (e.g. *finish*); (e) there is no morphology or subordination; (f) it relies on pragmatic (e.g. focus last) and semantic principles (e.g. agent first) for word order.

6.2.4 Processing the TL

In contrast to the nativists who argue for a special language capacity that comes into play in successful SLA, some scholars adopt a more functionalist or cognitive view of second language development (e.g. Klein 1986; von Stutterheim and Klein 1987). Cognitivists stress that adult L2 learners, unlike L1 learners, have a cognitive system at hand that guides language acquisition. Hence L2 and L1 acquisition cannot generally be compared. Adult L2 learners have access to sophisticated conceptions of temporality, modality and locality, which feature prominently in early SLA. Cognitivists do not focus on syntactic form alone, but stress semantic concepts and pragmatic functions (Lalleman 1996:42). There are a number of overlapping models that can be broadly characterised as cognitive; Ellis (1994:247–413) in an admirable survey includes the following proponents:

> Krashen (1977) – Monitor Model
> Bialystok (1978) – Second language learning model
> McLaughlin (1980) – Information processing model
> Ellis (1984) – Variable Competence model
> Tarone (1983) – Capability Continuum
> Schmidt (1990) – Consciousness vs noticing
> Preston (1989) – Sociolinguistic model
> Bates and MacWhinney (1987) – Competition model
> Clahsen, Meisel and Pienemann (1983) – Multidimensional model

Whereas there is a great deal of difference in emphasis amongst these models (e.g. in the role of input, in the representation of L2 knowledge and relationship of knowledge to output) they all have in common an emphasis on performance over competence. This should not be taken to imply a broad Chomskyan/non-Chomskyan bifurcation, since Chomskyans themselves are divided over the nature of SLA. Some simply study SLA as if it had the same properties of L1 acquisition (principles of Universal Grammar), while others simply ignore SLA beyond puberty on the assumption that it is outside the purview of the language acquisition device. This, of course, opens the door for non-UG accounts. In an unwitting way nativists (concerned with L1 acquisition) have enhanced the cognitive perspective for adult L2 acquisition.

It is therefore appropriate to highlight a functionalist approach that has been proposed by Jessica Williams (1987) for the study of New

Englishes. Williams attempts to account for the similarities across New Englishes in terms of production principles – i.e. a broad set of psycholinguistic strategies involved in learning and using an L2 under specific social conditions. An important foundation for this work comes from the psycholinguistic studies of first language acquisition by Dan Slobin. For Slobin (1977:186) '(the) needs and constraints of listener and speaker determine the structure of language'. He posited several 'operating principles' that enable children to comprehend and segment the input they receive and which controls how they organise and store linguistic information. Some principles (from Slobin 1973) are given below as an illustration:

   (i) Pay attention to the ends of words
  (ii) Pay attention to the order of words and morphemes
 (iii) Underlying semantic relations should be marked clearly and overtly.

Slobin (1985) identified forty such principles, answering to four general 'charges to language':

   (i) Be clear
  (ii) Be humanly processible in ongoing time
 (iii) Be quick and easy
 (iv) Be expressive

An attempt to adopt the processing principles for SLA was made by Andersen (1990), which included additional principles like 'transfer to somewhere' cited above. Williams adopted Slobin's work specifically to account for the overwhelming similarities amongst New Englishes of different backgrounds of the sort outlined in Chapter 2 – see also Platt, Weber and Ho (1984). She picks up specifically on Slobin's insistence that there is a constant competition between demands for explicitness and demands for economy in language. For New Englishes the two broad principles are 'economy of production' and 'hyperclarity' (the reduction of ambiguity).

(a) Economy of production: Williams points to features of early SLA and lower sociolects amongst New Englishes that are economical with grammatical elements of the TL: omission of pronouns, lack of verb and noun endings, variable deletion of the copula, of articles, etc. Whilst making production more economical, these deletions make processing more difficult, since it becomes reliant on contextual factors. In particular she identifies two strategies. The first involves regularisation of subsystems of the TL. A clear example is the use of an invariant tag, rather than the complex subsystem of TL tag questions (see section 3.2.5) like the following: *not so* (Cam Eng); *is it* (Zambian Eng, Mal Eng), *isn't it* (Ind Eng). Regularisation is also evident in the use of *be* + *-ing* with all verbs rather than just non-statives of the TL (e.g. *I am having a cold*), as is reported for WAf Eng, BlSAf Eng and Ind Eng. The second strategy identified by Williams is the selective production of redundant markers. Redundancy is meant as a technical rather than judgemental term: a TL phrase like *all the books* can technically be said to contain a redundancy, since the plural can be deduced from the quantifier *all* as well as the *-s* ending. Williams (1987:175) claims that in such instances the L2 learner focuses on, and produces, a single marker – usually the one that is perceptually more salient.

(b)   Hyper-clarity (reduction of ambiguity):   Williams claims that this principle follows from Slobin's 'charge' *be clear*. It involves two sub-principles – maximum transparency and maximum salience. Whereas the first principle (economy of production) refers to speech production, hyper-clarity takes into account the needs of the listener. It thus mediates between over-economy and over-redundancy. It is not entirely listener-oriented, as it helps speakers keep track of their own production (Williams 1987:179). The first sub-principle 'maximising transparency' strives for a one-to-one mapping of form and meaning. It involves replacing opaque markers of meaning by more transparent ones within the speaker's knowledge. The bulk of Williams' examples come from the lexicalisation of various elements of meaning. That is, salient grammatical/semantic categories are given overt stress-bearing forms. (This is the opposite of grammaticalisation, which we argue occurs in late SLA and language shift.) For a cognitivist the use of a TL form like *have* + *-en* (perfective aspect) goes against optimal processing principles since it makes use of discontinuous constituents and violates a one-to-one mapping of form to function. In early SLA and lower sociolects of New Englishes it is common to find adverbial forms like *before, finish* and *already* co-occurring with an unmarked verb for perfective aspect (see section 2.4.2). A related tendency is the form *use(d) to* mark habitual aspect in an un-TL way, since it focuses on the habitualness of the activity rather than whether it is past or completed, as in (9).

9.   My mother, she use(d) to go to Pulau Tikus market. (Sgp Eng)

As discussed in section 2.4.2 *use(d) to* in (9) carries no implication that 'she no longer goes' (Platt, Weber and Ho 1984:71).

The second sub-principle of hyper-clarity, 'maximising salience' refers to an increase in stress or duration of some linguistic form or the use of an extra morpheme. It has the effect of creating redundancy which is not there in the TL, as part of the process of clarifying meaning. Williams considers resumptive pronouns in relative clauses to be typical of this psycholinguistic strategy (e.g. *The guests who I have invited them have arrived* – EAf Eng and WAf Eng, Bokamba 1992). Another set of examples show double marking of semantic relationships like supposition or contrast across clauses:

10. Though the farmer works hard, but he cannot produce enough. (Ind Eng)
11. Although you are away, but you do not forget. (WAf Eng)

The strength of the cognitive approach is that it identifies similarities and posits plausible explanations for them. Its weak point is that the principles sometimes appear to cancel each other out, especially with regard to 'redundancy' and 'economy', making them appear somewhat ad hoc. This general criticism can be labelled at the outset at Slobin's work. Mesthrie (1992a:182) argues that though numerous examples can be found from IndSAf Eng illustrating each of Williams' principles and sub-principles, on the whole they do not account for a particularly large slice of the innovations in the dialect. In this regard it is necessary to turn to insights from Creolistics and to revisit aspects of the role of substrata, universals and the input. This we do in section 6.4.

6.3   DEGREES OF CONTACT AND TRANSMISSION

The study of Language Contact falls within the wider field of Bilingualism (or Multilingualism). The wider field stresses the fact that societies are rarely monolingual; languages exist amidst other languages. The field is concerned in the first place with how multilingualism is 'managed' by speakers at a microlevel (in actual speech) and at a macrolevel by societies (educational structures, administrative bodies, etc.). The subfield of language contact is particularly concerned with the ways in which speakers of different languages influence each other and how their languages are accordingly altered. Credit for the establishment of the field usually goes to Uriel Weinreich's *Languages in Contact* (1953). However, studies of pidgin and Creole languages predate this by a long way – e.g. van Name (1869–70), Schuchardt (1882) and Hesseling (1897).

A basic distinction in the cross-cutting fields of Language Contact, Creolistics and Historical Linguistics is made between borrowing and interference through shift (Thomason and Kaufman 1988). At its simplest level borrowing occurs when speakers of a language adopt a new word from another language, e.g. the English word *fever* is borrowed in Xhosa, a South African language, as *ifiva* (with the meaning 'cold, flu', as it happens). Such borrowing usually occurs under conditions of language maintenance: Xhosa continues to be spoken and is only slightly changed by the effects of occasional borrowing. Substratum interference, on the other hand, is associated with language shift, when a community adopts a new language (a TL) to the detriment of its own, without, however, replicating (or intending to replicate) all of the TL rules. Thomason and Kaufman (1988:39) hypothesise that vocabulary is the first part of the TL that is needed by speakers who are in the process of shift, and hence it is mastered relatively early. Phonology and syntax prove more susceptible to interference. Borrowing may result in extensive structural changes in the borrowing language. This usually takes centuries under conditions of stable bilingualism; interference through shift, on the other hand, may take as little as a generation (Thomason and Kaufman 1988:41).

Clearly not all language contact leads to the formation of a contact language, as the phenomenon of lexical borrowing makes clear. The prototypical contact language is the pidgin – one that is spoken initially only in situations of contact between speakers of two or more languages (usually the latter), and not as an in-group (ethnic) language. When pidgins creolise they do become (by definition, on most accounts of creolisation) native languages of a new community. This community is partly defined by its possession of the Creole as a primary shared language.

A further distinction made by Thomason and Kaufman (1988) between shift with 'normal' versus 'abnormal' transmission is central in characterising degrees of contact. In shift with normal transmission shifting speakers acquire the bulk of TL grammatical structures along with the TL vocabulary. Some of the grammatical features carried over from the original native language may cause significant changes in the TL as spoken in the shifting community. This variety is nevertheless recognisable as a version of the original TL (a social dialect of it). In shift without normal transmission shifting speakers acquire so few of the TL grammatical structures that the TL cannot be said to have been passed on to the new speaker group as a set of interrelated lexical, phonological, morphosyntactic and semantic structures. Rather a new language system has formed, a Creole. (The terms 'normal' and 'abnormal' were not intended to be judgemental).

Mufwene's (2001) reading of the typical Creole-engendering plantation scene is different. Drawing on traditions of enquiry begun by

Chaudenson (1992) and Alleyne (1980), Mufwene proposes that the restructuring of the TL into a Creole never involved a sharp disruption. Rather, it began with a colonial koine (see 6.3.3 below) spoken by Europeans in specific territories, which was adopted more or less intact by the earliest generations of houseslaves. This occurred before large plantations were developed, requiring larger numbers of slaves. Subsequent generations of incoming slaves gradually replicated this variety less and less perfectly resulting in a basilectal Creole at one extreme. Thomason and Kaufman's account draws a sharp distinction between Creoles and indigenised colonial varieties like Indian English; Mufwene's does not. In the latter account the broad principles of transmission are the same. A Creole involves increasingly imperfect replication over time; whereas the indigenised variety involves decreasingly imperfect replication over time, as education and adoption of English by local elites makes the TL more and more available.

Clearly the status of New Englishes in their many forms as contact languages is not as clear-cut as that of stable pidgins. On the other hand, they have similarities with certain types of contact languages which have been identified as resembling Creoles, whilst not being clear-cut Creoles themselves. In this vein Schneider (1990) speaks of a cline (or graded scale) of Creoleness.

6.3.1 Broad and narrow definitions of 'contact language'

For Thomason (2001b) a contact language is a new variety not totally relatable by techniques of historical linguistic classification to the original languages in contact. In Thomason and Kaufman's (1988) terms the new code would not be a result of continuous intergenerational transmission and would not have the same source language for crucial subsystems (like the lexicon versus grammar or subsystems within the grammar itself). This constitutes a narrow definition of language contact, for which only three varieties qualify: 'crystallised' pidgins, 'abrupt' Creoles and bilingual mixed-languages. Crystallised pidgins have a clear-cut structure (and hence count as new languages, even if they might not be nativised). Abrupt Creoles, according to Thomason and Kaufmann, are those which are formed without a prior stable pidgin stage. They exhibit contact-induced shift with imperfect learning. Bilingual mixed-languages are new codes resulting not from pidginisation–creolisation but from intimate borrowing in a situation of bilingualism, e.g. the intimate mixing of English and Afrikaans in Cape Town, described by McCormick (2004).

A broad definition of 'contact language' admits any new identifiable code (however ephemeral) arising out of multilingualism. The broad definition follows from the view that if 'imperfect learning' is a part of the definition of P/Cs (a cover term for pidgin and/or Creole), then there are degrees of 'imperfection'. The scale 'Creole–non-Creole' may therefore be a gradual one. The rest of this section provides an overview of non-canonical contact languages and phenomena that whilst not quite qualifying as 'full' languages, are relevant to situations of contact.

6.3.2 Creoloids

The term 'creoloid' dates to Platt's (1975) discussion of Singapore English, which arose under colonialism in a highly multilingual context that included several Chinese languages, Malay and Tamil. Although the variety owed its existence mainly to an educational setting in which the target language was made accessible, Platt noted several grammatical features of colloquial Singapore English that were reminiscent of creolisation:

(a) variable lack of copula
(b) more than one copula
(c) variable marking of 3rd person sg. for verbs
(d) variable marking of past tense

As checklists go this was a bit thin; though one should point out that this article appeared before Bickerton's (1981) *Roots of Language*, which posited twelve features of Creole grammars. (On the other hand Platt does not refer to features earlier noted by Taylor 1971.) Platt had put his finger on something significant which he was able to build on in subsequent work (e.g. Ho and Platt 1993). His adoption of the term 'basilect' for the sub-variety in question perhaps prejudged the issue of how similar early fossilised interlanguages were to Creoles. Further research did indeed show up major differences between basilect and the superstrate. Ritchie (1986), for example, emphasised substrate influences from Chinese which included the following:

(a) Topic–comment structure:

> 12. Certain medicine we don't stock – in our dispensary.

(b) Zero pronouns (or pro-drop):

> 13. _ can speak Cantonese also.

(c) Lack of dummy subjects:

> 14. In China, where _ got people go to English school. (='There aren't people who go to English school in China')

Ritchie argued for a typological difference between the basilect (topic–comment) and the superstrate (subject–predicate). The case is thus fairly strong that Sgp Eng, though always targeted towards the superstrate in an educational setting and presumably mutually intelligible with the superstrate, has more than passing resemblance to a Creole (i.e. is a creoloid in Platt's terms).

Holm (1988:10) expresses scepticism about the concept of a creoloid, seeing it as a temporary interlanguage phenomenon with limited grammatical interference. This is not the case with all ESLs. We argue in section 6.4 that certain ESL varieties that undergo language shift amidst limited access to the TL are relevant to Creolistics. Some clear-cut cases are Ir Eng, IndSAf Eng and Sgp Eng, which is also on its way to becoming a language of the home (Gupta 1994).

6.3.3 Koines

A koine is a variety essentially arising out of contact involving dialects of the same language. The result of such contact is typically a low-prestige lingua franca which is structurally continuous with its antecedents. The Greek prototype (*the* Koiné) was a mixed dialect (Thomson 1972) arising out of Greek territorial expansion in the third century BC. It was initially a second dialect or second language for a majority of its speakers, coexisting in Greece with other city-state dialects, before gaining prestige on account of its association with government and administration, and later as the language of the New Testament. It eventually became the basis for the modern colloquial dialects.

On most formulations koines and Creoles are easily distinguishable phenomena, the former arising largely from abrupt dialect shifts, the latter from abrupt language shifts. Koines thus have only passing relevance to Creole studies, as a foil for characterising how far-reaching the restructuring of the lexifier is under conditions of creolisation. However, Mufwene (2001) has suggested two reasons why koines are of greater significance than this. Firstly, the superstrates in the colonies were themselves possibly koines, i.e. distinct varieties arising from accommodation between dialects of English. Hence they would be an essential ingredient that preceded, and later participated in, the creolisation process. Secondly (and again not many analysts agree with Mufwene on this), initial creolisation was simply a continuation of the koineisation process. Only later when larger numbers of slaves arrived on the plantations with less access to the koine, significant imperfect replication of its norms amongst successive generations occurred, with each generation getting successively further away from rather than closer to the original koine.

For Mufwene (2001), colonial European koines, creolisation and second-language colonial varieties like New Englishes, etc., are all cut to the same cloth, involving recourse to substrata and superstrata as filtered by linguistic universals (the 'complementary hypothesis') and mediated by the 'founder principle', which gives prominence to the role of early socially significant groups of learners of the koine. Mufwene insists that all language learning and transmission is subject to this formulation. In order to develop and evaluate this claim in the context of New Englishes studies, it is necessary to turn to the field of Second Language Acquisition.

6.4   NEW ENGLISHES AND CREOLISTICS

New Englishes owe a great deal to classroom acquisition but are ultimately social phenomena showing a transformation of classroom language as learners begin to use the new code to converse with each other. This was sometimes done for reasons of prestige as new, Western-educated elites came into being. Also, colonialism frequently brought together people of different ethnic backgrounds, necessitating a new lingua franca at a somewhat rapid rate. This need for a new means of communication opens up possibilities of comparisons with, and insights from, the field of Pidgin and Creole Linguistics. Initially the fields of SLA and New Englishes did not have a great deal in common, as prototypically pidgins and Creoles seemed quite different from L2 varieties. This view was expressed forcefully by Bickerton (1983:238):

> No real connection exists between SLA and creolisation; they differ in almost every particular. SLA is done alone, creolisation is done in groups; SLA has a target, creolisation hasn't; SLA is done mainly by adults, creolisation mainly by kids ... SLA gives you a second language, creolisation gives you a first; SLA is done by people with a 'normal' background, creolisation with an 'abnormal' background.

For group SLA in colonial contexts Bickerton's argument is open to debate, as a closer examination shows:

(a) SLA gives you a second language, creolisation a first. Here Bickerton appeals to a notion of creolisation as a one-generation phenomenon. Work in the 1990s has suggested that such 'radical' Creoles are rare. More typically Creoles seemed to have developed gradually, over two generations at least. On the other hand, New

Englishes may become first languages by processes of language shift. In the case of IndSAf Eng this shift was well advanced a hundred years after the first immigration of speakers from India to South Africa, and within fifty years of the last immigrations. In Singapore some children are growing up monolingual in the New English, even while basilang varieties of the TL are in existence. That is, whilst these shifts are not abrupt, they are not very gradual either.

(b) SLA is done alone, creolisation in groups. This formulation is slightly disingenuous, since all language acquisition entails mastery of a system by individuals. Likewise all language learning involves 'negotiation' between acquirers and providers of the input. Bickerton's main point is that creolisation is a cohesive, focused process under specific sociohistorical conditions, whereas SLA involves isolated individuals trying to learn the dominant language around them. However, New Englishes are cohesive social phenomena too, not a loose aggregation of interlanguages of individuals learning the TL in isolation.

(c) SLA is done by adults, creolisation by children. Bickerton's promotion of an 'instantaneous' view of creolisation (from pidgin of adults to Creole of children) is rejected by most creolists today. Tok Pisin's evolution into a Creole in Papua New Guinea appears to be a gradual one, in which both children and adults actively participate in varying degrees.

(d) SLA involves a 'normal' linguistic background, unlike creolisation. Bickerton here appealed to a notion of a pidgin abruptly turning to Creole with minimal contacts with superstrate speakers. Subsequent research shows that some African languages did survive in the New World and that not all Creoles were preceded by a pidgin. The idea that SLA is linguistically and socially less traumatic than pidginisation and abrupt creolisation is uncontroversial. However, there are some New Englishes which are socially complex in that they involved a diverse, multilingual, immigrant populace. In Singapore the substrate languages are varieties of Chinese, Malay and Tamil, brought there by the movement of labour under British colonialism. For IndSAf Eng, indentured labourers spoke a number of languages and dialects belonging to two distinct language families, Indic and Dravidian (and therefore not mutually intelligible). For American Indian English, the boarding schools are cited as sites of genesis. These too were multilingual arenas in which a lingua franca must have had to emerge relatively rapidly. Note too that in many territories in which New Englishes emerged, pidgins or pidgin-like varieties did arise – e.g. Fanakalo pidgin in South Africa, Butler English in South India, Nigerian Pidgin in West Africa and American Indian Pidgin Englishes in the USA. However, these appear not to have been major inputs into the genesis of New Englishes and might well exist in a kind of 'complementary distribution' with the more developed New Englishes of specific territories.

(e) SLA has a target, creolisation does not. This is the only tenet from Bickerton's argument that stands up to scrutiny. Second-language learners, irrespective of ultimate success or failure, are goal-directed towards a TL. There is consensus that slaves in the colonial plantation era had to be more concerned with communi-cation than mastery of an antecedent TL. Baker (1995) argues that slaves of different ethnolinguistic backgrounds were not inter-ested in acquiring the language of other groups as much as in constructing a new 'medium for interethnic communication'. As such there was no antecedent TL. The only problem with this for-mulation is that the vocabulary of the Creoles that ensued tends to be overwhelmingly from the superstrate colonial language(s). The 'basic variety' approach stresses that despite the difference in TL availability, both early SLA and early pidgins rely on simi-lar strategies, namely using lexical rather than syntactic means (Siegel 2003).

In view of our reservation over Bickerton's position on language acquisition, it might be more feasible to go back to an earlier formu-lation of his (1977:49) that pidginisation was second-language learn-ing with restricted input, and creolisation was first-language learning with restricted input. While this makes 'input' the criterial variable, we would argue that 'targetness' is also crucial. In terms of input, Bickerton proposed that a ratio greater than 5 learners to 1 TL speaker would result in a Creole, rather than an L2. Certainly no New English classroom ever achieved this desideratum, nor did any English colony in its initial phase. However, the issue of targetness and the avail-ability of education is the important determinant between L2 and Creole.

Cognitivists like Slobin (1983:252) hold a different view from 'cre-ationists' like Bickerton:

> Wherever language users or language learners are pushed to devise a linguistic means of expression which is lacking or not evident in the language or languages at hand, the only source of materials lies within. These materials consist of prototypical notions of specifiable

form and content and preferred ways of mapping those notions onto linguistic expressions, striving for mapping that is maximally transparent and direct – again in specifiable ways.

As we noted earlier in 6.3 for the wider field of Contact Linguistics, Mufwene has argued vigorously that there is a continuum between what are traditionally thought of as 'Creoles' and 'non-Creoles'.

Our own view is that New Englishes and Creoles are prototypically clearly differentiable in their social circumstances and linguistic forms. Thus, most varieties of Indian English do not resemble Creoles and there is little insight to be gained in forcing the mould of one onto the other. On the other hand since there are pidgin-like Englishes in North India (Mehrotra 1977) as well as in the south (Butler English: Hosali 2000), it is an empirical question whether there is a continuum of varieties between pidgin and New English. No such investigation has been done, but it is likely that the tools of both SLA theory and Creolistics would be needed for such an enterprise. There are other less prototypical New Englishes which involved multiethnic learners at a crucial early stage who stabilised a basilectal variety, and later showed a propensity to language shift. For Sgp Eng and IndSAf Eng we would argue that perspectives from Creolistics are therefore crucial, especially if we view creolisation as the acquisition of a second language as a first language (see Andersen 1980).

A proponent of the 'SLA = creolisation' model is Schumann whose model of social and psychological distance in accounting for differential success in SLA is summarised in Table 6.1.

Though not designed for this purpose, Table 6.1 is a useful one for characterising the learning of English outside the classroom in colonial contexts. In this context the parameter of 'social distance' leaned by far to the negative (no social equality; no desire of assimilation; non-congruent cultures; negative attitudes of groups; few shared facilities). Only the last criterion (expectation of stay) is difficult to assess, as the colonial situation does not match up with the post-colonial metropolitan site that Schumann seems to have in mind. The yardstick of psychological distance seems to lean towards the 'positive' in the colonial situation, since the home languages of indigenous people and their cultures formed a buffer against culture shock. There was also high motivation to learn the languages of the colonisers. Again it is not clear whether 'low ego boundary' or its opposite are relevant to the group-learning situation of WE territories.

At various stages of his thinking Schumann has proposed that aspects of SLA can be viewed as pidginisation (Schumann 1974), in

Table 6.1. *Factors determining social and psychological distance* (based on Schumann 1978, and MacLaughlin 1987: 111)

Social distance	
Positive	Negative
Social equality between target- and second-language groups	No social equality
Both groups desire assimilation	No desire of assimilation
Second-language group is small and not cohesive	Second-language group is large and cohesive
Second-language group's culture is congruent with target-language group	Culture of second-language group not congruent
Both groups have positive attitudes towards each other	Groups do not have positive attitudes towards each other
Both groups expect second-language groups to share facilities	No expectation of shared facilities
The second-language group expects to stay in the target-language area for an extended period	No expectation by second-language group that they would stay in the target-language area for an extended period

Psychological distance	
Positive	Negative
No language shock	Language shock
No culture shock	Culture shock
High motivation	Low motivation
Low ego boundaries	High ego boundaries

terms of creolisation (Schumann 1974, also Andersen 1980) and in terms of decreolisation (Stauble 1978; Schumann and Stauble 1983). Schumann (1974) suggests that a number of processes of simplification occur in SLA that are reminiscent of pidginisation. In both SLA and pidgins word order tends to do the work of inflections, certain grammatical constructions like the passive tend to be absent, and the lexicon is reduced. He speculates that the early stages of SLA involve pidginisation in the sense of universal simplification processes. Such drastic reduction may suffice only if the interlanguage is used for communication at a rudimentary level (the referential function alone). Such a level is not feasible if the communication is intended to be integrative (with TL speakers or presumably even non-TL speakers) or expressive (the emotional or aesthetic uses of language). For these purposes the interlanguage must expand in ways analogous to the complication of linguistic structure when a pidgin creolises. In such cases 'redundancy will increase, obligatory tense markers will tend to develop, speed in speech will increase as a result of morphophonemic reductions and reductions in primary stress, and finally the lexicon will undergo extensive development' (Schumann 1974:147).

Schumann and Stauble (1983) and Andersen (1980) raise the possibility of equating the later stages of SLA with decreolisation. Stauble (1978) carried out a longitudinal study of the negation system of two L2 learners of English who acculturated well to the United States and who ultimately produced utterances showing standard English negation. She claimed that a series of developmental stages exhibited by the two learners was very similar to that produced in the decreolisation of Guyanese Creole negation as reported in Bickerton (1975).

These parallelisms seem to apply to IndSAf Eng, Sgp Eng and Ir Eng even more closely, since they have been not just nativised but adopted as first languages at a relatively early stage. Platt's (1975) initial espousal of a Creole continuum model to characterise Sgp Eng has already been cited (section 6.3.2). Platt, Weber and Ho (1984) suggested that the article system of Sgp Eng was essentially similar to that posited for Creoles by Bickerton (see section 2.3.1). Likewise Ho and Platt's (1993) analysis of copula verb phenomena showed parallels with the Creole continuum (see section 3.3). Platt's continuum model has been criticised by, *inter alia*, Gupta, who advocates a diglossia model instead, comprising Sgp Eng as a dialect fulfilling L functions, with standard English as the language of H functions. Prima facie we are doubtful whether a dialect versus standard situation could be called diglossia. Given the sociohistoric context, it would be unsurprising if Standard English and the basilect were to 'leak' into each other in a way disallowed by Ferguson's original model of diglossia.

Mesthrie's work on IndSAf Eng (1992a; shorter, chapter-length précis and update 2002) has been accepted as showing that some New Englishes do indeed fall somewhere between Creole and New English. His method was to interview a cross-section of the speech community in KwaZulu-Natal, and on the basis of their fluency group them into basilectal, mesolectal and acrolectal speakers. A fourth group turned up whose norms were makeshift and reflected a pidgin-like or early fossilised interlanguage. Although excluded from some parts of the analysis of the 'focused' new dialect, such pre-basilectal speakers form an important counterpoint for understanding the norms of basilectal speakers. The latter evince a coherent or focused system of norms that draw on a variety of sources: Indian substrates, English superstrate and properties of SLA and language contact. Acrolectal speakers, who are mostly members of a middle-class elite, use a variety that is close to the standard form of the TL, except for one or two syntactic constructions and in matters of accent.

It is clear that English was introduced in the community via schools initially run by missionaries, although some people had their first contacts with English outside the classroom. Why did language shift towards English occur relatively rapidly? It is likely that as a transplanted community, Indians in South Africa had to acculturate much faster to colonial English norms than had they remained in India to work on the land in villages. Moreover, no single Indian language could suffice as a lingua franca within the community because of their ethnic status (Hindi became associated with indentured North Indian Hindus, Tamil and Telugu with indentured South Indian Hindus, Urdu with indentured Muslims and Gujarati with trading-class Hindus and Muslims). English became relatively neutral in this context, while also being a statusful language of empire and colony. Why then does IndSAf Eng show so much variation that is clearly not derived from the TL? Issues of identity are again significant, with English needing to become something of an 'Indian' language (or at least an Indian dialect of English) to express certain cultural nuances. A second factor relates to access to TL speakers. Initially there was cultural and class segregation between colonial English settlers and their Indian employees. In 1948 at a time when Indians had shown a fair amount of linguistic and social acculturation and might have been set to acquire a more TL-like English, segregation was hardened with the official rise of apartheid. That is, social distance in Schumann's model actually increased in this period. The policy of apartheid thus contributed to a stabilising of interlanguage norms in a relatively fossilised form. IndSAf Eng thus affords the sociolinguist the opportunity of examining the processes of interlanguage formation in a community setting, rather than in the classroom alone. Processes that might have fallen by the wayside relatively rapidly in other social contexts were drawn out and fossilised. Although IndSAf Eng is slightly special as a New English (in having several substrate languages coming into sudden contact on the plantations and in emerging from language shift relatively rapidly), it exemplifies the processes of New English formation. Mesthrie (1992a:191–204) outlines the following strategies:

(a) Expansion of 'inner form'. The term 'inner form' is taken from Hymes (1971) and Valdman (1977:155) for the core or skeletal features of language structure – in this case, the generation of subordinate clauses, an elaborate tense-aspect system, etc. These do not necessarily accord with TL norms. Sentence (15) shows the generation of a subordinate clause by relatively paratactic means:

> 15. I don't like people must do things like that. (IndSAf Eng basilect = in Std Eng 'I don't like it that people do things like that')

(b) Complexification of 'outer form'. 'Outer form' (Hymes 1971, Valdman 1977) refers to the fleshing out of the syntax, by means of explicit markers of grammatical relations, like subordinators, question words and the double marking of clause relations. These are often realised by innovations involving the use of TL material in non-TL meaning, function and distribution. This is exemplified by the use of clause-final *too* in (16) to denote a hypothetical clause, with overtones of emphasis and disapproval:

> 16. It's a terrible house *too*, you have to live in it. (= 'Even if it's a terrible house, you have to live in it–IndSAf Eng basilect)
> 17. I made rice *too*, I made roti *too*. (= 'I made both rice and roti'–IndSAf Eng basilect)

Sentence (17) shows clause final co-ordination, on the analogy of substrate forms in Tamil and Hindi.

(c) Later accommodation of the basilect to TL norms. As speakers gained better access to the TL and were motivated to acquire it for better jobs and social mobility, the basilect was gradually restructured to TL norms. As in decreolisation, this was not a straightforward 'replacement' process. Some new (mesolectal) forms arise that mediate between basilect and TL. These sometimes retain the 'old' (basilectal) meaning, function and distribution of the forms they are meant to replace. Thus a mesolectal sentence like (18) could arise, which is meant as a more 'TL' version of (17), but in fact is still basilectal in structure.

> 18. My dad was a soccerite *as well*, he was a musician *as well*. (IndSAf Eng mesolect = 'My dad was both a soccer player and a musician')

Sentence (18) was uttered by a mesolectal speaker (so defined by social as well as linguistic characteristics), trying to avoid the basilectal clause final '*too...too*'.

IndSAf Eng thus does seem to support Mufwene's (2001) idea of a continuity between contact languages: that is, it has been subject to decreasing basilectalisation since its formation; whereas other varieties bearing the label 'Creoles' were subject to increasing basilectalisation as conditions on slave plantations decreased rather than increased access to the TL.

6.5   HISTORICAL RETENTIONS IN NEW ENGLISHES

We conclude this chapter with a plea for more historical research in the area of New Englishes. The field of creolistics has shown how detailed archival research can illuminate earlier forms of contact languages and offer a firmer foundation against which to test characterisations of Creoles and theories of creolisation. In particular the relative contributions of the superstrate, substrate and universals is very much an area of intense research and debate. Our emphasis in this chapter has been on transfer from substrates to New English, one of their important characteristics. Yet transfer is not unconstrained. We hypothesise that at an earlier 'adding to the pool of variants' stage transfer is unconstrained. This is at the stage of what Siegel (2002) calls 'use' (without 'acquisition'). The later selection stage is constrained by principles like 'transfer to somewhere' discussed above. At this stage 'use' turns into 'acquisition' and a new (second language) dialect is born. At the same time we have seen that there appear to be universal strategies of simplification and complexification. These have thus far been characterised at the level of cognitive processes (Williams 1987; Mesthrie 1992a); we await a plausible model from generative linguistics.

We should however, not take the notion of superstrate for granted. Many New Englishes are compared to standard British English for reasons of convenience (as we have done in our occasional glosses of rare constructions from New Englishes). However, we should not take the use of modern standard British English as a metalanguage to imply that this is the only relevant variant of the superstrate for New English study. For historical veracity we need to keep in mind the following: (a) that Standard English of the period of exploration, trade and colonisation was slightly different from English in the twentieth and twenty-first centuries; and (b) that Standard English was not the only input in the formation of New Englishes.

The superstrate was also shaped by sailors, soldiers, adventurers, hunters, missionaries, tradespeople, indentured workers, plantation owners, overseers, settlers, schoolteachers, and – in some island and coastal contexts – divers and whalers. This was a rather varied input, that reminds us that the notion of a TL is an idealisation. More often – and certainly outside the classroom – the TL was a varied and 'moving' target.

6.5.1 Archaic Standard English

In what ways did early modern Standard English (i.e. from the sixteenth to the eighteenth century onwards) differ from modern Standard British English? This is clearly too great a task to do justice to here; though a few pointers of relevance to New English studies are necessary. Consider the following four constructions of seventeenth- and eighteenth-century English:

(a) unstressed *do* was still prominent at this time and occurs in most travel narratives:

> 19. ...Thee 11. day of Iune, the King did anoint the Generall with ritch ointment, and called him his son (Governors & Assistants of the East India Merchants 1603)

(b) the use of *for... to* infinitives as in (20)

> 20. A Billet is a piece of Cleft Wood for to Burn (R. Holme, 1688, cit. *Oxford English Dictionary*)

(c) the dative of advantage as in (21):

> 21. I got me a servant at Harwich (Defoe 1724, cit. Visser 1963: 630)

(d) use of *you was* for singular and *you were* for plural (in eighteenth-century Eng at least).

Some of these rules may have stabilised in one or other WE, as we show later on. We now turn to less standard superstratal input in the periods of exploration and colonisation:

6.5.2 Regional English of Settlers

In order to establish continuity between superstrate and New English convincingly, features must be shown to emanate from the right speakers at the right time. In this vein Mesthrie and West (1995) undertook a survey of settler English of the Eastern Cape, South Africa, of the 1820s, focusing on unpublished archival letters by new settlers to the governors. As was common at the time, people leaving Britain for the colonies were largely from the working class. The handwriting of such speakers sometimes gives a clear indication of their unfamiliarity with the practice of writing; but since problems in the new colony were pressing they felt the urgency of communicating with the governor in Cape Town. One such barely literate settler (Jeremiah Goldswain, a sawyer from Buckinghamshire) outdid everyone in keeping a detailed diary, which was eventually published in two volumes. The archival materials give a fascinating view of language variation in the first generation of settlers; many of the features did not survive the process of koineisation in South Africa. But several did, including a few that have been mistakenly imputed to Afrikaans influence (e.g. the adjective 'with infinitive' as in (22):

> 22. The leaves.... quite capable to withstand even the severest frost.

Of greater interest to WE studies are two types of features in the input: (a) morphological features that are variably absent or involve levelling of grammatical distinctions; (b) non-standard morphosyntactic forms that also recur in New Englishes; and (c) some features of syntax that were lost in white Settler English but not before they passed on to one New English variety. We exemplify these below.

(a) Omissions in Settler grammar: These include the following: determiners in certain contexts (23–25); prepositions after certain verbs (26–28); particles (29–31); possessive 's (32–34); and -s inflection with 3rd sg. verbs (35).

> 23. in order to procure Φ living for my wife and family
> 24. 24. most probably Φ great part of those potatoes are by this time unfit for use
> 25. this was Φ matter of fact
> 26. could I be permitted here to receive the third of my deposit which government proposed to be repaid me on landing
> 27. He promised him leave to go to Cape Town to complain me his Excellency
> 28. relative to our colonial passes which were sent from your office Φ Cape Town to Grahamstown [*in* omitted]
> 29. and that the finding Φ personal security may not be required [*of* omitted]
> 30. But on attending at the office this morning I learn with much regret Φ your indisposition [*of* omitted]
> 31. at the Government expence
> 32. on hearing of your Lordship design to visit the frontier
> 33. which has totally exhausted your Memorialist finances
> 34. your Memorialist humbly hope your Excelency will be so kind ...
> 35. the total impossibility of procuring flour or bread ... induce your Memorialists ...

(b) **Variable non-standard morphosyntactic forms that recur in the Settler corpus:**

  (i) double negation;
  (ii) variation in the use of complementisers, especially zero after verbs like *request, expect, state, conceive* which require an overt complementiser in the standard today;
  (iii) use of *is* and *was* with plural subjects; singular form *you was*;
  (iv) *have* with 3rd sg. subjects; and *has* with 3rd pl. subjects;
  (v) use of *-s* endings with verbs following a plural subject;
  (vi) plural endings for non-count nouns like *progresses, evidences, sufferings; hopes.*

For examples see Mesthrie and West (1995:127-9).

(c) **Constructions lost in Settler English but retained in a New English:** The dative of advantage is the clearest example here. This construction survives in CFl Eng, where it is frequently misdiagnosed by purists as an incorrect use of the reflexive:

36. I'm gonna buy me a car.

This usage (also known as the ethical dative in Middle English studies) implies that the action expressed by the verb accrues some advantage to the subject (which is historically the dative case). Although many of the sentences appear to admit a reinforcive reflexive nuance, this is not always the case, as Christian (1991) suggests in another context (L1 Appalachian English):

37. I'm gonna write me a letter to my cousin Tom. (Christian 1991:16)

Here the writing of the letter accrues some advantage (like personal satisfaction) to the subject: the reflexive interpretation *I'm gonna write myself a letter to my cousin Tom* is inadmissible. That people who are classified 'Coloured' in South Africa and have English as L2 use the construction has led teachers to stigmatise the construction as simply non-standard. However, the construction was once standard and brought to South Africa by a large number of settlers (Mesthrie and West 1995), who in their reports to the Governor in Cape Town frequently wrote lines like:

38. ... your memorialist then built him a house on a spot of Ground. (Mesthrie and West 1995:124)

This construction was soon lost in Settler speech as people went up in the social world in South Africa (especially after the capital accumulation consequent on the precious metals boom of the 1860s onwards). But before it did so, it stabilised in one L2 variety of the country. A challenge to WE studies is to ascertain why certain superstratal features stabilised in some territories but not others. Is there a reversal of Andersen's (1983b) 'transfer to somewhere' principle? That is, will a superstratal feature survive better if there is some reinforcement in a prominent substrate language? This is conjecture at this stage.

Regional dialects of especial interest in New English studies are Scots and Irish English. The Scots were influential as schoolteachers in many colonies, whilst the Irish often occupied a lower status as indentured labourers working side by side with locals or imported slaves, especially (but not exclusively) in New World contexts. The diffusion of features like *youse* (pl. of you) in CFl Eng and other Englishes originates in Ir Eng whilst *to fright for* ('to be afraid of') and *mines* ('mine') in IndSAf Eng probably come from Scots English. The Ind Eng pl. pronoun *who-all*, noted in section 2.5.3, does not have a Std Eng equivalent but has parallels in Ir Eng (Montgomery 2004:318). It is not clear whether the Ind Eng form derives from this source, however: it could be an independent innovation based on substrate morphology.

6.5.3 Sailors:

Bailey and Ross (1988) carried out a survey of 'Ship English' (as recorded in the logs of the British Navy) between 1631 and 1730, with a view to ascertaining which features of New World Creoles might be attributable to this sociolect. As many of the sailors and some captains and masters were illiterate, a fair picture of this sociolect emerges. Ship English may not have been an entirely autonomous, monolithic or stable variety: it must have drawn on non-standard English, English regional dialects and English slang. Bailey and Ross demonstrate how Ship English differed from early modern Standard English of the times in respect of present tense marking; forms of the verb *be*; past tense form of weak verbs and strong verbs; *a*-prefixing with participles and so forth. The present tense of verbs has the endings Φ, -*s* and -*th*, but the distribution of these was different from the contemporary standard. Bailey and Ross (1988:199) found that 3rd sg. forms are sometimes unmarked:

39. . . . the Comondore [sic] who arrived here this Day and seem to be very well pleased.

More common is the occurrence of -s on verbs that are not 3rd sg. forms:

40. ... gross corall Racks which makes you ride with a short scope. (*Racks* = 'rocks')

Such examples give pause for thought even for New English studies, as absence of -s is a frequently remarked upon characteristic of some varieties. CFl Eng has a rule that favours – Φ for 3rd sg. verbs and -s for 3rd pl. (We called this the '-s plural symmetry' rule in section 2.4.4.) Was the inherent variability in the input a contributing factor? Clearly the shape of the superstrate needs to be studied carefully for specific New English varieties. Amongst Bailey and Ross' (1988:206) examples are an intriguing use of *use to* (41 below) in a combination with present tense *do* that is reminiscent of the habitual *use to* cited for Sgp Eng (section 6.2.4(b)).

41. ... in this bay vessels do use to stop for want of a wind.

The use of the present tense *do* (serving a habitual function, according to the authors) here implies 'they used to stop and still do'. While we are not advocating that such constructions are necessarily superstratal, we are cautioning for a less substratophile interpretation of New English variability.

One researcher who does take a conservative view of the New Englishes is Jim Davy (2000). Davy argues that in New English studies it has become common to deduce, falsely, that deviation from modern Standard English is prima facie evidence of linguistic and/or 'normic newness'. In the field of lexis he shows from careful use of the *OED* (*Oxford English Dictionary*) that features thought to be unique to parts of Africa have a long history in the UK. Alleged West Africanisms like *how now?*, *not so?*, and *trinket* (for 'a precious thing, a jewel'), and *to move with a group* are recorded in the *OED* with British sources, from respectively *c.* 1838–1878; 1606–1978; 1533–1774; 1967. Similarly, Bamgbose (1992:156) cites the Nig Eng lexical archaisms *dress* 'move at the end of a row so as to create room for additional persons' and *station* for 'town or city in which a person works'. The latter also occurs in Ind Eng. Davy conjectures that some syntactic constructions reported as distinctively New English like single comparatives (e.g. *than* for *more than*, as in (39), and use of *be* + *ing* with statives, as in (43), may turn out to have L1 trajectories too.

42. He values his car than his wife.
43. He is knowing how to drive a car.

To Davy's Nigerian examples we can add from the sailors' records forms like *beeves* (plural of *beef* in the sense of 'a cow, a head of cattle'). According to the *OED* this was a part of British English up till the nineteenth century (sg. *beef*, pl. *beeves*, for 'any animal of the ox-kind'). The form *beef* meaning 'cow, cattle' survives in West African Pidgin English. A scrutiny of sailors' logs for different territories is a desideratum for future research.

6.5.4 Missionaries

Missionaries were an important presence in most colonies and formed an important linguistic link as introducers of Western education (and in some territories, also, as early recorders of indigenous languages). As there have been few studies of their own varieties, the default assumption is that they were speakers or proponents of standard English. Mesthrie (1996) shows that for at least one colony this assumption is unwarranted for the period when English was first introduced. In the Cape Colony (South Africa) British rule was established first in 1795 and then again in 1806. Missionary and army activity preceded the arrival of a British civilian element by a good twenty years. The first missionaries from the London Missionary Society were sent over in 1799 with the aim of converting the local people and introducing Christian and Western concepts via education. What the missionaries lacked in numbers they made up for in terms of contact with, influence over and interest in the local populace (Khoi Khoi in the western Cape, Xhosa in the eastern Cape). A survey of the unpublished letters and journals of the first generation of missionaries reveals a surprising number of them to be continental Europeans with little knowledge of English, or working-class L1 English speakers with little familiarity with the conventions of literacy and standard English. As an example of the first we supply the first sentence in the journal of Revd Kayser (born in Saxony, 1800) addressed to his employers at the London Missionary Society:

44. I hope that you my universal letter, dated the 22nd of June, which our safe
     arrival in Capetown mentioned, with the extract of my diary, which I the
     6th of August too Mr. Beck who embarked with the Ferrie for London
     delivered have, in safely have recieved. (12 Oct. 1827)

Clearly, Kayser himself was an interlanguage English user who at the time of his arrival was so unsure of his English as to resort to a literal translation from his mother tongue (German) in his written English. Although his journals give an indication of gradual improvement in

English, he cannot really be said to have mastered it. Yet he started a school for Xhosa children and was its English teacher. (Though he seems to have wisely delegated most of these teaching responsibilities to his wife and daughter.) Kayser was a slight exception; there were other Dutch and German missionaries labouring in the Cape at this time, whose English varied from mid-interlanguage (like Kayser's) to a much closer version of the TL. Surprisingly some *English* missionaries also felt uncomfortable in writing English. Missionary work was not always dictated by other-worldly concerns alone. For some it was a source of employment and an avenue for a better life overseas than as a craftsman in England with little education (Warren 1967:11–12). Revd Ayliff, for example, who originally came over as a settler, kept a diary which has been described by its editors (Hewson and van der Riet (1963:9) as containing 'errors in grammar, spelling and punctuation on almost every page, and the use of clichés'. Whilst this characterisation describes his lack of literacy and literary skills, his diary reveals a great deal of variation between standard and non-standard forms of concord (*was* versus *were*), prepositions, relative pronouns and the like. Note the double negative, and the non-standard auxiliary inversion within the subordinate *wh*-clause in (45):

45. What have I done this last year what have I done doesn't amount to nothing. Can only speak a few words of Dutch instead of being a sufficient master to speak it with Freedom? (Ayliff 1823, cit, Mesthrie 1996:150)

The average English missionary's skill in his native language was superior to that of Ayliff, yet he was not alone in being uncomfortable in the grammatical and discourse conventions of the standard form of his own language. It is not yet known whether South Africa's mission field was exceptional in this regard, and if so, why this should be so. Preliminary investigation of the repertoires of missionaries elsewhere suggests that in India whilst some English missionaries were of the working class, this was not widespread (Piggin *c.* 1984:34). Of 550 missionaries based in India in the period 1789–1859 Piggin lists 114 as of the working class (p. 37); on the other hand he mentions 88 as skilled artisans, mechanics, shop assistants, labourers, etc.

> The teachers who became missionaries in India then, were drawn from the better educated, professionally conscious, ranks of teachers. Only a few were like Joseph Fletcher who had yet to discover punctuation.

It seems that missionaries who were not L1 speakers were also prominent enough in India to warrant a caustic sketch entitled *Our German*

Missionary in Atkinson's *Curry and Rice* (5th edn of 1911: sketch 12) satirising a German missionary and his family's L2 English as follows:

> A very excellent little fellow is our Fruitz but it is to be hoped that his orations in the oriental vernacular are couched in language more intelligible to his hearers than are his efforts in English...
>
> ... You will find Mrs Fruitz who with smiles and much broken English will be delighted to show you the establishment...
>
> ... Those were the orphans you saw in the Fruitz' verandah, and for whom little Fruitz pleaded in broken English...

For good measure the sketch also satirises a Maltese Roman Catholic priest for his 'bad Italian, broken French, a smattering of Hindustani, and dislocated English...' Whilst we should be sceptical about the obvious chauvinism in this comic sketch, it should be acknowledged that there is a great deal of self-mockery in the book as well. Hence the negative stereotype about the L2 English of missionaries might have a basis in reality.

For West Africa, Moorhouse (1973:324) draws an engaging picture of linguistic diversity in the superstrate, citing a letter from the 1860s by Bishop Towzer:

> 'There was Kelleway,' he [= Bishop Towzer] wrote home to his sister, 'teaching Devonshire of the broadest kind, Sivill the most undoubted Lincolnshire, and Adams indulging in low cockney slang where "grub" stands habitually for "food" and "kid" for "child". The effect was that the boys who heard all this jargon were naturally puzzled and, with the exception of a few such sentences like "O, my Eye" and the like, made but a small advance in speaking English.'

Such dialect phonology is sometimes claimed to have passed on to the emergent local dialects of English, though it is not clear that they could have been widespread or long-lasting within the 'pool of variants'. Our third quote, from Kirk-Greene (1971) concerning West Africa, reinforces the view of Bishop Towzer in a slightly more optimistic vein:

> There is...scope for research into how enduring is the effect of the regional accent of the English teacher on the West African student. Can the trained listener perceive traces of the long line of German and Swiss teachers of English in Ghana and Nigeria? For how long will so many of the Northern Nigerian secretarial grade speak with a Glaswegian intonation acquired from their sole instructor for eleven years? Now comes a new influence. This is the steady flow of American Peace Corps teachers to West African schools, over a thousand in the past few years. (Kirk-Greene 1971:129)

Schmied (1991:11) is more cautious in suggesting that 'both the missionaries in the West and the settlers in the South still looked upon

England as their model in matters pertaining to the language standard (although most of them did not speak Standard English themselves)'. Despite the extreme variability, the missionaries' influence must have been considerable as the ones who converted locals to Christianity and to the use of some English. Mesthrie (1996) argues that the survival of unstressed *do* in Cape Flats English is most likely to be due to the influence of the continental European missionaries who used it not only in their preaching styles based on the King James Bible (e.g. 48), but in their letters and journals too:

46. We did go to the beach yesterday. (CFl Eng)
47. But some did wait till I had finished. (Revd Kayser: 1833)
48. And they did beat the gold into thin plates. (Exodus 39:14; King James Bible).

Although unstressed *do* was once standard, it waned in the standard variety from the eighteenth century onwards and does not occur in the South African Settler corpus of the 1820s (though a more formal perlocutionary legal or affective *do* is used as part of the written style as in *I do declare in the most solemn manner that...*). The semantics of unstressed *do* in the missionaries' correspondence, on the other hand (highlighting a salient or new VP activity) fits very well with present-day New English norms on the Cape Flats. A reinforcing effect may well be from the Afrikaans substrate (McCormick 1995, Mesthrie 1999a).

6.5.5 Soldiers

In characterising the superstrate via its intermediaries the teachers (British as well as locals) should not be forgotten. Some of the earliest teachers were soldiers. Shivachi (1999) discusses the significance of the King's African Rifles in disseminating a knowledge of English in East Africa in the early twentieth century. In nineteenth-century Natal, in an early attempt to provide education to Indians on some sugar estates, discharged soldiers from the Indian army were recruited, since they had acquired some knowledge of an Indian language. This project was soon abandoned, for as the Superintendent's report of 1880 put it, 'their conduct was not such as to command the respect of those among whom their work lay' (Brain 1983:205). The role of soldiers in the dissemination of English has still to be studied. Andersen (1988:100) describes an advertisement from a magazine version of *The History of the English Speaking People* which shows a picture of a white soldier in colonial uniform with pith helmet, rifle and bayonet. It is accompanied by an ironic comment 'Come see how we taught the world English.' This irony may not be entirely off the mark. The Indian Army composed largely of battalions drawing on Hindus, Sikhs and Muslims from various regions was involved in the initial conquests that led to the colonisation of many adjacent Asian territories. What was their role in spreading a local South Asian variety of British English? What was the role of the famous Gurkha battalions in establishing English in their own country (Nepal) and adjacent territories where they fought? And finally, although the officers spoke standard English (RP at the highest levels), what was the English of the British rank and file like? These are interesting questions that archival research must answer in the future.

6.5.6 Teachers

An important intermediary of the superstrate was Indian English itself. As one of the earliest colonies and the jewel in the imperial crown, India often supplied English teachers when new Asian colonies were established. This applies especially to Sri Lanka, Malaysia and Singapore, though other territories were also influenced in this way (Brunei, Hong Kong and Fiji; see section 1.4.1). Currently Indian teachers are influential in the Middle East and north-east Africa. Some New English features are likely to have diffused in this way. Mesthrie (1992a:20) describes four features that were passed on from teachers to pupils in IndSAf Eng and which are likely to have come from India:

(a) *alphabets* ('letters of the alphabet')
(b) *by-heart* ('to learn off by heart')
(c) *tuition(s)* (= 'special classes outside of school for which one pays a tutor')
(d) *further studies* (= 'higher education')

Again we await more careful sociohistorical work in this area on the role of teachers in disseminating features of WEs.

6.6   CONCLUSION

This chapter has tried to show ways in which Pidgin and Creole studies can illuminate the study of New Englishes, even though the two classes of phenomena can be broadly separated. At the same time we have argued for a greater interface between the fields of Second Language Acquisition and New Englishes than is historically the case. We also suggested ways in which New Englishes can contribute to these neighbouring disciplines. This chapter has also argued for greater historical continuity between the early modern English superstrate and its New English colonial offspring than is generally appreciated. We stress, however, that we are not advocating a largely superstratal view of the formation of New Englishes. Rather, they are the result of a synthesis between superstrate(s), substrates, cognitive processes and linguistic universals. Although we have focused inevitably on features that distinguish New Englishes from other varieties, from the viewpoint of modern linguistics the differences are largely on the surface. This applies especially to educated varieties of New Englishes in, say, India, Nigeria and the Philippines. Although generativists have had little to say about the status of New Englishes vis-à-vis Universal Grammar, it would be well to remind ourselves that New Englishes are analysable, from a psycholinguistic viewpoint, as 'ordinary' languages which are the targets of acquisition themselves. Children growing up in Singapore are acquiring the rules of Sgp Eng, using the principles of Universal Grammar and the cultural rules of their social networks.

STUDY QUESTIONS

1. In terms of their sociohistorical backgrounds how are Creoles different from New Englishes?
2. In terms of their linguistic structure how are Creoles different from New Englishes?
3. What is a creoloid?
4. Distinguish between a pidgin and early interlanguage. Which of these is more relevant to New English studies?
5. What is a parameter in syntax; and why is parameter setting of relevance to second-language acquisition?

Further reading

All works mentioned here are fully referenced in the bibliography.

A good introduction, among many, to Pidgin and Creole studies is Sebba's *Contact Languages: Pidgins and Creoles* (1997), while a good overview of SLA is Ellis' *Understanding Second Language Acquisition* (1985). A more comprehensive update of the latter is Ellis' *The Study of Second Language Acquisition* (1994). Studies of New Englishes within some of the frameworks proposed in this chapter are Mesthrie's *English in Language Shift: The History, Structure and Sociolinguistics of South African Indian English* (1992a) and Ho and Platt's *The Dynamics of a Contact Continuum*, dealing with Singaporean English (1993).

7 Conclusion: current trends in the spread of English

7.1 INTRODUCTION

This chapter rounds off the study of WEs by examining them in the context of linguistic aspects of globalisation and some practical issues surrounding it. The main areas covered are WEs in education, special purpose international communication like air traffic control, the growing call-centre industry in the Outer Circle and the further spread of English in Europe.

7.2 SOME EDUCATIONAL ISSUES

In previous chapters we focused on the characteristics of New Englishes that set them apart from metropolitan varieties. These structural and discourse characteristics lead us to characterise individual New Englishes as varieties in their own right. That is, they are treated as relatively autonomous varieties, or dialects with a special status, namely being L2 varieties, not frequently used in the home. Crucially a New English like that of Sri Lanka is not invented anew with each generation of learners. Earlier generations are responsible for effectively laying down tracks that subsequent generations were to follow and modify. Thus Sri Lankan English is not simply 'English in Sri Lanka', but a variety with a certain regional and social identity, one of its characteristics being, as Kachru (1982) and others have stressed, acculturation to the languages, environment and sociopolitical activities in the society. A relevant question that has arisen is whether the New English should be overtly recognised within the educational system, if it is the tacit norm that people follow. This has spawned an interesting debate that goes beyond purely linguistic matters, touching on resources, attitudes and perceptions of the role of English. These are issues related to the hegemonic power of standard varieties. In this chapter we begin by looking at the 'Kachru–Quirk controversy' over the role of New English and Standard English in classrooms. We examine some crucial pedagogical questions arising from each of these positions. We also highlight some studies that attempt to use New Englishes as classroom resources.

7.2.1 The Kachru–Quirk controversy

Two prominent scholars of worldwide English have come to diametrically opposed conclusions about which English should be inculcated in post-colonial classrooms. The theoretical positions have been disparagingly labelled by the proponents themselves as 'liberation linguistics' (Quirk 1990 – referring obliquely to Kachru's position) and 'deficit linguistics' (Kachru 1991a, responding directly to Quirk's position). Quirk (1985, 1990) argues for a global standard to maintain comprehensibility among different nations. Although in earlier work he had written positively about the possibilities of stable and institutionalised varieties arising in Asia and Africa, Quirk (1985) later takes the position that regional, social and ethnic variation were being overvalued in educational contexts. In this he was iterating the position of the Kingman Report (1988) on the Teaching of English in the UK and extending it to Outer Circle contexts. Quirk recognises that different national varieties of English are developing in the Outer Circle, but does not find any overt support for them from policy-makers. He cites some educationists and political leaders who equate the rise of a local variety with a failure of the educational system. He points out further (1985:6) that 'the relatively narrow range of purposes for which the non-native needs to use English (even in ESL countries) is arguably well-catered for by a single monochrome standard form that looks as good on paper as it sounds in speech'. For Quirk Standard British or American English should be the norm for international communication and hence the ones to be inculcated in Outer Circle classrooms. Quirk (1990:9) equates the New Englishes with lower standards as follows:

> It is neither liberal, nor liberating to permit learners to settle for lower standards than the best, and it is a travesty of liberalism to tolerate low standards which will lock the least fortunate into the least rewarding careers.

B. B. Kachru (1991a) criticises Quirk's position as involving applied linguistics divorced from its context. Such a position equates linguistic differences with language deficit, a theory outlined for working-class L1 speakers of British English (Bernstein 1974). Bernstein's theory that different linguistic codes of the same language are generated and sustained by class differences has been rejected by most sociolinguists (see Labov 1969; Edwards 1979). Kachru notes that for the Outer Circle the theory is further inapplicable, since people already have a stable L1, with English being an additional language. Although the local variety has little overt and official authority, Kachru (1991a:8) refers to 'invisible language planning' which gives it recognition despite the attitudes of elites and officialdom. Invisible language planning is determined by the attitudes and expectations of parents towards a language, the role of the media, the role of peer groups amongst middle-class youth, etc. For every critic of a New English (see Quirk 1990:8–9), there is a creative writer insisting on the need for an English that is adapted to the local context to best express its cultural and intellectual milieu (see Kachru 1991a:6–7). That is, internal communication and creativity is just as important as international communication. The starting point of such an undertaking, of using endo-normative models, will be the codification of regional varieties, extending their uses and preparing learners to cope with variation (see Fairman 1992). By contrast Kachru (1986) insists on allowing non-native teachers to develop their own models using local communicative, pragmatic and pedagogic competence. Using local linguistic resources is seen as more authentic and appropriate (see also Seidlhofer and Widdowson 1998; Canagarajah 2005).

The debate has implications for issues concerning the most appropriate qualifications of teachers. Who are the best teachers: monolingual speakers of English who embody the standard norm, or bilingual teachers who might not always command the metropolitan standard but who are familiar with the pupils' mother tongues? Once again Quirk (1990:8) comes down on the side of the native speaker, stressing the inadequacies of some teachers:

> No one should underestimate the problem of teaching English in such countries as India and Nigeria, where the English of the teachers themselves inevitably bears the stamp of locally acquired deviation from the standard language...

For Kachru and others the reverse is the case. Kachru points out that the resources needed to promulgate the British or American norm are unlikely to be fulfilled in the vast territories of Africa and Asia. These resources include trained teachers, availability of native speakers, appropriate educational technology, etc. The prominence of native speakers in traditional (ELT) methodologies has obscured the distinctive contribution of successful second-language users. It has, instead, defined them as failed native speakers by focusing on what they are not (see further Kramsch 1998; Cook 1999).

The third issue pertains to the nature of teaching materials. Here the standard has traditionally been used. Yet, the existence of recognisably local but 'educated' varieties gives reason to re-examine the issue of whose norms should be codified. Bamgbose (1998:1) puts the two sides of the issue as follows:

> In spite of the consensus on the availability of non-native Englishes, there are issues that still remain unsettled. These include the status of innovations in the nativisation process, the continued use of native norms as a point of reference, the ambivalence between recognition and acceptance of non-native norms, the adequacy of pedagogical models, and the overwhelming need for codification. Underlying these issues is the constant pull between native and non-native English norms. Innovations in non-native Englishes are often judged not for what they are or their functions within the varieties in which they occur, but rather according to how they stand in relation to the norms of native Englishes.

There is a strong tradition within ideological studies of language to critique the way in which the need for British (or American) norms in World Englishes serves hegemonic purposes relating to power and economics in the centre–periphery relation. The alleged need for native teacher support is challenged in Phillipson (1992). Romaine (1997:426) equates it with the 'the maintenance of hegemony and the continuation of an ideological and practical dependence of other countries on native-speaking countries for expertise, books, teachers, etc.' The power and political symbolism of the variety to be chosen for education and the use of education as a hegemonic site has been shown in analyses of the very content of grammar books (let alone literary texts prescribed). Singh (1987) analysed four grammar books prescribed in India in different periods: Nesfield's *Idiom, Grammar, and Synthesis for High Schools* (1895); Tipping's *Matriculation High School English Grammar of Modern English Usage* (1933), Wren and Martin's *High School English Grammar and Composition* (1954) and Sidhu's *An Intensive Course in English* (1976). Singh shows a close correlation between the sociopolitical ethos and example sentences in the texts. Nesfield's grammar of 1895 promotes British supremacy and naturalises empire in examples like *A viceroy is one who rules for a king or queen*. Tipping, writing in 1933, promotes a localised view of India and attempts to naturalise English within this context (e.g. in inviting students to make a relative clause out of the pair: *India is a great peninsula in Asia; India is our land*). In Wren and Martin (revised edn. 1954, originally written in the 1930s), Indian characters carry the brunt of the grammatical messages. According to Singh (1987:257), the authors appear to be symbolically handing over power

to the Empire's Indian 'subjects'. The final post-independence grammar of Sidhu (1976) reflects a transformation of the role of English.
Sentences like the following are used to teach auxiliary verbs: *Luckily,
my desire to learn English is strong enough. I want to make good friends,
and after my B.A., I want to get a good job. My good English can help me in
this...*' As Singh concedes, even though the examples in this book are
Indocentric, there is a sense of neocolonialism in the uncritical equa-
tion of English with economic and educational progress. It is not our
intention in citing this study to criticise the different textbook writers for being products of their times. Rather it is to illustrate how
the power and allure of Standard English is reinforced in diverse
ways, down to the very grammar lessons. The Kachruvian position that
such cultural hegemony has to be deconstructed and hence resisted is
accordingly given credence.

Chelliah (2001) examines a similar phenomenon among local, Indian
English author-grammarians. She shows, for example, how *Common
Errors in Indian English* guidebooks in India – designed to prepare students for various English proficiency examinations – still promote the
native-speaker norm. Chelliah argues that the problems that these
local authors-experts attempt and promise to eradicate are salient
Indian English features. This raises the question of 'whose English'
is really being developed and for what reason. Chelliah makes it clear
that in colonial times English was being made to serve the interests of
those in power, rather than those who were acquiring the language.
She quotes the work of local ELT practitioners that demonstrates the
effects of discourses of native ELT experts:

> The cleavage [between Indian and British English] that is established
> becomes more and more pronounced with time, and it is not difficult
> to imagine, that if this process goes on, there will develop in course
> of time *a real Indian English which* will have so many expressions and
> peculiarities characteristic of our people that it *will be unintelligible to
> an Englishman.* (Sood and Bright, n.d.:6; emphasis added)

Things look rather different from the viewpoint of the learner, as Paul
Christophersen (1992:16) recounts in relation to his experience teaching English in Nigeria:

> After giving a lecture on the phonetics of English to students at
> Ibadan, Nigeria, I was consulted by one of them who said, 'If I try
> outside the College to use the kind of English you teach us, people
> will ask, "Why do you speak English in the white man's way? Why
> don't you speak it like an African?"'

The Kachru–Quirk controversy may ultimately be an *academic* polarity. In the real world there is space for both viewpoints, and many compromises are inevitably made in classrooms. These arise from the availability of resources, the attitudes and perceptions of parents and pupils, the availability of English teachers (of whatever background) etc. Ruth Petzold (2002:423) reminds us that a pedagogical model for any language is an idealised or slightly simplified language system that aims to capture the language that is common among educated speakers of that variety. It seldom reflects the rich variety of individual differences or the innovations among speakers of the model. She also stresses that the pedagogical model to be accessed and used has to be codified and used in dictionaries, educational materials and other resources. There also have to be recognised proficiency measurement instruments.

Turning to attitudes, sociolinguists need to acknowledge that community attitudes and expectations are important. Kachru himself (1992:60) acknowledged that where language attitudes are concerned there were many ambiguities:

> The non-native speakers themselves have not been able to accept what may be termed the 'ecological validity' of their nativised or local Englishes. One would have expected such acceptance, given the acculturation and linguistic nativisation of the new varieties. On the other hand, the non-native models of English (such as RP or General American) are not accepted without reservations. There is thus a case of linguistic schizophrenia…

Attitudes, of course, can change in response to new circumstances. Kachru (1976) reported in the 1970s that a majority of Indian graduate students surveyed expressed a preference for a British model of English as a medium of instruction. By the 1990s Sahgal (1991) suggests a growing preference for 'Ordinary Indian English'. We propose in fact that conditions are now favourable for the emergence of a standard Indian English with overtly prestigious norms of its own, as exemplified in its national and international television networks, the English of Indian film stars, cricketers and other prestigious role models, etc.

Quirk's confidence in the monochrome standard also needs to be tempered by practical issues relating to the availability of L1 speakers, the costs involved in hiring them, etc. The issue of resources cuts both ways. Many countries are unable to attract and pay sufficient numbers of teachers from the Inner Circle. However, those same countries sometimes find it easier to import educational materials from the West, rather than devise and produce their own. Many Outer Circle students learn and are tested in Inner Circle territories like India, Singapore and the Philippines. In Chapter 1 we mentioned the movement of students from South-East Asia to India in search of access to English in an environment deemed less costly and more in tune with their cultural values. This pragmatism thus undercuts the dichotomy between local versus metropolitan varieties. Lowenberg (2002:434) examined enrolment patterns at the Center for Language Learning at De La Salle University in Manila, the Philippines. Of 152 students the majority were from Outer Circle countries: 52 from Korea, 44 from mainland China, 16 from Taiwan and 12 from Japan. Lowenberg suggests that teaching materials from these settings de facto propagate Outer Circle, rather than Inner Circle norms: 'When these learners return to their home countries and often become leaders in English language teaching there, they introduce many of these Outer Circle norms, which then become more widespread and influence Expanding Circle nativisation.'

Furthermore, we caution that there is always a gap between formal educational standard and informal speech. Even if there were an earnest and dedicated directive to inculcate, say, Indian English in the classroom, with all its salient grammatical features, there is no guarantee that that is what the pupils will necessarily acquire. We should always expect an approximation of the target variety, rather than full replication. And students may signal their individuality and changing identities by further innovations. The sociolinguistic universe is not a static one, even in the Outer Circle.

Kimberley Brown (1995:241) argues that the internationalisation of English language teaching is long overdue. She proposes that the World English perspective be integrated as part of teacher training: 'it is imperative that students work with actual data from around the world; otherwise the whole concept of a World Englishes perspective remains abstract and potentially divorced from young teachers' lives'. Two educational programmes discussed in the literature are of relevance here, showing the possibilities and problems associated with using WE materials in education. This time the theme revolved around educating students about the varieties of English, rather than the choice of the very medium of instruction. Baik and Shim (2002) wished to promote the idea of World Englishes as a medium of worldwide communication. They argued that the standard for World Englishes should not come from just one hegemonic variety of English (for EFL countries) nor solely from the local variety (for ESL countries). The authors describe a fourteen-week internet-based course that introduced a wide range of Englishes from the three circles. Sample materials were of two sorts: (a) speech data from radio broadcasting stations in the different territories and (b) newspaper articles. In this first taste of the field for Korean students (run in Korean) the choice is wisely on the more formal and standardised varieties, rather than the full lectal and stylistic ranges possible in any one territory. The authors considered the course a successful one.

However, this success was not matched in an Inner Circle environment. Kubota (2001) investigated the attitudes of Anglo high-school students in a southern US state to the English of foreign teaching-assistants and professors. She found a great deal of prejudice against foreign accents inside and outside the classroom. Kubota tried to overcome such prejudice in a short eight-lesson unit covering variation within US English and extending it to a study of materials from other territories like India and Mexico. She included video and written materials as well as live presentations by professors from territories like India and Nigeria (Outer Circle varieties) and Ecuador, France and China (Expanding Circle varieties). Kubota reports that her intervention was not very successful – she found it difficult to overcome prejudice in the short term by educating students directly about cultural and linguistic relativism.

The Kachru–Quirk disagreement can be evaluated in the light of dialect versus standard debates for English. At one level the role of New English in a multilingual society is not very different from that of L1 dialects in a largely monolingual English society. Similar issues arise as to whether schools should accept some of the localised and colloquial linguistic norms that pupils bring to the classroom. Should dialect be used to facilitate access to the standard; and can schools inculcate the formal standard without denigrating the class dialects of some pupils? Trudgill (1975) has made trenchant observations about the place of dialect in the school, arguing for greater sociolinguistic sensitivity on the part of teachers. Varieties that are frequently silenced in the educational system can contain a wealth of local linguistic resources in vocabulary, grammar, discourse conventions and accent. Whilst sociolinguists recognise that the empowerment of pupils includes the inculcation of the standard, they insist that it should not lead to the devaluation of the local norms. The debate between the traditional guardians of the standard and the supporters of variation can be an acrimonious one (see Honey 1997; Trudgill 1998). One attempt to validate a social dialect within the education system generated an enormous amount of controversy that went beyond the ivory tower – the Ebonics debate of the 1990s in the USA. The Ebonics proposal arose from the lack of recognition of African American English within the educational system. Pupils using features of this stigmatised variety were diagnosed as learning-disabled and hence unprepared for their next grade level. In 1996 the schoolboard in Oakland, California, proposed that the students' home dialect (labelled *Ebonics*, from *Ebony* plus *phonics*) be integrated into the school system. The board cited the uniqueness of the variety, stressing that it was not a sub-standard, defective version of Standard English, but a different linguistic system. It accordingly proposed a bilingual system of education, using dialect and standard. Initially the home dialect would be used, and instruction offered in the standard dialect. The standard was expected to be phased in as medium of instruction at a later stage. There were both local and national objections to this policy. Although some community leaders and many sociolinguists and linguists supported the experiment, it was the more vociferous objectors who won the day and the Ebonics proposal was never fully implemented (see Baugh 2000; Mesthrie *et al.* 2000:378–82).

There are lessons here for propagators of Outer Circle Englishes to bear in mind. Ultimately the Kachru–Quirk controversy can only be resolved outside the ivory tower, by the attitudes and actions of parents, pupils, teachers, administrators and the like. Linguistic hegemony power can be contested, but it is seldom dismantled by reason alone.

7.3 THE EXPANDING CIRCLE AGAIN

We began this book with an overview of the spread of English. We return to this theme in this section, with a focus on new developments, especially in the Expanding Circle. EFL has been underplayed in this book, since our main concern has been on common linguistic structures in focused varieties, especially ones that began as (and mostly remain) ESL varieties. By contrast EFLs are more diffuse and do not yet lend themselves to systematic comparisons with each other. In Kachru's terms (1985:16) they are 'norm dependant'. For EFLs there has been no one defining encounter with British or American rule. English is restricted to being a subject studied in the classroom and an important means of international communication, and interaction with tourists. This sense of the 'global connectivity' afforded by English to the Outer Circle is effectively captured in a Microsoft commercial on French television (Martin 2002:11):

(Written online English-language 'chat' in Microsoft commercial for French audiences (from Martin 2002:11))
A: Hi! I'm Francois.
B: Hey, Francois. Hi Bill, Hi Kimoko.
C: What's it like in Paris now?
A: It's Spring. The tourists are blooming.
B: Same here. What's going on in Russia?
D: Confusion, political upheaval, the usual.
C: I'm in Indonesia.
E. I'm in Newark.
A. That's nice.

As we note later, the crisp simple language used and the play on *blooming* is effective as advertising copy, but need not reflect actual EFL norms.

For internal communication in EFL territories, English is less important, since individual countries are united in having a majority official language (e.g. Japanese) or in having a lingua franca (e.g. Mandarin Chinese). However, globalisation and the increasing use of English as its vehicle has meant that EFL countries face certain common changes and challenges. We discuss some of these in outline.

7.3.1 Airline communication and the spread of English

Of especial concern in EFL countries is the need to fill key positions requiring international communication with people having a general level of proficiency in English as well as English for Special Purposes (special proficiency in specific registers). For a discussion of Essential English for International Maritime Use (or 'Seaspeak') see Crystal (1997:97–8). We take as our example the language of Air Traffic Control (ATC). Air travel is, of course, closely intertwined with globalisation and requires not just the highest technological expertise, but clarity of communication too. Given the birth of the industry in the USA, it is unsurprising that English has been the language predominantly used in aviation, established in this position by the International Civil Aviation Organization in 1950 (Tajima 2004:453). English is still not the mandatory official language in ATC, with countries like France, Italy and those of the former Soviet Union permitting the use of their own languages besides English for their domestic ATC. However, the vast majority of air-traffic controllers whose mother tongue is not English have to acquire English during their flight training, which frequently takes place in the USA. Tajima (2004) provides a detailed – and alarming – analysis of cases of major airline accidents. Whilst most of these occurred because of some technological and environmental difficulty, a compounding factor in many of them was a failure between pilot and air-traffic controller to communicate adequately. A brief synopsis of some problems relating to the topic of ESL and EFL follows:

(a) *Insufficient basic English proficiency:* In connection with a major 1996 accident, Indian air-traffic controllers complained that pilots from the former Soviet Union had a poor command of English, whilst the Kazakhstan pilots might not have understood the instructions given by the Indian controller. Here we see the normal difficulties of ESL and EFL communication compounded by the degree of clarity and precision required in aviation communication. The difficulties are, of course, compounded by the quality of sound on the channels of communication and of the general noise levels at airports.

(b) *Insufficient proficiency to cope with unusual events:* A 1995 accident was partly due to the lack of intermediate to advanced English proficiency of the Columbian air-traffic controller to whom the content of the radio transmission from the American pilots did not make much sense. However, he also acknowledged that he would have questioned the pilots or discussed the situation further if the pilots had been Spanish speakers. He said that 'their request made no sense, that their request was illogical, incongruent, but I did not know how to convey those thoughts to the American flight crew... in English' (Lunsford 1996, cited by Tajima 2004:457).

(c) *Local English vs international English:* Tajima outlines another tragic case where an air-captain from Holland experiencing difficulty on a foggy runway said after some discussion with the ATC, 'Ah, roger sir, we are cleared to Papa Beacon, flight level niner zero...We are at takeoff.' The controller responds 'OK, standby for take-off. I call you', but is then interrupted by another radio transmission. By this time, however, the plane is already in motion for takeoff and a serious accident ensues. Tajima (2004:460) suggests that the main reason for the miscommunication was not the Dutch captain's fluency in English, but the use of one phrase 'We are now at takeoff' with a Spanish-speaking controller. In Tajima's analysis this is possibly a feature of Dutch EFL influenced by mother-tongue usage, whose intended meaning is 'We are now taking off.' It is unlikely that the captain used this construction frequently, as he had extensive experience in aviation English and was himself chief examiner of a pilot training programme. Tajima suggests that out of frustration and fatigue (from being grounded for a long time) the captain inadvertently backslid to a construction influenced by transfer from Dutch. The controller (who himself had earlier contributed some confusion in giving detailed instructions for the take-off and subsequent altitude) understood him in the standard sense of being ready for take-off rather than actually taking off.

It is not the case, however, that the communication problems are *all* caused by the use of EFL. Tajima cites another misunderstanding between pilot and controller who were both native speakers of English. The captain had inadvertently got the plane into gradual descent, instead of a holding position. Noticing this, but not aware that the pilot had done this accidentally, the controller asks in colloquial English '*Eastern, ah, four oh one, how are things coming there?*' The captain responded '*Okay, we'd to turn around and come, come back in.*' Then the plane crashed. Tajima argues that the accident illustrates the danger of using ambiguous and colloquial English, instead of the more formal Airspeak '*Confirm you are descending*' or '*Report your altitude.*' Tajima concludes (2004:462) 'Hypothetically and ironically, if at least one of the participants had been a non-native speaker of English who could use only set expressions...the accident could have been avoided.'

A final point of relevance to EFL studies is Tajima's suggestion, based on the experiences and opinions of an experienced US airline captain, that English-speaking pilots have to become accustomed to the special characteristics of local Englishes in EFL countries. 'When he started flying to Japan and China, he had experienced many difficulties and problems in his ATC communication with Japanese and Chinese controllers. However, he now experiences almost no problem in communicating with them' (Tajima 2004:265). We note finally that in many of the instances it is not language that is the fundamental problem, but the congestion of airspaces and uncontrollable weather conditions.

7.3.2 The changing face of English in Europe

In the airline miscommunication example above we cited the English of the Dutch captain as (technically) EFL. Anyone familiar with Dutch speakers of English would realise that this technical description seems odd, given the high level of competence in the 'foreign language' of many Dutch people. The question could well be asked whether certain European countries like Norway, Sweden and Holland lie somewhere in between ESL and EFL (or Outer Circle and Expanding Circle). In this vein, Truchot (1997) accepts that English is an 'expanding circle' type in Europe, since the use of English is mostly determined by international purposes. In some specific countries like Belgium and Switzerland, however, there is also an internal role for English across linguistic communities. Moreover English is beginning to be used more intensively in certain domains in some countries. In many European countries English has become a compulsory subject, elevated from its previous position of competing with other 'foreign' European languages. Although not quite 'ESL' in the sense that the term has been defined in Applied Linguistics (see section 1.2), English is sometimes described as a second language of the educational system in places like Scandinavia. A more accurate formulation might be 'first foreign language' (van Essen 1997:97); and this might in fact be the characterisation of English in almost all parts of the Expanding Circle.

The term 'Euro English' is currently a somewhat disparaging term, suggesting less than full competence amongst some public speakers in the European Union. However, Modiano (2003) and others consider that the rise of a distinctly Euro English out of the current diversity is a distinct possibility. Modiano speculates that some features that are accepted in Sweden might become part of such a core. Sweden's status as somewhat intermediate between ESL and EFL can be seen from examples given by Modiano which confirm that as the use of English increases, it shows some signs of indigenisation with new idioms like *blue-eyed* 'naïve, innocent', rather than its more usual Std Eng reference to 'someone's favourite' – see Modiano (2003:39) for more examples. Kachru's (1982) documentation and assessment of the penetration of English into new cultural contexts and its assimilation therein seems to be repeating itself in the Expanding Circle.

Even countries previously colonised by other European powers like France (e.g. the Ivory Coast) or Portugal (e.g. Mozambique) have lobbyists for English over other European and local languages. Truchot (1997) suggests that in places like Holland and Denmark a near-diglossic situation in the future is not out of the question. In the 1990s Holland came close to accepting (but ultimately rejected) English as the sole language of higher education. The role of English in this domain is particularly strong in countries like Norway, Denmark, Holland and Germany. As Truchot notes (1997:74) France takes a stronger line than, say, Germany in trying to safeguard the national language in higher education. In France, theses must be written in French by law; in Germany, by contrast, the attitude seems to be that English is preferable for wider dissemination of the results of graduate theses in certain disciplines.

7.3.3 Euro English: a composite force? ▬▬▬▬▬▬▬▬▬

Euro English is a fascinating topic which is likely to rise in prominence in the next decade of WE studies. Although the spread of English in Europe is not qualitatively different from the spread of EFL in, say, Asia, several factors make the spread particularly salient. Firstly, western Europe covers a relatively small area (not much more than India, and far less an expanse than Asia). Secondly, proximity to the UK and the rise of the European parliament makes English relatively accessible. Thirdly, cultural similarities make it easier to absorb English into the local ethos. Finally, the hegemony of English is sealed by the popularity of US youth culture and entertainment. In a sense, as we suggest in Chapter 1 (with a fair bit of historical and geographical licence), where northern Europe is concerned (especially parts of Scandinavia and north Germany) Anglo-Saxon is coming back home – much changed, of course, and much more refined via contacts with Latin and French, not to mention its enrichment by the languages of the colonies. Hoffman (2000:20) remarks on the irony that 'the language that has acquired such wide currency is the tongue which originated in what is now Europe's most reluctant, and linguistically least adventurous member'.

However, it is American rather than British English that has been influential since the second World War, initially in Germany and Austria via American soldiers, and subsequently via the dominant economic, political and scientific position of the United States (Hoffman 2000:7). We might add 'and Hollywood'. This influence predates Britain's late entry into the Common Market in the 1970s. For Hoffman terms like 'internationalisation', 'globalisation' and 'modernisation' could just as well be read as meaning 'Americanisation'. Recent loan words into European languages, she argues, come from American English, whilst neologisms in Euro English emanate more from the USA than the UK. Hoffman appears to downplay the influence of England by its very proximity (just under two hours from most airports). This makes it a more viable destination for German students to travel to with the intention of improving their spoken English than the long trans-Atlantic crossing to the United States. British literature and culture also have prestige value for many German university students.

'Euro English' is a cover term for two types of English. The first is sometimes called 'mid-Atlantic', an extension of an old term used to describe any intermediate variety between US and British English – e.g. the accommodations made by people from one side of the Atlantic who have lived in the other territory for a long period of time, or the 'stage American' of British actors and vice versa. In WE studies it is notable that a new kind of mid-Atlantic might be arising, spoken by neither US nor UK residents, but in continental Europe. This variety occurs under conditions of 'elite bilingualism', with well-educated and well-travelled speakers (to the UK and USA, at least) commanding a variety that is, in the terms we used in earlier chapters, 'acrolectal'. Some such speakers are claimed to use a variety that mediates between prestige varieties of American and British English. For example, on a Euro sports channel that we occasionally listen to, one of the announcers uses a general sporting register, with the intonation and accent patterns that are close to RP, with some clear exceptions. The BATH vowel is generally [æ] as in US English, not RP. Moreover, there were subtle signs of an independence reflecting a specifically European variety, rather than a mere admixture of the two varieties. The most notable feature was the devoicing of final consonants, giving a slight Germanic flavour to the accent. Perhaps this is the formula for prestige varieties of Euro English: RP, plus certain salient American segments like [æ] in BATH and postvocalic /r/, plus some localised features from Europe. Our characterisation of Euro English should indicate that we do not accept the sometimes disparaging overtones of the term, usually when associated with the language of bureaucrats from the EU. It is probably too soon to claim that there is a single entity called Euro English, anymore than there can be said to be a single Asian English or African English, despite the many similarities that do occur within those continents.

There is a second strand to the emergent Euro English, which is coming to be called 'English as a Lingua Franca' (James 2000). This refers to the increasing use of English in conversations between people from different language backgrounds who are still in the process of mastering the language. Whereas the mid-Atlantic described above is an acrolectal variety, 'Lingua Franca English' falls more on the basilectal (or basilang) side of the scale. James (2000:22) gives a snippet from an Austrian/Italian/Slovenian conversation overheard in Central Europe: A: *I don' wanna drink alcohol.* B: *Me too.* C: *I also not.* James comments: 'Such and similar uses of English may be recorded countless times daily throughout Europe. It shows English being created 'on-line' for immediate communication purposes in a relatively ad hoc way by speakers who have no doubt had at least four years of formal training in the language in their respective school systems.'[1]

---

[1] From this fragmentary evidence it is only speaker C who shows divergence from L1 colloquial norms. Speaker A diverges in idiom – a native speaker would probably say something like *I don't feel like a drink today.*

This is interlanguage development in a context in which the TL is not spoken natively; it appears to be more of a performance variety (see section 1.2.1). This process is not, of course, a European phenomenon alone and has been played out in many colonial situations in previous times – see Mesthrie (1992a:26) for IndSAf Eng.

Meierkord (2004) studied the patterns of interaction between students of different WE backgrounds at dinner in halls of residence in the UK, with a view to ascertaining what accommodations speakers made to each other's varieties. The broader field of inquiry that this kind of study relates to is koineisation (see Siegel 1985), which analyses processes of levelling and change as speakers of related dialects come into contact in a new environment. In the globalising world this process is particularly salient in that non-native speakers might predominate in such interactions. In Meierkord's studies there were thirty speakers from the Expanding Circle (Europe, North Africa, South-East Asia) of whom twelve were competent in English, and eighteen not. In addition there were nineteen from the Outer Circle (South Asia and sub-Saharan Africa). Meierkord found that the ESL speakers tended to retain salient features of their New English varieties, whilst speaking a variety that was overall not very far removed from the grammatical rules of Std Eng. There was, moreover, a sharp distinction in the database between ESL and EFL, with the latter speakers speaking an unfocused interlanguage, with utterances corresponding to the classic utterances associated with a developing interlanguage continuum. Her study shows the relatively focused nature of ESLs and suggests that a lingua franca English on a global scale has not (yet) developed.

7.3.4 The spread of English as a company language ▬▬▬▬▬

Large international companies in Europe (Ericsson, Philips, Volvo) have institutionalised the use of English as a company language. This makes it compulsory for any form of oral and written communication intended for a multilingual audience within such companies. In domestic advertising and marketing English phrases are also used to heighten the prestige of products. Truchot (1997:76) points to the spread of English as a consequence of the internationalisation of society and the globalisation of exchanges:

> Seen globally, these consequences are social as well as economic. Some of them are linguistic. Very few languages share the market of international linguistic exchanges. To get a fair share of that market it is necessary for a language to fulfil a number of conditions, that is, an important demographic weight, strong economic support, a previously established international spread, and a high level of

modernization. Only English fulfils all these conditions; German and French fulfil some of these conditions; Russian has lost several of them; Spanish and Chinese may acquire more potential in the future. But most languages are more or less excluded from the 'linguistic market'.

The use of English in industry includes a crucial role for it in advertising. McArthur (1998:14–15) has referred to the use of English as a 'decorative language' in situations where its use is more symbolic than literal. Since a large number of readers or viewers may not be fully familiar with English, its value lies in its overtones (promising quality, success, style, modernity, etc.) rather than in the literal wording. Sometimes the wording in fact makes little sense within English semantics. Consider the following examples of public signs in Japan (from Hyde 2002).

> Shop names: *Tasty Plaza*
> *Your: Jazz and lunch*
> *Sandwiches and Café.*
>
> Soft drink name: *Pocari sweat*

As Hyde (2002:12) stresses, such examples of 'emblematic English' found in Japanese public signs are not primarily meant for the scrutiny of native users of English. The medium is a message in itself, serving to index Japanese participation in the global village.

7.4 METROPOLIS, OUTER CIRCLE AND GLOBAL COMMUNICATION

In this section we examine briefly two aspects of globalisation in contact between an Inner and Outer Circle English. These involve (a) the re-entrance of the metropolitan varieties into Outer Circle territories, via new communication technologies and (b) the acculturation of New English speakers in the metropolis, via the age of jetplane migration. In both cases the Outer Circle variety is expected to accommodate to the more powerful Inner Circle norms, but as we discuss, there is a necessary degree of give and take, since the Outer Circle variety (Indian English) has a clearly defined identity.

7.4.1 Call-centre industries

An aspect of the distributed nature of work in the era of globalisation that is of direct interest to WE studies is the growing call-centre industry in the Outer Circle. Large multinational companies origi-nating in the USA and UK find it economical to outsource certain services to ESL countries in Asia, notably India. Since the 1990s voiced-based services like customer queries and enquiries in the UK and USA have been outsourced to call centres set up in places like Bangalore. The customer dials a local number to check the status of his or her account (say), not knowing that the call is rerouted to Bangalore, where a trained Indian employee deals with the query. The novelty of speak-ing to someone halfway round the world about a product manufac-tured and purchased in one's own locality in the West has attracted a great deal of popular attention in the media. This interaction typ-ically involves speakers of a metropolitan English with New English speakers. It thus proves fertile testing ground for some of the ideas about World Englishes discussed in this book. As this is a relatively new phenomenon there is not much sociolinguistic research to draw on, although there is a growing literature on the subject from the viewpoint of business studies (see Chadha 2004; Taylor and Bain 2005). Like other issues discussed in this book the phenomenon of accent and grammar accommodation in call-centre encounters cannot be treated as a linguistic issue alone. Issues of power and authority are at stake too. That outsourcing has led to job losses in the West means that customers are not always well disposed to call centres. Claire Cowie (2007) has studied the expectations and training offered in Bangalore to call-centre employees. She was interested in what changes employ-ees were advised and trained to make in accommodating to their cus-tomers. In particular this raised questions about the status of their own varieties of English (educated Indian English), perceptions about the differences between British and American English, and whether a new 'call centre' brand of international English is emerging. Cowie found that the popularly reported accounts of employees taking on a new identity like the following were often exaggerated: 'workers serv-ing UK customers are often given accent training, and taught about pubs, football and running story lines in popular soap operas, to be able to hold conversations with British customers' (BBC news website, 7 March 2003). Since a typical training session lasts from three to six weeks, this is clearly not enough to effect a large-scale accent and identity change. Cowie notes that trainees were assertive about the validity of their own kind of English, which they saw as based on a sound education. Cowie was keen to ascertain whether accent training was focused on the elimination of stigmatised Indian English features in favour of a more conservative Indian English, or on the introduc-tion of the salient features of a metropolitan accent. If the latter, she was interested in whether an American or British norm was being inculcated. Cowie reports (in press): 'A term that anyone involved in accent training in India would have heard more than any other is "neutralization". A direct question put to anyone in the accent training business about what accent they were aiming for produced the same (puzzled) answer: a neutral accent.' There is no core list of features of such a neutral accent, since different training manuals and training agencies have different ideas on the subject. They do, however, call attention to the more stigmatised features of Indian English, like [v] and [w] being interchanged occasionally. A manual put out by Roma Chadha advises (2004:117–18) trainees to listen to the BBC rather than CNN, even if they have American customers, since 'the British speech pattern is much closer to the Indian'. Furthermore 'If we try and fake the American accent, it starts to sound artificial and fake because it does not fit in with our existing speech framework and only ends up causing more miscommunication.' Another manual (Gupta 2003) promotes and exemplifies a 'neutral accent', which does have some very obvious American features like rhoticity, yod-dropping and t-flapping. Cowie reports that younger trainers are more comfortable with promoting such a neutral accent that leans slightly towards US English. Older trainers tended to favour a British-oriented norm. Since trainees themselves were not insecure about their own accents, call centres are obviously interesting grounds for further studies of how varying WE ideologies are being played out, keeping in mind, of course, that success depends on keeping the distant customer satisfied.

7.4.2   A New English in the metropolis

Devyani Sharma's (2005b) study of the English of migrants from India in the San Francisco Bay Area offers a more concrete opportunity of studying the dynamics of a New English in contact with the superstrate language. Like many Asian immigrants in the USA, Indians in the Bay Area retained a strong sense of identity, based on their ancestry and their new lives in the host society. Sharma studied the attitudes of adult speakers to their own variety of English forged in India and its relation to the English of the Bay Area. The subjects in her sample generally had a positive opinion of their own English, some even rating it as in some ways superior to that of US English. These speakers felt that US English diverged much more from the 'Queen's English' than their own. Sharma studied whether this value judgement (and rare example of the overt prestige of a New English) was upheld in the actual speech of the Indian settlers. She demonstrates that many syntactic variables of Ind Eng like subject–verb concord, variability in copula usage and variability in past tense marking are treated like language-learning features, in that they are corrected when immersed in an L1 environment. This does not appear to be true of the Ind Eng article system, which appears to have stabilised and be shared and transmitted by the speakers in the study. Phonological variables, on the other hand, do not correlate with speaker proficiency (unlike the first set of syntactic variables). Sharma argues that features like rhoticity, *l*-velarisation and variable aspiration correspond to speakers' personal experiences of cultural and dialect contact, reflecting both personal choice and the ideological stance to US English cited above.

7.5 LANGUAGE SPREAD, PURISM AND CULTURAL IMPERIALISM AGAIN

The idea of English as 'a killer language' has been raised many times in connection with its spread (see Edwards 1986). The 'glottophagic' (or language-devouring) power of English over languages of the European Union is criticised by Chiti-Batteli (1987) and others concerned with the effects of linguistic globalisation. On the other hand, Pulcini (1997:81) claims that there is little support for this idea in Italy, citing a poetic piece of anti-purism from Beccaria (1988:24) in translation:

> Language is the social and cultural property of the people, but it is
> not like the environment which should be protected because
> polluting effluents and garbage are illegally discharged in it.
> Language is not a monument which deteriorates in contact with air.
> It is not like the Ara Pacis Augustae to keep in a glass tower. It has to
> live in the streets, in academies and in narrow lanes, in books and in
> songs, in isolated valleys and busy metropoles. Its 'Babelic' spirit
> forcefully reflects the composite community it is the expression of.
> To talk of corruption is foolish.

Pulcini also proposes that the influence of English over Italian declines with increasing proficiency in the former. Processes like calquing and translation increase with greater bilingualism. This is noticeable, for example, in the register of sports terminology, with some English loan words even being replaced by Italian words.

Despite the significant changes occurring in the EU, it is China which appears to show the most dramatic changes in an EFL territory. China had been closed to Western cultural and linguistic influence for most of the twentieth century. The foreign language most studied in that period was Russian. With the break-up of the Soviet Union as a major power bloc in the 1990s, Russian has taken a back seat as a potential world language. The Chinese government has given its backing to English over other foreign languages, making it a compulsory subject nationwide from the third year of primary school (Yajun 2003:3). Given China's large population, this effort has seen the country propelled into becoming the major growth point for EFL. For example, the number of learners of English in China is larger than the number of English speakers in the USA (Taylor 2002, cited by Yajun). The education system aims to change the role of English from foreign language to second language (Qiang and Wolff 2003). As in Europe, 'second language' in this context does not refer to 'ESL' in the sociolinguistic sense; rather it refers to what we termed the 'first foreign language'. China is dogged by problems familiar to other EFL territories, especially the availability of sufficient input from mother-tongue and other fluent speakers of English. The eagerness to acquire English has seen the acceptance of foreign graduates even if they do not have teaching qualifications, or experience in language teaching. The commitment of some of these teachers from the West and the training they receive is criticised by Qiang and Wolff (2003). A second problem to be faced is that of possible cultural erosion, as Qiang and Wolff (2003:10) suggest:

> the nationwide ESL campaign brings with it an immersion in Western concepts, including social, cultural, business and political thought. It is inevitable that a certain amount of traditional Chinese thought will give way to a certain amount of Western thought, which translates into a society with confusing input.

A third problem identified by the authors is the implications for the indigenous Chinese languages, especially Mandarin. Why is China forsaking Mandarin for English, they ask pointedly, when 25 per cent of the world's population already speaks Mandarin, which is also one of the six working languages of the United Nations?

Cultural erosion can be seen in the new practice of Chinese children being given an additional English name, to facilitate contacts with people from the West. On the other hand critics of the Anglicisation policy may be overstating the case, since the Chinese case does not appear to be very different from other situations in Asia. Taking India as a parallel (with a similar large and multilingual population), who is to argue that the synthesis between East and West could not be a positive one – with the possibility of continuing influence *from* the West as well as influencing *of* the West. In earlier chapters we suggested that English has undergone something of an incarnation in India – as an

Indian language, with its reduplications, echo-constructions, calques, its culturally laden lexis and specific registers. It is likely that the same trajectory could apply to China in the long run.

We do not believe that the worst-case scenario, language endangerment and death applies to Asian and African countries. Statistics on language death worldwide are alarming, and it does seem to be the case that many of the smaller and less powerful languages of the globe will face increasing pressure as their speakers accommodate to (or are assimilated into) larger languages (see Grenoble and Whaley 1998; Romaine and Nettle 2000). In former times it was the brute force of colonisation and conquest that destroyed viable language and cultural groupings in the Americas and Australasia. It is doubtful that economic globalisation would have the same catastrophic impact in Europe, Asia and Africa. For this to be the case something like the following stages would have to occur in an EFL territory like Denmark or China:

$$\text{English} = \text{EFL} \rightarrow \text{'1st foreign lg'} \rightarrow \text{ESL} \rightarrow \text{'2nd first lg'} \rightarrow$$
$$\text{first lg serving H functions} \rightarrow \text{sole first lg.}^2$$

The posited line of influence of English here is as follows. Initially it is a foreign language, necessary for international trade and communication vying for this role with other international languages like French, Spanish or (previously) Russian. It then becomes the 'first' (or main) foreign language, explicitly designated so and promoted in the education system. A situation then develops in which some people start using some English internally, perhaps academics and scientists amongst each other, perhaps some youngsters influenced by Western pop culture. As Hoffman (2000:14) argues 'it has become clear that the teaching of English in mainstream schools, when combined with additional opportunities for input and motivation, do provide a favourable basis for bilingualism with English'. In time this would have to spread to the general population, which starts to use English outside the English classroom. If this is done regularly classroom English could become ESL. That is, EFL would turn into 'bilingualism with English' or, as Kachru (1983a:264) calls it in New English phraseology, 'English-knowing bilingualism'. In time speakers could become so fluent that they consider English to be their second first-language, rather than a second language. English could be associated more with formal and

---

[2] H here stands for the language or variety deemed appropriate for use in 'High' domains, like education and administration.

H registers, the local languages more with L functions, though the diglossia model need not apply rigorously. Finally, the local language(s) would recede amongst the population and become associated with rural, less educated and less 'modern' people. The scene is set for a gradual process of language shift.

This trajectory is reminiscent of the stages posited by Schneider (2003) described in section 1.5. It is possible that individual cases like Singapore (where language shift is ongoing) or Ireland (where it is virtually completed) might fit this formulation. But it is hard to see countries like Japan, India and China from Asia; Nigeria, Somalia and Kenya from Africa; and Sweden, Holland and Poland from Europe going all the way. Berg, Hult and King (2001) suggest that Sweden is in the fourth stage above: English is a 'second first language', in a relation with Swedish that cannot be considered diglossia, but perhaps 'pre-diglossia' (since Swedish does serve several H functions as in education and politics). There is a sense, though, in which Swedish is already subordinate in so far as it is appropriate for local and regional (Scandinavian) politics but less so for Euro- or international politics.

7.6 CONCLUSION

Not for the first time in its history there is an excitement about the diversity of English, the vast number of territories into which it is spreading, and the prospects of a global means of communication. David Graddol (1997, 2003) has warned that this is but one of the stories of English (a 'rags to riches fable'), and that in language history nothing is certain. Graddol is of the view that English may have reached saturation point as a world language; and that the prospects for other world languages like Spanish and Chinese should not be underestimated. Our perspective on this topic is also one of caution. Like many thoughtful writers on the topic (notably David Crystal 1997, 2004) we do not support the triumphalist stories of English that are wittingly and sometimes unwittingly presented. Our main concern has been to examine the linguistic underpinnings of the spread (from the perspective of Sociolinguistics and other branches of Linguistic Theory), and to place the spread of English in a global context as well as in various local contexts. The tools we tried to present in this book to characterise the spread of English are what matter, and would not be invalidated, we believe, were Spanish or Chinese to overtake English as the language of the globe. These tools would then be used for a comparative study of spreading world languages. Still, we hope that we have also shown that the details of the history of the spread of English, its multifarious linguistic forms worldwide, the cultural diversity of its habitual users, the questions it poses for Linguistic Theory and the practical and sociopolitical implications of the spread are of immense scholarly interest.

STUDY QUESTIONS

1. Differentiate between Euro English, Mid-Atlantic and Lingua Franca English in Europe.
2. Review the common characteristics of educated Euro English.
3. What are the positive and negative consequences of the spread of English to an Outer Circle country like China?
4. Find out more about the special 'register' characteristics of Air Traffic Control language and *Seaspeak*.
5. Is the Ebonics debate entirely relevant to the issue of using New Englishes in classroom contexts?

Further reading

All works mentioned here are fully referenced in the bibliography.

On specific territories within the Expanding Circle, see Bolton *Chinese Englishes: A Sociolinguistic History* (2005), and Cenoz and Jessner (eds.) *English in Europe: The Acquisition of a Third Language* (2000). On the globalisation of English, see Crystal *English as a Global Language* (1997) and McArthur's *The English Languages* (1998).

Glossary

Terms that are part of the core discipline of World Englishes (and which often feature in the *Study Questions*) are not given here; they can be extracted from the text via the index, in which '(*defn.*)' indicates the page number in which these key terms are first defined and discussed. The terms that are defined here come from other areas of Linguistics, and cover grammatical, phonetic, language contact and general sociolinguistic terms that are not defined in the text.

abrupt Creole – see *Creole*.

acrolang – see *basilang*.

acrolect – see *basilect*.

adjunction – a syntactic operation in generative grammar where an element is adjoined to a node.

affricate – type of consonant like the 'ch' in *choose*, which is produced when the airstream in the oral cavity is blocked and then released with friction.

antilanguage – sub-varieties of a language that embody a degree of rebellion or resistance to the norms of the prestige varieties of a language – e.g. the language of prisoners or teenage slang.

approximant – type of consonant produced when two articulators come together but do not touch, so that no friction accompanies the sound – e.g. the 'y' sound in *yet*.

aspect – a grammatical term for a verb category that expresses information about the duration, completion, repeatedness, etc. of the event expressed by the verb, e.g. *I often go to town* expresses **habitual aspect**; while *I am going to town* expresses **continuous aspect**.

aspiration – accompaniment of a consonant sound by a puff of air – e.g. that of the 'p' in *pit* but not in *spit* in many varieties of English.

aux-inversion – the inversion of an auxiliary verb like *can* in the formation of questions like *Can Peter bat?*

backsliding – the recurrence of a linguistic feature in second-language acquisition previously thought to have been eradicated by the speaker in earlier stages.

basic variety – a simple system characteristic of early acquisition of second language and **pidgins**.

basilang – a term used to characterise the relatively unstable type of **interlanguage** of an early L2 learner, on the analogy of the term **basilect** in Creole studies. A basilang is in fact unlike a basilect, which is a stable first language of a Creole-speaking community. The term 'basilang' contrasts with **acrolang**, which is relatively stable and close to the target language. **Mesolang** denotes the interlanguage stages intermediate between these two.

basilect – in its original sense the variety of a **Creole** language showing a grammatical system maximally distant from the **superstrate** (or colonial European) language that it drew its vocabulary from. In WE studies the term has been extended to cover an L2 sub-variety that is maximally different from the **target language**. The term contrasts with **acrolect** which refers to the version of the Creole (or the L2) which closely approximates the super-strate. The term **mesolect** refers to a number of intermediate sub-varieties that arise when a basilect becomes influenced by the acrolect.

calque – a type of borrowing in which words or expressions are trans-lated from one language to another, e.g. French *lune de miel* to English *honeymoon*. Also known as 'loan translation'.

c-command – refers to a relation between two categories. Informally, if a catgory *x* c-commands *y*, then the category *x* must not be lower in the syntactic structure than the category *y*.

cleft – a type of construction where a single clause is divided into two, each with its own verb. A sentence such as *John is eating a banana* can be clefted as *It is John who is eating a banana* or *It is a banana that John is eating*.

clefting – see *cleft*.

code-switching – the alternate use of two or more languages (or dialects or styles) within a sentence (intra-sentential code-switching) or between sentences (inter-sentential code-switching).

cognate object predicates – a phrase made up of a verb and a noun which are an expansion of a basic verb of standard English, e.g. *take possession* from *possess*.

Comp – short for complementiser; also position in clause structure where English complementisers appear in subordinate contexts, e.g. '*I know **that** John is sick.*'

complement – refers to an expression that combines with a word (head) to constitute a larger structure of essentially the same kind, e.g. in the expression *open the window*, *the window* is the complement of the verb *open*.

compound – a word made up of two free morphemes, themselves capable of functioning as words, e.g. *egg-plant*.

constraint hierarchy – a term used in Optimality Theory to denote a grammar that is based on the notion of relative importance (ranking) of constraints for a particular language; i.e. all the constraints in a given language are in principle violable (= not categorical), but the constraints that are relatively more important (less violable) than others are ranked higher relative to others that are less important (more violable). A grammar of a language under this view is a list of constraints ranked relative to each other in terms of their violability.

continuous aspect – see *aspect*.

copula – a verb denoting a member of a set, typically a form of the verb *be*, e.g. *She **is** a doctor*. Adjective form: **copular**.

correlative – a type of sentence in which two clauses have a parallel structure, rather than the more usual main clause-subordinate clause relation. E.g. the indirect indefinite relative clause in *Whoever comes first to my funeral, let him or her have my best CDs*.

count noun – see *mass noun*.

Creole – a language believed to have arisen by the expansion of a **pidgin**, or to have been created afresh as an **abrupt Creole**, without a pidgin preceding it.

declarative – a sentence having the form and function of a statement, rather than a question, e.g. *The boy is at school today*.

diphthong – see *monophthong*.

directive – an utterance whose purpose is to get other people to do something for the speaker.

discourse particles – elements in an expression appearing at the beginning or the end of a sentence signalling to the hearer how the expression must be interpreted. E.g. *of course, anyway*.

do-support – the use of the 'carrier' verb *do* in negatives, questions and other sentence forms lacking an auxiliary. Compare *He can sing* and *He can't sing* versus *He sings* and *He doesn't sing*, where the second sentence of the second pair shows *do*-support.

echo construction – the repetition of the latter part of a word, with the first syllable changed to convey a sense of plurals, e.g. in Indian English *petrol-vetrol* for 'petrol and other such fuels'.

face – is generally defined following Goffman's work as an image of 'self', the positive social value a person effectively claims for him-/herself by the stance others assume he/she has taken in a given interactional context. Brown and Levinson (1987) discuss politeness in terms of two notions of face: **negative face**, which refers to the basic claim to freedom of action and freedom from imposition, and **positive face**, which refers to the positive consistent self-image or 'personality' claimed by interactants.

fricative – a sound like the 's' in *send*, produced with audible friction as two articulators come close together.

foreigner talk – the special way in which **native speakers** of a language speak to those who lack a command of the language.

fossilisation – the stabilisation of some features of an interlanguage, which are not part of the target language.

glide – a sound considered to be intermediate between a vowel and a consonant, e.g. the 'y' in *yet*.

hegemony – rule or the exercise of power with the consent of the ruled, because of the dominance of particular ideologies.

hypercorrection – the overgeneralisation of linguistic forms which carry social prestige. This may be **quantitative** when a social group shows a greater frequency of prestige forms in formal situations than members of higher status groups; or it may be **qualitative**, when speakers misapply linguistic rules which are considered prestigious, e.g. *heggs* for *eggs*, in an effort to avoid *h*-dropping.

hyponym, hyponomy – a relation of subordination between two words, with the meaning of one being included in the other, e.g. *rose* is a hyponym of *flower*. Their relation is one of hyponomy, rather than, say, synonymy.

implicational scale – a method of data presentation, showing how the presence of one element in the data set presumes (or implies) the presence of others, thus forming a chain.

instrumental motivation – see *integrative motivation*.

integrative motivation – the learning of a new language or dialect with the intention of interacting frequently or integrating with its speakers. Contrasts with **instrumental motivation**, in which the new language is learnt more for work or educational reasons.

interference – see *transfer*.

interlanguage – a version of a language produced by a second- or foreign-language learner. The term draws attention to the learner's unstable but continually developing system, equivalent to neither the learner's first language nor the **target language**.

intonation – systematic variation in pitch of an utterance, as when pitch is changed to produce a question rather than a statement.

inversion – the rule of English that puts the auxiliary verb before the subject in direct questions and *yes/no* questions.

koine – a new variety of language that arises out of the amalgamation of different dialects of the language, typically under patterns of migration.

l-**velarisation** – the production of the 'l' in words like *lot*, in which the influence of the vowel causes the tongue to be retracted in articulating the 'l'. Velarisation refers to the direction of the velum or hard palate. In words like *let*, the 'l' is produced in a more forward position (at the gum ridge).

language shift – the gradual switch in a community's primary language in the face of competition from a regionally or socially more powerful language.

language spread – a process during which the uses and/or users of a language increase, often under conditions of political expansionism, prestige or technological influence.

learner variety – a form of a second language which is unstable because the user is still in the process of acquiring it. Same as (early) **interlanguage**.

lexeme – the linguistic unit that underlies related words, e.g. *cry*, *cried*, *crying* are all part of the same lexeme *cry*. A lexeme is not the same as word, and may include a phrasal unit like *try out*.

lexical set – a means of labelling vowels for phonetic purposes, without using phonetic symbols. Thus the KIT vowel is the entire set of words pronounced the same as the 'i' in *kit* in a particular dialect – thus bit, fit, myth, build, English, etc.

liquid – a sound like 'l' or 'r', so-called because they form a set in many languages, whose elements are variable (or 'fluid') with respect to syllable structure.

loanblend – a **compound** word in a language made from one element from that language in combination with one from another, e.g. *team-geist*, the name of the 2006 World Cup soccer ball (*geist* being German for 'spirit').

locative – a form of a word or phrase expressing location, e.g. the Xhosa word, *e-khaya* 'at home' (from -*khaya* 'home') or the English phrase *in town*.

marked – a linguistic element that is more special than a related (**unmarked**) one in terms of carrying additional form and meaning. E.g. *unhappy* is marked in relation to *happy*; *lioness* is marked in relation to *lion*. The relation between such elements is called markedness, and applies to other levels of linguistic structure like syntax and phonology.

markedness – see *marked*.

mass noun – a noun that denotes an uncountable whole, e.g. *water*, *imagination*, *electricity*. These typically do not take plural forms.

mesolang – see *basilang*.

modal – a verb or auxiliary verb form that expresses **mood** or **modality**, i.e. ways in which speakers express attitudes to, beliefs about, and degrees of certainty about the action expressed by the verb. E.g. *She works hard* does not contain a modal element (and is sometimes described as indicative mood) in contrast to *She **might** work hard* or *If she **were** to work hard*... which express possibility and supposition respectively (or subjunctive mood).

modality – see *modal*.

monophthong – a simple vowel, e.g. the 'e' in *get* which is distinguishable from a **diphthong** or combination of simple vowels as is *gate*.

mood – see *modal*.

morpheme – minimal meaning-bearing unit in a word, *dog* is a single morpheme, wheareas *dogs* is made of two morphemes 'dog' + plural -*s*. **Morphology** is the study of the morphemic structure of languages.

morphosyntax – elements that belong to either the **morphology** or **syntax** of a language (or are on the margins of both).

nasal – consonant or vowel produced with air allowed to flow through the nose; e.g. the sounds /m/ and /n/.

native speaker – one who has acquired a particular language (**a native language**) from birth to early childhood via interaction with family and community members, rather than through more formal means like education. The definition has proved controversial because it assumes that only one language exists within a community.

Negative politeness – see *positive politeness*.

Northern Subject rule – a rule found in northern English dialects in which -*s* occurs with verbs having plural, non-pronoun subjects (*They eat fish* vs *The polar bears eats fish*). The -*s* suffix is, however, permissible if the verb is separated from its plural pronoun subject (*They eat and comes back for more*).

operators – refers to expressions (e.g. interrogatives and negatives in English) that have the syntactic properties of triggering auxiliary inversion.

OV – word order in some languages having the verb consistently following the direct object. Most of these languages have the order **SOV**. (**S** = *subject*; **O** = *object*; **V** = *verb*.) Languages may also be characterised as **SVO, VSO, VO**, etc.

parameter setting – an approach to syntax which focuses on how rules can be related to each other as a set and how they are acquired as a set, rather than on the properties of individual constructions.

past participle – form of a verb that occurs when a verb expresses **continuous** or **perfective aspect**, rather than the simple present or past tense, e.g *I am playing* (continuous) vs *I play* (simple present); *I have thrown* (perfective) vs *I threw* (simple past) respectively.

perfective – form of verb or auxiliary focusing on an event or action as completed, rather than on the tense as such, e.g. *I have eaten* is in the perfect tense, *I ate*, simple past.

phrasal verb – consists of two-word verbs that form a meaning chunk, such as *come across* (roughly paraphrasable by *found*) in a sentence like *John came across an interesting review of my article*.

pidgin – a new and initially simple form of language that arises out of language contact between two or more groups of people who do not share a common language. A pidgin is initially no one's **native language**.

pool of variants – a set of linguistic elements that are derived from different sources in a language contact situation, and which are used in an ad hoc manner, before one or more are selected as a norm.

positive politeness – a communicative strategy of being polite by recognising the interlocutor's desire to be respected, emphasising goodwill and camaraderie. Positive politeness is thus concerned with demonstrating closeness and affiliation. This strategy is usually contrasted with **negative politeness** that respects the interlocutor's rights and privileges. Negative politeness is thus concerned with distance and formality.

pragmatics – the study of the role played by non-linguistic (contextual) knowledge in the use of language.

prepositional verb – refers to verbs that appear with a preposition-like particle, such as *look over, eat up, fired up* in sentences such as as *I want you to look over this report, John ate up his apple* and *The coach fired up his team*. These particles can be moved to the end of the clause as, for example, in *The coach fired his team up*.

pro-drop – the absence of subject or object pronouns in a sentence, especially in those contexts where the identity of the 'dropped' pronoun is easily recoverable from the context (or, as in languages like Spanish, Hindi, etc., from the morphology of the verb). Occurs occasionally in special English idioms such as *Works every time*.

prosody – refers informally to a collective variation in pitch, loudness, tempo and rhythm.

postvocalic /r/ – the occurrence of 'r' after a vowel e.g. *park*. This is pronounced in some dialects of English (e.g. many US English varieties) but not in others, e.g. **RP**.

punctual verb – verb that denotes an action conceived of as occurring at a single point in time, e.g. *touch, strike, glance*. Contrasts with **non-punctual** verbs expressing duration (e.g. *cry, fly, think*) or iteration (e.g. *cut, roll*).

RP – or Received Pronunciation, the prestige variety associated with the middle and upper classes of the UK. Also known as *Oxford English, BBC English*, the *Queen's English*, etc.

rank-reduction – the reduction of a full phrase to a structural element of lower rank, e.g. *a fish that eats man* to *a man-eating fish* shows the reduction of a relative clause to an adjectival compound.

reduplication – the repetition of a morpheme with the effect of denoting plurality, intensity, iteration, etc., e.g. *hot-hot potatoes*.

register – variation in language according to the context in which it is being used, e.g. the register of legal language vs the register of chit-chat.

register shift – the use of items of language associated with one register in another with which it is not usually associated, e.g. the use of legal language like *You are hereby asked to appear before me tomorrow* in speaking to friends.

relexification – the replacement of the words of one language with those of another, without changing the underlying grammar.

resumptive pronoun – a pronoun used to fill the gap inside a relative clause, as the use of **he** in a non-standard English sentence like *This is the man that no one believed **he** would amount to anything*.

rhotic – used to describe dialects in which **postvocalic** /r/ is pronounced.

rhoticisation – the property of being *rhotic*.

scope – refers to the range of influence that a category may have over other constituents, e.g. the part of a phrase or clause modified by a negative is referred to as the scope of negation.

semantic feature – recurring components of meaning which make up the semantics of words, e.g. the word *girl* is made up of the semantic features 'human', 'female' and 'young'.

semantic shift – a slight change of meaning of a word, e.g. the change from Middle English word *lust* denoting a simple or moderate pleasure to sexual desire in modern English.

semantic widening – the broadening of the meaning of a term, e.g. *lady* as a term for an upper-class woman to its more modern sense as a synonym for 'woman'.

SOV – see *OV*.

speech act – a communicative activity (e.g. a request or greetings) that is defined with reference to the intention of the speaker while speaking (the illocutionary force of the utterance) and the effects he/she achieves on the listener (the perlocutionary effect of the utterance).

style switching – see *code-switching*.

substrate – the less dominant language of a multilingual community. **Substrate influence** upon the **superstrate** language is quite common among bilinguals.

superstrate – the socially and/or politically dominant language in a multilingual society.

s-plural symmetry – the occurrence of *-s* with plural subjects and not with the singular as expected in Standard English, e.g. *the boy eat* vs *the boys eats*.

Spec-CP – the left-most position in the clause structure where topics and question (*wh-*) phrases appear.

stative – a category associated with verbs, denoting a state or situation, rather than an activity. In Standard English non-stative verbs may take the continuous present (*I am eating it*), non-stative verbs may not (**I am knowing it*).

syntax – the study of how words combine to form sentences; the structure of sentences.

t-flapping – the pronunciation of 't' between two vowels, the first of which occurs in a stressed syllable as a tap or flap, rather than a plain stop consonant, e.g. in many US dialects the 't' in *city* is flapped while the 't' in *sit* is not.

tag question – a question attached to the end of a statement, of the form *She's rather tall, isn't she?*

tone – the pitch level of a syllable, usually 'high', 'mid' or 'low', used to differentiate words or grammatical forms in some languages, though not English.

topicalisation – the use of a particular word order to highlight the topic rather than necessarily the subject of a sentence and make a comment about it, e.g. in *Dogs, I love them*, the noun *dogs* is topic, but not subject.

topicalised construction – see *topicalisation*.

transfer – the influence of a speaker's first language upon a subsequently learnt language. Also known as **interference**.

undeletion – the occurrence of an element in some varieties that is typically deleted in Standard English syntax, e.g. *I'll have you to know*, rather than *I'll have you know*.

universals – abstract patterns of language believed to be common to all human languages, and hence acquirable by all children.

VARBRUL – a computer programme for analysing sociolinguistic variation statistically. The programme correlates linguistic variants with the social characteristics of speakers.

VS – see *OV*.

violable constraints – see *constraint hierarchy*.

wh-movement – the rule of generative grammar that removes the *wh*-question word/phrase from its original position (indicated by a trace 't') to clause-initial position, e.g. '*What is John watching t?*'

wh-question – see *yes–no* question.

x-bar theory – a system of phrase structure representation where every word (hence the use of variable 'x') category, e.g. noun, determiner, verb, etc. has the same template: where the word category and its complement appear as sisters, dominated (c-commanded) by a position called the specifer (Spec) position. This template is diagrammed below:

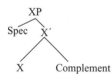

yes–no question – a question to which the expected answer is *yes* or *no* (or *I don't know*), e.g. *Is she your best friend?* These typically involve **aux-inversion**. Contrasts with **wh-questions**, which begin with a word like *who*, *what* and *when* and which require information rather than *yes–no* answers, e.g. *Who did that?*

yod-dropping – the non-occurrence of a 'y' sound (phonetically [j] or *yod*) in some dialects in words like *tune*, *duke* and *tuna*.

Bibliography

(no author): Governors and Assistants of the East India Merchants, 1603, reprint 1968. East Indian Trade. London: Gregg Press.

Achebe, C. 1965. English and African writer. *Transition* 18: 27–30.

1966. *Things Fall Apart*. London: Heinemann.

1969. *Arrow of God*. New York: First Anchor Books.

1975. *Morning yet on Creation Day*. London: Heineman.

Adey, A. D. 1977. South African Black English. *English Usage in Southern Africa* 8/1: 36–9.

Agnihotri, R. 1991. Acquisition of articles in learning English as a second language: a cross-cultural study. *South Asian Language Review* 1/2: 67–80.

Agnihotri, R., Khanna, A. L., and Mukherjee, A. 1988. *Tense in Indian English: A Sociolinguistic Perspective*. New Delhi: Bahri.

Alexander, N. 2000. English unassailable but unattainable: the dilemma of language policy in South African education. *PRAESA Occasional Papers* 3. Cape Town: University of Cape Town.

Algeo, J. 1988. The tag question in British English: it's different, i'n'it? *English World-Wide* 9/2: 171–91.

1990. The Briticisms are coming! How British English is creeping into the American language. *Journal of English Linguistics* 23: 123–40.

Alleyne, M. 1980. *Comparative Afro-American*. Ann Arbor: Karoma.

Alo, M. A., and Mesthrie, R. 2004. Nigerian English: morphology and syntax. In Kortmann, B., Schneider, E. W., Burridge, K., Mesthrie, R., and Upton, C. (eds.), *A Handbook of Varieties of English*, Vol. II, 813–27. Berlin: Mouton de Gruyter.

Alsagoff, L., and Lick, H. C. 1998a. The grammar of Singapore English. In Foley, J. A. *et al.* (eds.), *English in New Cultural Contexts: Reflections from Singapore*, 127–51. Oxford: Oxford University Press.

1998b. The relative clause in colloquial Singapore English. *World Englishes* 17/2: 127–38.

Andersen, R. W. 1980. Creolization as the acquisition of a second language as a first language. In Valdman, A., and Highfield, A. (eds.), *Theoretical Orientations in Creole Studies*, 273–95. New York: Academic Press.

(ed.) 1983a. *Pidginization and Creolization as Language Acquisition*. Rowley, MA: Newbury House.

1983b. Transfer to Somewhere. In Gass, S., and Selinker, L. (eds.), *Language Transfer in Language Learning: Issues in Second Language Research*, 177–201, Rowley, MA: Newbury House.

1990. Models, processes, principles and strategies: second language acquisition inside and outside the classroom. In Van Patten, B., and Lee, J. F. (eds.), *Second Language Acquisition/Foreign Language Learning*, 45–68. Clevedon: Multilingual Matters.

Andersen, R. 1988. *The Power and the Word: Language, Power and Change*. London: Paladin.

Angogo, R., and Hancock, I. 1980. English in Africa: emerging standards or diverging regionalisms. *English World-Wide* 1: 67–96.

Anttila, A. 1995. How to recognise subjects in English. In Karlsson, F., Voutilainen, A., Heikkilä, J., and Anttila, A. (eds.), *Constraint Grammar: A Language-Independent System for Parsing Unrestricted Text*, 315–58. Berlin: Mouton de Gruyter.

Appel, R., and Muysken, P. 1987. *Language Contact and Bilingualism*. London: Edward Arnold.

Archangeli, D. B., and Langendoen D. T. 1997. *Optimality Theory: An Overview*. Malden: Blackwell Publishing.

Arends, J. 1993. Towards a gradualist model of creolization. In Byrne, F., and Holm, J. (eds.), *Atlantic Meets Pacific*, 371–80. Amsterdam: John Benjamins.

Arua, A. E. 1998. Some syntactic features of Swazi English. *World Englishes* 17/2: 139–51.

Atkinson, G. F. 1911. *Curry and Rice (on Forty Plates) or The Ingredients of Social Life at 'Our' Station in India*. 5th edn. London: W. Thacker and Co.

Baik, M. J. and Shim R. J. 2002. Teaching World Englishes via the Internet. *World Englishes* 21/3: 423–30.

Bailey, C.-J. N., and Maroldt, K. 1977. The French lineage of English. In Meisel, J. M. (ed.), *Langues en Contact – Pidgins – Creoles – Languages in Contact*. Tübingen: TBL Verlag.

Bailey, G., and Ross, G. 1988. The shape of the superstrate: morphosyntactic features of Ship English. *English World-Wide* 9: 193–212.

Bailey, R. W. 1991. *Images of English*. Ann Arbor: University of Michigan Press.

Bailey, R. W., and Görlach, M. (eds.) 1982. *English as a World Language*. Ann Arbor: University of Michigan Press.

Bailey, R. W., and Robinson, J. L. (eds.) 1973. *Varieties of Present-Day English*. New York: Macmillan.

Baker, P. 1990. Off target? *Journal of Pidgin and Creole Languages* 5: 107–19.

1994. Review of R. Mesthrie, *Language in Indenture: A Sociolinguistic History of Bhojpuri-Hindi in South Africa*. *Journal of Pidgin and Creole Languages* 9: 168–72.

1995. Motivation in Creole genesis. In Baker, P. (ed.), *From Contact to Creole and Beyond*, 3–15. London: University of Westminster Press.

2000. Theories of creolization and the degree and nature of restructuring. In Neumann-Holzschuh, I., and Schneider E. (eds.), *Degrees of Restructuring in Creole Languages*, 41–63. Amsterdam: John Benjamins.

Baker, P., and Corne, C. 1982. *Isle de France Creole: Affinities and Origins*. Ann Arbor: Karoma.

Bakhtin, M. M. 1981. *The Dialogic Imagination: Four Essays*, ed. M. Holquist, trans. C. Emerson, and M. Holquist, Austin: University of Texas Press.

Bakker, P., and Muysken, P. 1995. Mixed languages and language intertwining. In Arends, J., Muysken, P., and Smith, N. (eds.), *Pidgins and Creoles: An Introduction*, 41–52. Amsterdam: John Benjamins.

Bakker, P., and Papen R. A. 1995. Michif: a mixed language based on Cree and French. In Thomason, S. G. (ed.), *Contact Languages: A Wider Perspective*, 295–363. Amsterdam: John Benjamins.

Bamgbose, A. 1971. The English language in Nigeria. In Spencer, J. (ed.), *The English Language in West Africa*, 35–48. London: Longman.

1992. Standard Nigerian English: issues of identification. In Kachru, B. B. (ed.), *The Other Tongue: English across Cultures*, 148–61. Urbana, IL: University of Illnois Press.

1998. Torn between the norms: innovations in World Englishes. *World Englishes* 17/1: 1–14.

Bamgbose, A., Banjo, A., and Thomas, A. (eds.) 1997. *New Englishes: A West African Perspective*. Trenton: Africa World Press.

Bamiro, E. O. 1995. Syntactic variation in West African English. *World Englishes* 17/2: 189–204.

1992. Standard Nigerian English: issues of identification. In Kachru, B. B. (ed.), *The Other Tongue: English across Cultures*, 148–61. Urbana: University of Illinois Press.

Bao, Z. 2005. The aspectual system of Singapore English and the systemic substratist explanation. *Journal of Linguistics* 41: 237–67.

Bao, Z., and Wee, L. 1999. The passive in Singapore English. *World Englishes* 18/1: 1–11.

Baskaran, L. 1994. The Malaysian English mosaic. *English Today* 37: 27–32.

2004. Malaysian English: phonology. In Kortmann, B., Schneider, E. W., Burridge, K., Mesthrie, R., and Upton, C. (eds.), *A Handbook of Varieties of English*, Vol. I, 1034–46. Berlin: Mouton de Gruyter.

Bates, E., and MacWhinney, B. 1987. Competition, variation and language learning. In Macwhinney B. (ed.), *Mechanisms of Language Acquisition*, 157–93. Hillsdale: Lawrence Erlbaum.

Baugh, A. C., and Cable, T. 1978. *A History of the English Language*. 3rd edn. Englewoods Cliffs: Prentice-Hall.

Baugh, J. 1980. A re-examination of the Black English copula. In W. Labov (ed.), *Locating Language in Time and Space*, 85–106. New York: Academic Press.

2000. *Beyond Ebonics: Linguistic Pride and Racial Prejudice*. New York: Oxford University Press.

Baumgardner, R. 1993. The indigenisation of English in Pakistan. In Baumgardner, R. (ed.), *The English Language in Pakistan*, 41–54. Karachi: Oxford University Press.

Baumgardner, R. J. and Kennedy, A. E. H. 1994. Measure for Measure: terms of measurement in Pakistani English. *English World-Wide* 15: 173–93.

Bayles, K. A., and Harris, G. A. 1982. Evaluating speech-language skills in Papago children. *Journal of American Indian Education* 21/2: 11–19.

Beccaria, G. L. 1988. *Italiano Antico e Nuovo*. Milan: Garzanti.

Bellugi, U. 1967. The acquisition of negation. Unpublished PhD dissertation, Harvard University.

Berg, C., Hult, F., and King, K. 2001. Shaping the climate for language shift? English in Sweden's elite domains. *World Englishes* 20/3: 305–20.

Bernstein, Basil. 1974. *Class, Codes and Control*, Vol. I. London: Routledge.

Bhatt, R. 1995. Prescriptivism, creativity, and World Englishes. *World Englishes* 14/2: 247–59.

1999. *Verb Movement and the Syntax of Kashmiri*. Dordrecht: Kluwer Academic Press.

2000. Optimal expressions in Indian English. *English Language and Linguistics* 4: 69–95.

2002. Experts, dialects, and discourse. *International Journal of Applied Linguistics* 12/1: 74–109.

2004. Indian English: syntax. In Kortmann, B., Schneider, E. W., Burridge, K., Mesthrie, R., and Upton, C. (eds.), *A Handbook of Varieties of English*, Vol. II, 1016–30. Berlin: Mouton de Gruyter.

Bhatt, R., and B. Hancin-Bhatt 2002. Structural minimality, CP and the initial state in Second Language Acquisition. *Second Language Research* 18/4: 348–92.

Bialystok, E. 1978. A theoretical model of second language learning. *Language Learning* 28: 69–84.

Biber, D., Johansson, S., Leech, G., Conrad, S., and Finegan, E. 1999. *Longman Grammar of Spoken and Written English*. Harlow, Essex: Pearson Education Ltd.

Bickerton, D. 1971. Inherent variability and variable rules. *Foundation of Language* 7: 457–92.

1975. *The Dynamics of a Creole Continuum*. Cambridge: Cambridge University Press.

1977. Pidginisation and creolisation: language acquisition and language universals. In Valdman A. (ed.), *Pidgin and Creole Linguistics*, 49–60. Bloomington: Indiana University Press.

1981. *Roots of Language*. Ann Arbor: Karoma.

1983. Comments on A. Valdman, Creolisation and second language acquisition. In Andersen R. (ed.), *Pidginisation and Creolisation as Language Acquisition*, 235–40. Rowley, MA: Newbury House.

Bierswisch, M. 1997. Universal grammar and the basic variety. *Second Language Research* 13/4: 348–66.

Blakemore, D. 2002. *Relevance and Linguistic Meaning: The Semantics and Pragmatics of Discourse Markers*. Cambridge: Cambridge University Press.

Blom J. P., and Gumperz J. J. 1972. Code-switching in Norway. In Blom J. P., and Gumperz J. J. (eds.), *Directions in Sociolinguistics*, 407–34. New York: Holt, Rinehart and Winston.

Blum-Kulka, S., House, J., and Kasper, G. (eds.) 1989. *Cross-Cultural Pragmatics: Requests and Apologies*, Norwood, NJ: Ablex.

Bokamba, E. G. 1992. The Africanization of English. In Kachru, B. B. (ed.), *The Other Tongue: English across Cultures*, 125–47. 2nd edn. Urbana: University of Illinois Press.

Bolinger, D. 1989. *Intonation and its Uses: Melody and Grammar in Discourse*. Stanford: Stanford University Press.

Bolton, K. 2000. The sociolinguistics of Hong Kong and the space for Hong Kong English. *World Englishes* 19/3: 265–85.

2005. *Chinese Englishes: A Sociolinguistic History*. Cambridge: Cambridge University Press.

Bourdieu, P. 1977. The economics of linguistic exchanges. *Social Science Information* 16: 645–68.

1991. *Language and Symbolic Power*. Cambridge: Polity Press.

Bright, W. 1968. Toward a cultural grammar. *Indian Linguistics* 29: 20–9.

Brown, A. 1988. Vowel differences between Received Pronunciation and the English of Malaysia and Singapore: which ones really matter? In Foley, J. (ed.), *New Englishes: The Case of Singapore*, 129–47. Singapore: Singapore University Press.

Brown, G., and Yule, G. 1983. *Discourse Analysis*. Cambridge: Cambridge University Press.

Brown, K. 1995. World Englishes: to teach or not to teach? *World Englishes* 14: 233–45.

Brown, P., and Levinson, S. 1987. *Politeness: Some Universals in Language Usage*. 2nd edn. Cambridge: Cambridge University Press.

Bruthiaux, P. 2003. Squaring the circles: issues in modeling English worldwide. *International Journal of Applied Linguistics* 13/2: 159–78.

Brutt-Griffler, J. 2000. *World English: A Study of its Development*. Clevedon: Multilingual Matters.

Burns, A., and Coffin C. (eds.) 2001. *Analysing English in a Global Context*. London: Routledge.

Canagarajah, A. S. 1993. Critical ethnography of a Sri Lankan classroom: ambiguities in student opposition to reproduction through ESOL. *TESOL Quarterly* 27: 601–26.

1996. 'Nondiscursive' requirements in academic publishing, material resources of periphery scholars, and the politics of knowledge production. *Written Communication*. 13/4: 435–72.

1999. *Resisting Linguistic Imperialism in English Teaching*. Oxford: Oxford University Press.

(ed.) 2005 *Reclaiming the Local in Language Policy and Practice*. Mahwah: Lawrence Erlbaum.

Cane, G. 1994. The English language in Brunei, Darussalam. *World Englishes* 13/3: 351–60.

Carden, G., and Stewart, W. A. 1988. Binding theory, bioprogram and creolization: evidence from Haitian Creole. *Journal of Pidgin and Creole Languages* 3: 1–67.

Cenoz, J., and Jessner, U. 2000. *English in Europe: The Acquisition of a Third Language*. Clevedon: Multilingual Matters.

Chadha, R. 2004. *Taking the Call: An Aspirant's Guide to Call Centres*. New Delhi: Tata Macgraw-Hill.

Chang, J. 1987. Chinese speakers. In Swann, M., and Smith, B. (eds.), *Learner English: A Teacher's Guide to Interference and Other Problems*, 224–37. Cambridge: Cambridge University Press.

Chaudenson, R. 1992. *Des îles, des hommes, des langues*. Paris: Harmattan.

Chelliah, S. 2001. Constructs of Indian English in language 'guidebooks'. *World Englishes* 20: 161–78.

Cheng, W., and Warren, M. 2001. 'She knows more about Hong Kong than you do, isn't it': Tags in Hong Kong conversational English. *Journal of Pragmatics* 33: 1419–39.

Cheshire, J. (ed.) 1991. *English around the World*. Cambridge: Cambridge University Press.

Chew, P. G. L. 1995. Lectal power in Singapore English. *World Englishes* 14/2: 163–80.

Chinebuah, J. K. 1976. Grammatical deviance and first language interference. *West African Journal of Modern African Languages* 1: 67–78.

Chiti-Batelli, A. 1987 *Communication Internationale et Avenir des Langues et des Parles en Europe*. Nice: Presses d'Europe.

Choi, Y. H. 1988. Text structure of Korean speakers' argumentative writing in English. *World Englishes* 7/2: 129–42.

Chomsky, N. 1971. Deep structure, surface structure and semantic interpretation. In Steinberg, D., and Jakobovits, L. (eds.), *Semantics: An Interdisciplinary Reader in Philosophy, Linguistics and Psychology*, 183–216. Cambridge: Cambridge University Press.

1976. Conditions on Rules of Grammar, *Linguistic Analysis* 2/4: 303–351.

1981. *Lectures on Government and Binding*. Dordrecht: Foris.

1986. *Knowledge of Language: Its Nature, Origin and Use*. New York: Praeger.

1995. *The Minimalist Programme*. Cambridge, MA: MIT Press.

Christian, D. 1991. The personal dative in Appalachian English. In Trudgill, P., and Chambers, J. K. (eds.), *Dialects of English: Studies in Grammatical Variation*, 11–19. London: Longman.

Christophersen, P. 1992. 'Native' models and foreign learners. *English Today* 31: 16–18.

Clahsen, H., Meisel, J., and Pienemann, M. 1983. *Deutsch als Zweitsprache: der Spracherwerb auslandischer Arbeiter.* Tübingen: Gunter Narr.

Clyne, M. 1987. Constraints on code-switching: how universal are they? *Linguistics* 25: 739–64.

Coe, N. 1987. Speakers of Spanish and Catalan. In Swann M., and Smith, B. (eds.), *Learner English: A Teacher's Guide to Interference and Other Problems*, 72–89. Cambridge: Cambridge University Press.

Coelho, G. 1997. Anglo-Indian English: a nativized variety of Indian English. *Language in Society* 26/4: 561–89.

Cohen, A. 2005. Strategies for learning and performing L2 speech acts. *Intercultural Pragmatics* 2/3: 275–301.

Cohen, A. and Olshtain, E. 1981. Developing a measure of sociocultural competence in the case of apologies. *Language Learning* 31: 113–34.

Combrink, J. G. H. 1978. Afrikaans: its origins and development. In Lanham L. W., and Prinsloo K. P. (eds.), *Language and Communication Studies in South Africa*, 69–95. Cape Town: Oxford University Press.

Comrie, B. 1989. *Language Universals and Linguistic Typology*. 2nd edn. Oxford: Basil Blackwell.

Condry, I. 2000. *The Social Production of Difference: Imitation and Authenticity in Japanese Rap Music*. New York: Berghan Books.

Cook, M. J., and Sharp, M. A. 1966. Problems of Navajo speakers in learning English. *Language Learning* 16: 21–9.

Cook, V. 1999. Going beyond the native speaker in language teaching. *TESOL Quarterly* 33: 185–209.

Coovadia, I. 2002. *The Wedding*. New York: Picador.

Coppieters, R. 1987. Competence differences between native and fluent non-native speakers. *Language* 63: 544–73.

Cote, S. 1996. Grammatical and discourse properties of null arguments in English. PhD dissertation, University of Pennsylvania.

Cowie, C. 2007. Attitudes to accent in the Indian call-centre industry. Paper presented at the 13th Annual Conference of the International Association for World Englishes, University of Regensburg, 4–6 October.

Crystal, D. 1997. *English as a Global Language*. Cambridge: Canto.

—— 2001. The future of Englishes. In Burns, A., and Coffin C. (eds.), *Analysing English in a Global Context*, 53–64. London: Routledge.

—— 2004. *The Stories of English*. New York: Overlook Press.

Darling, M. 1988. Canadian writing 1987: a review. In Metcalf, J., and Rooke, L. (eds.), *The Macmillan Anthology*, Vol. I, 277–96. Toronto: Macmillan of Canada.

Das Gupta, P. 1986. On the sociolinguistics of English in India. *Indian Journal of Linguistics* 13: 61–8.

Davies, A. 1996. Ironising the myth of linguicism. *Journal of Multilingual and Multicultural Development* 17/6: 485–96.

—— 2003. *The Native Speaker: Myth and Reality*. Clevedon: Multilingual Matters.

Davy, J. 2000. A conservative view of the New Englishes. Paper presented at the First International Conference on Linguistics in Southern Africa, 12–14 January 2000, University of Cape Town.

de Camp, D. 1971. Toward a generative analysis of a post-creole speech continuum. In Hymes, D. (ed.), *Pidginization and Creolization of Languages*, 349–70. Cambridge: Cambridge University Press.

de Klerk, V. 2004. Expressing levels of intensity in Xhosa English. *English World-Wide*. 26/1: 77–96.

2005. Procedural meanings of *well* in a corpus of Xhosa English. *Journal of Pragmatics*, 37/8: 1183–205.

Delbridge, A. 1981. *The Macquarie Dictionary*. Sydney: Macquarie Library.

Dendrinos, B. 1999. The conflictual subjectivity of the periphery ELT practitioner. In Christidis, A.-F. (ed.), *'Strong' and 'Weak' Languages in the European Union: Aspects of Linguistic Hegemonism*, 711–17. Proceedings of an international conference, Thessaloniki, 26–28 March, Thessaloniki: Centre for the Greek Language.

Derwing, T., and Munro, M. 1997. Accent, intelligibility, and comprehensibility. *Studies in Second Language Acquisition* 19: 1–16.

Dobson E. J. 1955. Early modern standard English. *Transactions of the Philological Society*: 25–54.

Domingue, N. Z. 1975. Another Creole: Middle English. Paper presented at the 1975 International Conference on Pidgins and Creoles, University of Hawaii, Honolulu.

D'souza, J. 1988. Interactional strategies in South Asian languages: their implications for teaching English internationally. *World Englishes* 7/2: 159–72.

1991. Speech acts in Indian English fiction. *World Englishes* 10/3: 307–16.

2001. Contextualizing range and depth in Indian English. *World Englishes* 20: 145–60.

Dulay, H., and Burt, M 1973. Should we teach children syntax? *Language Learning* 23: 245–58.

Eades, D. 1991. Communicative strategies in Aboriginal Australia. In Romaine, S. (ed.), *Language in Australia*, 84–93. Cambridge: Cambridge University Press.

Eagleson, R. D. 1982. English in Australia and New Zealand. In Bailey, R. W., and Görlach, M. (eds.), *English as a World Language*, 415–38. Ann Arbor: University of Michigan Press.

Edwards, J. R. 1979. *Language and Disadvantage*. London: Arnold.

1986. Did English murder Irish? *English Today* 6: 7–14.

Ellis, R. 1984. *Classroom Second Language Development*. Oxford: Pergamon.

1985. *Understanding Second Language Acquisition*. Oxford: Oxford University Press.

1994. *The Study of Second Language Acquisition*. Oxford: Oxford University Press.

Emeneau, M. B. 1956. India as a linguistic area. *Language* 32: 3–16.

Ervin-Tripp, S. 1968. An analysis of the interaction of language, topic and listener. In Fishman, J. (ed.), *Readings in the Sociology of Language*, 192–211. The Hague: Mouton. (Reprinted from: *American Anthropologist* 66: 86–102.)

Fairman, T. 1992. Ergo lingua mihi deficit. *English Today*, 29, 23–6.

Ferguson, C. A. 1971. Absence of copula and the notion of simplicity: a study of normal speech, baby talk, foreigner talk, and pidgins. In Hymes, D. (ed.), *Pidginisation and Creolisation of Languages*, 141–50. Cambridge: Cambridge University Press.

1977. Baby talk as a simplified register. In Snow, C., and Ferguson, C. A. (eds.), *Talking to Children: Language Input and Acquisition*, 219–35 Cambridge: Cambridge University Press.

1982. Foreword. In Kachru, B. B. (eds.), *The Other Tongue: English across Cultures*, xii–xvii. London: Pergamon.

Ferguson, C., and Heath, S. B. 1981. Introduction. In Ferguson, C. A., and Heath, S. B. (eds.), *Language in the USA*, xxv–xxxviii. Cambridge: Cambridge University Press.

Filppula, M. 1999. *The Grammar of Irish English: Language in Hibernian Style*. London: Routledge.

Finegan, E., and Besnier, N. 1989. *Language: Its Structure and Use*. Orlando: Harcourt, Brace, Jovanovich.

Finn, P. 2004. Cape Flats English: phonology. In Kortmann, B., Schneider, E. W., Burridge, K., Mesthrie, R., and Upton, C. (eds.), *A Handbook of Varieties of English*, Vol. 1, 964–84. Berlin: Mouton de Gruyter.

Firth, A., and Wagner, J. 1997. On Discourse, communication, and (some) fundamental concepts in SLA Research. *Modern Language Journal* 81: 285–300.

Fishman, J. 1991. *Reversing Language Shift: Theoretical and Empirical Foundations of Assistance to Threatened Languages*. Clevedon: Multilingual Matters.

Fisiak, J. 1995. *An Outline History of English*, Vol I, *External History*. Poznan: Kantor Wydawniczy Saww.

Flannigan, B. 1984. Language variation among native Americans: reflections on Lakota English. Ms.

Flynn, S. 1989. The role of the head-initial/head-final parameter in the acquisition of English relative clauses by Spanish and Japanese learners. In Gass, S., and J. Schachter (eds.), *Linguistic Perspectives on Second Language Acquisition*, 89–108. Cambridge: Cambridge University Press.

Flynn, S., and Espinal, I. 1985. Head-initial/head-final parameter in adult Chinese L2 acquisition of English. *Second Language Research* 1: 93–117.

Foley, J. (ed.) 1988. *New Englishes: The Case of Singapore*. Singapore: Singapore University Press.

Foucault, M. 1972. *The Archaeology of Knowledge*. London: Tavistock.

Fox, J., and Wood, R. 1968. *A Concise History of the French Language*. Oxford: Blackwell.

Fraser, B. 1999. What are discourse markers? *Journal of Pragmatics* 31: 931–52.

Friedrich, P. 2002. Teaching World Englishes in two South American countries. *World Englishes* 21/3: 441–4.

Gardner, R. C., and Lambert, W. E. 1972. *Attitudes and Motivation in Second-language Learning*. Rowley, MA: Newbury House.

Gargesh, R. 2004. Indian English: phonology. In Kortmann, B., Schneider, E. W., Burridge, K., Mesthrie, R., and Upton, C. (eds.), *A Handbook of Varieties of English*, Vol. I, 992–1002. Berlin: Mouton de Gruyter.

Gass, S., and Varonis, E. 1984. The effect of familiarity on the comprehensibility of nonnative speech. *Language Learning* 34: 65–8.

Goffin, R. W. 1934. Some notes on Indian English. *S.P.E. Tract* No. 41. Oxford: Clarendon.

Gonzalez, A. 1983. When does an error become a feature of Philippine English. In Noss, R. B. (ed.), *Varieties of English in South-East Asia*, 150–72. Singapore: RELC/Singapore University Press.

Görlach, M. 1988. *Even More Englishes: Studies 1996–1997*. Amsterdam: John Benjamins.

1990. *Studies in the History of the English Language*. Heidelberg: Carl Winter.

1991. *Englishes*. Amsterdam: John Benjamins.

1995. Heteronomy in International English. In Görlach, M. *More Englishes*, 93–123. Amsterdam: John Benjamins.

1998. *Even More Englishes*. Amsterdam: John Benjamins.

2002. *Still More Englishes*. Amsterdam: John Benjamins.

Gough, D. 1996. Black English in South Africa. In de Klerk, V. (ed.), *Focus on South Africa*, 53–77. Amsterdam: John Benjamins.

Gough, D., and de Klerk, V. 2002. Black South African English. In R. Mesthrie, R. (ed.), *Language in South Africa*, 356–78. Cambridge: Cambridge University Press.

Graddol, D. 1997. *The Future of English*. London: British Council.

2003. Shifting the Centre: how global English is redefining Centre–Periphery relationships. Paper presented at 15th International ASNEL Conference (Association for the Study of New English Literatures), Otto von Guericken University, Magdeburg, Germany, 28–31 May.

Gramley, E. 2001. *The Vocabulary of World English*. London: Arnold.

Grant, N. 1987. Swahili speakers. In Swann, M., and Smith, B. (eds.), *Learner English: A Teacher's Guide to Interference and Other Problems*, 184–211. Cambridge: Cambridge University Press.

Greenberg, H. 1966. *Universal Language*. 2nd edn. Cambridge, MA: MIT Press.

Grenoble, L. A., and Whaley, L. J. 1998. *Endangered Languages: Current Issues and Future Prospects*. Cambridge: Cambridge University Press.

Grimshaw, J. 1991. Extended projection. Ms., Brandeis University.

1997. Projection, heads, and optimality. *Linguistic Inquiry* 28: 373–422.

Grimshaw, J., and Samek-Lodovici, V. 1995. Optimal Subjects. *University of Massachusetts Occasional Papers in Linguistics (UMOP)*: 589–605.

Gumperz, J. J. 1982. *Discourse Strategies*. Cambridge: Cambridge University Press.

Gumperz, J. J., and Wilson, R. 1971. Convergence and creolisation: a case from the Indo-Aryan/Dravidian border. In Hymes, D. (ed.), *Pidginisation and Creolisation of Languages*, 151–67. Cambridge: Cambridge University Press.

Gupta, A. F. 1992. The pragmatic particles of Singapore Colloquial English. *Journal of Pragmatics* 18: 31–57.

1994. *The Step-Tongue: Children's English in Singapore*. Clevedon: Multilingual Matters.

Gupta, V. 2003. *Comdex Call Center Training Course Kit*. New Delhi: Dreamtech.

Gut, U. B. 2004. Nigerian English: phonology. In Kortmann, B., Schneider, E. W., Burridge, K., Mesthrie, R., and Upton, C. (eds.), *A Handbook of Varieties of English*, Vol. I, 813–30. Berlin: Mouton de Gruyter.

Hakluyt, R. 1598–1600. *The Principal Navigations, Voyages, Traffiques and Discoveries of the English Nation*. London: Dent and Sons (1927 reprint).

Halliday, M. A. K. 1978. *Language as a Social Semiotic*. London: Arnold.

Hancock, I., and Angogo, R. 1982. English in East Africa. In Bailey, R. W., and Görlach, M. (eds.), *English as a World Language*, 306–23. Ann Arbor: University of Michigan Press.

Hancock, J., and Kobbah, E. 1975. Liberian English of Cape Palmas. In Dillard, J. (ed.), *Perspectives on Black English*, 248–71. The Hague: Mouton.

Hankin, N. B. 1994. *Hanklyn-Janklin*. New Delhi: Banyou Books.

Harkins, J. 2000. Structure and meaning in Australian Aboriginal English. *Asian Englishes* 3/2: 60–81.

Harris, J. 1984. Syntactic variation and dialect divergence. *Journal of Linguistics* 20: 303–27.

Harris, S. 1984. Questions as a mode of control in magistrates' courts. *International Journal of the Sociology of Language*, 49: 5–27.

Hartford, B. 1996. The relationship of New Englishes and Linguistic Theory: a cognitive-based grammar of Nepali English. In Baumgardner, R. (ed.), *South Asian English: Structure, Use, Users*, 88–103. Urbana: University of Illinois Press.

Hayden, M., and Hartog, M. 1909. The Irish Dialect of English: its origins and vocabulary. *Fortnightly Review* 85: 775–85, 933–47.

Hesseling, D. 1897. *Het Hollandsch in Zuid-Afrika. De Gids*, 60: 138–62.

Heugh, K. 2002. Recovering multilingualism: recent language policy developments. In R. Mesthrie (ed.), *Language in South Africa*, 449–75. Cambridge: Cambridge University Press.

Hewson, L. A., and van der Riet, F. G. (eds.) 1963. *The Journal of 'Harry Hastings', Albany Settler*. Grahamstown: Grocott and Sherry.

Hickey R. 1995. An assessment of language contact in the development of Irish English. In Fisiak, J. (ed.), *Linguistic Change under Contact Conditions*, 109–30. Berlin: Mouton de Gruyter.

(ed.) 2004a. *Legacies of Colonial English*. Cambridge: Cambridge University Press.

2004b. Development and diffusion of Irish English. In R. Hickey (ed.), *Legacies of Colonial English*, 82–120. Cambridge: Cambridge University Press.

2004c. South-East Asian Englishes. In R. Hickey (ed.), *Legacies of Colonial English*, 559–85. Cambridge: Cambridge University Press.

Hilles, S. 1987. Interlanguage and pro-drop parameter. *Second Language Research* 3/1: 33–52.

Hinnenkamp, V. 1984. Eye-witnessing pidginisation?: structural and sociolinguistic aspects of German and Turkish foreigner talk. *York Papers in Linguistics* 11: 153–66.

Ho, M. L., and Platt, J. T. 1993. *The Dynamics of a Contact Continuum*. Oxford: Clarendon.

Hoffman, C. 2000. The spread of English and the growth of multilingualism with English in Europe. In Cenoz, J., and Jessner, U. (eds.), *English in Europe: The Acquisition of a Third Language*, 1–21. Clevedon: Multilingual Matters.

Holm, J. 1988. *Pidgins and Creoles: Theory and Structure*, Vol. I. Cambridge: Cambridge University Press.

2000. Semi-creolization: problems in the development of theory. In Neumann-Holzschuh, I., and Schneider, E. W. (eds.), *Degrees of Restructuring in Creole Languages*, 19–40. Amsterdam: John Benjamins.

Honey, J. 1997. *Language Is Power: The Story of Standard English and its Enemies*. London: Faber and Faber.

Hornberger, N. H. 1996. Language and education. In McKay, S. L., and Hornberger, N. H. (eds.), *Sociolinguistics and Language Teaching*, 49–73. Cambridge: Cambridge University Press.

Hosali, P. 2000. *Butler English: Form and Function*. Delhi: B. R. Publishing.

Huang, C.-T. J. 1984. On the distribution and reference of empty pronouns. *Linguistic Inquiry* 15: 531–74.

Huber, M. 2004. Ghanaian English: phonology. In Kortmann, B., Schneider, E. W., Burridge, K., Mesthrie, R., and Upton, C. (eds.), *A Handbook of Varieties of English*, Vol. I, 842–65. Berlin: Mouton de Gruyter.

Huber, M., and Dako, K. 2004. Ghanaian English: morphology and syntax. In Kortmann, B., Schneider, E. W., Burridge, K., Mesthrie, R., and Upton, C. (eds.), *A Handbook of Varieties of English*, Vol. II, 854–65. Berlin: Mouton de Gruyter.

Huddleston, R., and G. K. Pullum 2002. *The Cambridge Grammar of the English Language*. Cambridge: Cambridge University Press.

Hudson, R. A. 1975. The meaning of questions. *Language* 51: 1–31.

Huebner, T. 1983. *A Longitudinal Analysis of the Acquisition of English*. Ann Arbor, MI: Karoma.

Hyams, N. M. 1986. *Language Acquisition and the Theory of Parmeters*. Dordrecht: D. Reidel.

Hyde, B. 2002. Japan's emblematic English. *English Today* 18/3: 12–20.

Hyltenstam, K. 1984. The use of typological markedness conditions as predictors in second language acquisition: the case of pronominal copies in relative clauses. In Andersen, R. (ed.), *Second Languages: A Cross-Linguistic Perspective*, 39–58. Rowley, MA: Newbury House.

Hymes, D. 1971. Introduction to Section III. In Hymes, D. (ed.), *Pidginisation and Creolisation of Languages*, 151–67. Cambridge: Cambridge University Press.

Ihalainen, O. 1994. The dialects of English since 1776. In Burchfield, R. W. (ed.), *The Cambridge History of the English Language*, Vol. V: *English in Britain and Overseas: Origins and Development*, 197–274. Cambridge: Cambridge University Press.

Ionin, T., Ko, H., and Wexler, K. 2004. Article semantics in L2 acquisition: the role of specificity. *Language Acquisition* 12: 3–69.

Jackendoff, R. S. 1972. *Semantic Interpretation in Generative Grammar*. Cambridge, MA: MIT Press.

Jaeggli, O., and Safir, K. 1989. The null subject parameter and parametric theory. In Jaeggli, O., and Safir, K. (eds.), *The Null Subject Parameter*, 1–44. Boston: Kluwer.

Jain, D. 1973. Pronominal usage in Hindi: a sociolinguistic study. Doctoral dissertation, University of Pennsylvania.

James, A. 2000. English as a European lingua franca. In Cenoz, J., and Jessner, U. (eds.), *English in Europe: The Acquisition of a Third Language*, 22–38. Clevedon: Multilingual Matters.

Janda, R. D., and Auger J. 1992. Quantitative evidence, qualitative hypercorrection, sociolinguistic variables – and French speakers 'eadaches with English h/Φ. *Language and Communication* 12: 195–236.

Jenkins, J. 2003. *World Englishes: A Resource Book for Students*. London: Routledge.

Johnson, H. 1992. Defossilizing. *ELT Journal* 46: 180–9.

Joseph, C. A. B. 2005. Language in contact and literatures in conflict: text, context and pedagogy. *World Englishes* 24/2: 131–43.

Jowitt, D. 1991. *Nigerian English Usage: An Introduction*. Lagos: Longman Nigeria.

Kachru, B. B. 1976. Models of English for the Third World: white man's linguistic burden or language pragmatics? *TESOL Quarterly* 10/2: 221–39.

 1982. South Asian English. In Bailey, R., and Görlach, M. (eds.), *English as a World Language*, 353–83. Ann Arbor: University of Michigan Press.

 1983a. *The Indianization of English*. New Delhi: Oxford University Press.

 (ed.) 1983b. *The Other Tongue: English across Cultures*, Oxford: Pergamon.

 1983c. The bilingual's creativity: discoursal and stylistic strategies in contact literatures in English. *Studies in the Linguistic Sciences* 13/2: 37–55.

 1983d. Cross-cultural texts and interpretation. *Studies in the Linguistic Sciences* 13/2: 57–72.

 1985. Standards, codification and sociolinguistic realism: the English language in the Outer Circle. In Quirk, R., and Widdowson, H. (eds.), *English in the World: Teaching and Learning the Language and Literatures*, 11–30. Cambridge: Cambridge University Press.

1986. The *Alchemy of English: The Spread, Functions and Models of Non-native English*. Oxford: Pergamon Institute Press. (Reprinted 1990, Urbana: University of Illinois Press.)

1987. Cross-cultural texts, discourse strategies and discourse interpretation. In Smith, Larry E. (ed.), *Discourse across Cultures: Strategies in World Englishes*, 87–100. Englewood Cliffs: Prentice-Hall.

1988. The sacred cows of English. *English Today* 16: 3–8.

1991a. Liberation linguistics and the Quirk concern. *English Today* 7: 3–13.

1991b. Speech acts in world Englishes. *World Englishes* 10/3: 299–306.

1992. Models for non-native Englishes. In Kachru, B. B. (ed.), *The Other Tongue: English across Cultures*, 48–74. 2nd edn. Urbana: University of Illinois Press.

1996. Language and cultural meaning: expository writing in South Asian English. In Baumgardner, R. (ed.), *South Asian English: Structure, Use and Users*, 127–40. Urbana: University of Illinois Press.

1997. World Englishes and English-using communities. *Annual Review of Applied Linguistics* 17: 66–87.

2001. Discourse competence in World Englishes. In Thumboo, E. (ed.), *The Three Circles of English*, 341–55. Singapore: UniPress.

2005. *Asian Englishes: Beyond the Canon*. Hong Kong: Hong Kong University Press.

Kachru, B. B., Kachru, Y., and Nelson, C. (eds.). 2006. *A Handbook of World Englishes*. Oxford: Blackwell.

Kachru, B. B., and Nelson, C. L. 1996. World Englishes. In McKay, S. L., and Hornberger, N. H. (eds.), *Sociolinguistics and Language Teaching*, 71–102. Cambridge: Cambridge University Press.

Kachru, Y. 1983. Linguistics and written discourse in particular languages: contrastive studies – English and Hindi. *Annual Review of Applied Linguistics* 3: 50–77

1987. Cross-cultural texts, discourse strategies and discourse interpretation. In Smith, L. E. (ed.), *Discourse across Cultures: Strategies in World Englishes*, 87–100. London: Prentice-Hall.

1991. Speech acts in World Englishes: toward a framework for research. *World Englishes* 10: 299–306.

1996. Kachru revisits contrasts. *English Today* 12: 41–4.

1997a. Cultural meaning and contrastive rhetoric in English Education. *World Englishes* 16: 337–50.

1997b. Culture and augmentative writing in world Englishes. In Smith, L. E., and Forman, M. L. (eds.), *World Englishes 2000*, 48–67. Honolulu: University of Hawaii Press.

2001a. Discourse competence in world Englishes. In Thumboo, E. (ed.), *The Three Circles of English*, 341–55. Singapore: UniPress.

2001b. World Englishes and rhetoric across cultures. *Asian Englishes: An International Journal of the Sociolinguistics of English in Asia/Pacific*. Winter: 54–71.

Kahane, R. 1992. American English: from a colonial substandard to prestige language. In Kachru, B. B. (ed.), *The Other Tongue: English across Cultures*, 211–19. 2nd edn. Urbana: University of Illinois Press.

Kaye, A. 1990. Observations on pidginistics and creolistics. *Semiotica* 78: 285–348.

Kidwai, A. 1997. *Only* in Indian English only. *18th South Asian Language Analysis Roundtable*, New Delhi, India.

King, R. D. 2004. A review of Jeffrey Kallen, Focus on Ireland. *World Englishes* 20: 107–9.

Kingman, J. (chairman) 1988. Report of the committee of inquiry into the teaching of English language. [The Kingman Report]. London: Her Majesty's Stationery Office.

Kirk-Greene, A. 1971. The influence of West African Languages on English. In Spencer, J. (ed.), *The English Language in West Africa*, 123–44. London: Longman.

Kirkpatrick, A., and Zhichang, X. 2002. Chinese pragmatic norms and 'China English'. *World Englishes* 21/2: 269–79.

Klein, W. 1986. *Second Language Acquisition*. Cambridge: Cambridge University Press.

Klein, W., and Perdue, C. 1997. The basic variety, or: Couldn't language be much simpler? *Second Language Research* 13/4: 301–47.

Knapp, K. 1991. *Linguistische Aspekte intercultureller Kommunikations fahigkeit*. Habilitation thesis. University of Düsseldorf.

Kong, Lily. 1997. Popular music and a sense of place in popular music in Singapore. Ms. National University of Singapore.

Kortmann, B., Schneider, E. W., Burridge, K., Mesthrie, R., and Upton, C. (eds.), *A Handbook of Varieties of English*, Vol. II. Berlin: Mouton de Gruyter.

Kramsch, C. 1998. The privilege of the intercultural speaker. In Byram, M., and Fleming, M. (eds.), *Language Learning in Intercultural Perspective: Approaches through Drama and Ethnography*, 16–31. Cambridge: Cambridge University Press.

Krashen, S. 1977. Some issues relating to the Monitor Model. In Brown, H., Yorio, C., and Crymes, R. (eds.), *On TESOL '77*, 144–58. Washington: TESOL.

Kubota, R. 2001. Teaching world Englishes to native speakers of English in the USA. *World Englishes*. 20: 47–64.

Kuno, S. 1978. Japanese: a characteristic of language. In Lehmann, W. P. (ed.), *Syntactic Typology: Studies in the Phenomenology of Language*, 57–138. Sussex: Harvester Press.

Kwan-Terry, A. 1978. The meaning and the source of the 'la' and the 'what' particles in Singapore English. *RELC Journal* 9/2: 22–36.

1992. Towards a dictionary of Singapore English: issues relating to making entries for particles in Singapore English. In Pakir, A. (ed.), *Words in a Cultural Context*, 62–72. Singapore: Unipress.

Labov, W. 1969. The logic of non-standard English. *Georgetown Monographs in Languages and Linguistics*, 22. (Reproduced in W. Labov, 1972 *Language in the Inner City: Studies in the Black English Verncaular*, 201–40. Philadelphia: University of Pennsylvania Press.)

1972a. *Sociolinguistic Patterns*. Philadelphia: University of Pennsylvania Press.

1872b. *Language in the Inner City: Studies in the Black English Vernacular*: Philadelphia: University of Pennsylvania Press.

2001. *Principles of Linguistic Change*, Vol II: *Social Factors*. Oxford: Basil Blackwell.

Labov, W., and Harris, W. 1986. De facto segregation of black and white vernaculars. In Sankoff, D. (ed.), *Diversity and Diachrony*, 1–24. Amsterdam: John Benjamins.

Lalleman, J. 1996. The state of the art in second language acquisition research. In Jordens, P., and Lalleman, J. (eds.), *Investigating Second Language Acquisition*, 1–64. Berlin: Mouton de Gruyter.

Lambert, W. E. 1978. Some cognitive and sociocultural consequences of being bilingual. In Alatis, J. E. (ed.), *Georgetown University Round Table on Languages and Linguistics*, 214–29. Washington, DC: Georgetown University Press.

Langacker, R. 1883. *Foundations of Cognitive Grammar*. Bloomington: Indiana University Linguistics Club.

Lardiere, D. 1998. Case and tense in a 'fossilized' steady state. *Second Language Research* 14: 1–26.

Larsen-Freeman, D., and Long, M. H. 1991. *An Introduction to Second Language Acquisition Research*. New York: Longman.

Leap W. 1993. *American Indian English*. Salt Lake City: University of Utah Press.

Lee, J. S. 2005. Global and local fusion: semiotic creativity in Korean and Japanese pop music. Paper presented at the Linguistics Seminar, University of Illinois at Urbana, 7 April.

Lefevbre, C. 1986. Relexification in creole genesis revisited: the case of Haitian Creole. In Muysken, P., and Smith. N. (eds.), *Substrata Versus Universals in Creole Genesis*, 279–300. Amsterdam: Benjamins.

Leith, D. 1997. *A Social History of English*. 2nd edn. London: Routledge.

Le Page, R., and Tabouret-Keller, A. 1985. *Acts of Identity*. Cambridge: Cambridge University Press.

Levinson, S. C. 1983. *Pragmatics*. Cambridge: Cambridge University Press.

Li, C. N., and Thompson, S. 1976. Subject and topic: a new typology of language. In Li, C. N. (ed.), *Subject and Topic*, 457–89. New York: Academic Press.

Loke, K. K., and Low, M.-Y. J. 1988. A proposed descriptive framework for the pragmatic meanings of the particle *la* in colloquial Singaporean English. In McCarthy, B. (ed.), *Asian–Pacific Papers, Occasional Papers Number* 10: 150–61 (Applied Linguistics Association of Australia).

Long, M. 1981. Input, interaction and second language acquisition. *Native Language and Foreign Acquisition: Annals of the New York Academy of Sciences* (ed. H. Winitz) 379: 259–78.

Lowenberg, P. 1990. Standards and norms for world Englishes: issues and attitudes. *Studies in the Linguistic Sciences* 20: 123–37.

    1992. Testing English as a world language: issues in assessing non-native proficiency. In Kachru, B. B. (ed.), *The Other Tongue: English across Cultures*, 108–21. Urbana: University of Illinois Press.

    1993. Issues of validity in tests of English as a world language: whose standards? *World Englishes* 12:96–106.

    2002. Assessing English proficiency in the Expanding World. *World Englishes* 21/3: 431–5.

Lukmani, Y. 1972. Motivation to learn and language proficiency. *Language Learning* 22: 261–73.

Lunsford, L. J. 1996. 'Flight position confused pilots in Columbia crash'. *Dallas Morning News*, 17 April.

MacLaughlin, B. 1987. *Theories of Second-Language Learning*. London: Edward Arnold.

Magura, B. 1984. Style and meaning in African English: a sociolinguistic analysis of South African and Zimbabwean English. Unpublished PhD thesis, University of Illinois (Urbana-Champaign).

Mahboob, A. 2004. Pakistani English: morphology and syntax. In Kortmann, B. Schneider, E. W., Burridge, K., Mesthrie, R., and Upton, C. (eds.), *A Handbook of Varieties of English*, Vol. II, 1045–57. Berlin: Mouton De Gruyter.

Mahboob, A., and Ahmar, N. H. 2004. Pakistani English: phonology. In Schneider, E., Burridge, K., Kortmann, B., Mesthrie, R., and C. Upton (eds.), *A Handbook of Varieties of English*, Vol. II, 1003–16. Berlin: Mouton de Gruyter.

Makalela, L. 2004. Making sense of BSAE for linguistic democracy in South Africa. *World Englishes* 23/3: 355–66.

Malcolm, I. G. 2004. Australian creoles and Aboriginal English: morphology and syntax. In Kortmann, B., Schneider, E. W., Burridge, K., Mesthrie, R., and Upton, C. (eds.), *A Handbook of Varieties of English*, Vol. II, 657–81. Berlin: Mouton de Gruyter.

Martin, E. 2002. Cultural images and different varieties of English in French television commercials. *English Today* 18/4: 8–20.

Mazrui, A. A., and Mazrui, A. M. 1998. *The Power of Babel: Language and Governance in the African Experience*. Oxford: James Currey.

Mbangwana, P. 2004. Cameroon English: morphology and syntax. In Kortmann, B., Schneider, E. W., Burridge, K., Mesthrie, R., and Upton, C. (eds.), *A Handbook of Varieties of English*, Vol. II, 898–908. Berlin: Mouton de Gruyter.

McArthur, T. 1987. The English Languages? *English Today* 11: 9–11.

    1998. *The English Languages*. Cambridge: Cambridge University Press.

2003a. World English, Euro English, Nordic English? *English Today* 19/1: 54–8.

2003b. English as an Asian language. *English Today* 19/2: 19–22.

McCafferty, K. 2004. '[T]hunder storms is verry dangese in this country they come in less than minnits notice...': the Northern Subject Rule in Southern Irish English. *English World-Wide* 25/1: 51–80.

McCarthy, J. 1995. Some misconceptions about Optimality Theory. Ms. University of Massachusetts, Amherst.

McCarthy, J. J., and A. Prince. 1995. Faithfulness and reduplicative identity. In Beckman, J., *et al.* (eds.), *Papers in Optimality Theory*, 249–384. (*University of Massachusetts Occasional Papers in Linguistics*, 18.) Amherst: University of Massachusetts.

McCormick, K. 1995. Code-switching, code-mixing and convergence in Cape Town. In Mesthrie, R. (ed.), *Language and Social History: Studies in South African Sociolinguistics*, 193–208. Cape Town: David Philip.

2002. *Language in Cape Town's District Six*. Oxford: Oxford University Press.

2004. Cape Flats English: morphology and syntax. In Kortmann, B., Schneider, E. W., Burridge, K., Mesthrie, R., and Upton, C. (eds.), *A Handbook of Varieties of English*, Vol. II: 993–1005. Berlin: Mouton de Gruyter.

McLaughlin, B. 1980. Theory research in second language: an emerging paradigm. *Language Learning* 30: 331–50.

McLaughlin, B. 1987. *Theories of Second Language Learning*. London: Edward Arnold.

Medgyes, P. 1994. *The non-native teacher*. London: Macmillan.

Mehrotra, R. R. 1977. English in India: the current scene. *English Language Teaching Journal* 31: 163–70.

1982. Indian English: a sociolinguistic profile. In J. B. Pride (ed.), *New Englishes*, 150–73. Rowley, MA: Newbury House.

1998. *Indian English: Texts and Interpretation*. Amsterdam: John Benjamins.

Meierkord, C. 2004. Syntactic variation in interactions across international Englishes. *English World-Wide* 25/1: 109–32.

Meisel, J. 1997. The L2 basic variety as an I-language. *Second Language Research* 13/4: 374–85.

Melchers G., and Shaw, P. 2003. *World Englishes*. London: Arnold.

Mesthrie, R. 1987. From OV to VO in language shift: South African Indian English and its OV substrates. *English World-Wide* 8/2: 263–76.

1992a. *English in Language Shift: The History, Structure and Sociolinguistics of South African Indian English*. Cambridge: Cambridge University Press.

1992b. *Language in Indenture: A Sociolinguistic History of Bhojpuri-Hindi in South Africa*. London: Routledge.

1993. Koineization in the Bhojpuri-Hindi diaspora, with special reference to South Africa. *International Journal of the Sociology of Language* 99: 25–44.

1994. Standardisation and variation in South African English. *Stellenbosch Papers in Linguistics* 26: 181–201.

1996. South African Indian English. In de Klerk, V. (ed.), *Varieties of English around the World: Focus on South Africa*, 79–98. Amsterdam: John Benjamins.

1997. A sociolinguistic study of topicalisation phenomena in Black South African English. In Schneider, E. W. (ed.), *Englishes around the World*, Vol. II: *Caribbean, Africa, Asia, Australasia (Studies in Honour of Manfred Gorlach)*. Amsterdam: John Benjamins.

1999a. Fifty ways to say 'I do': tracing the origins of unstressed *do* in Cape Flats English. *South African Journal of Linguistics* 17: 58–71.

1999b. The study of new varieties of English. Inaugural lecture. Cape Town: University of Cape Town.

2001. Male workers' English in the Western Cape: interlanguage, code-switching and pidginisation. In Ridge, S., Ridge, E., and Makoni, S. (eds.), *Freedom and Discipline: Essays in Applied Linguistics from Southern Africa*, 85–104. New Delhi: Bahri.

2002. Mock languages and symbolic power: the South African radio series *Applesammy and Naidoo*. *World Englishes* 21: 99–112.

2003. Children in language shift: the syntax of fifth-generation South African Indian English speakers. *South African Journal of Linguistics and Applied Language Studies* 21/3: 119–26.

2004a. Synopsis: the phonology of English in Africa and South and South-east Asia. In Kortmann, B., Schneider, E. W., Burridge, K., Mesthrie, R., and Upton, C. (eds.), *A Handbook of Varieties of English*, Vol. I, 1099–110. Berlin: Mouton de Gruyter.

2004b. Indian South African English: phonology. In Kortmann, B., Schneider, E. W., Burridge, K., Mesthrie, R., and Upton, C. (eds.), *A Handbook of Varieties of English*, Vol. I, 953–63. Berlin: Mouton de Gruyter.

2006. Anti-deletions in a second language variety: a Study of Black South African English mesolect. *English World-Wide* 27/2: 111–46.

Mesthrie, R., and Dunne, T. 1990. Syntactic variation in language shift: the relative clause in South African Indian English. *Language Variation and Change* 2/1: 31–56.

Mesthrie, R., Swan, J., Deumert, A., and Leap, W. 2000. *Introducing Sociolinguistics*. Edinburgh: Edinburgh University Press.

Mesthrie, R., and West, P. 1995. Towards a grammar of proto-South African English: English World Wide. *English World-Wide* 16/2: 105–34.

Milroy, L., and Milroy, J. 1991. *Authority in Language: Investigating Language Prescription and Standardization*. London: Routledge.

Mistry, R. 1987. *Tales from Firozsha Baag*. Toronto: McLelland and Stewart.

Mitchell, A. G., and Delbridge, A. 1965. *The Pronunciation of English in Australia*. 2nd edn. Sydney: Angus and Robertson.

Moag, R. 1992. The life-cycle of non-native Englishes: a case study. In Kachru, B. B. (ed.), *The Other Tongue: English across Cultures*, 270–88. 2nd edn. Oxford: Pergamon.

Modiano, M. 2003. Euro-English: a Swedish perspective. *English Today* 19/2: 35–41.

Montgomery, M. 2004. Solving Kurath's puzzle. In Hickey, R. (ed.), *Legacies of Colonial English*, 310–25. Cambridge: Cambridge University Press.

Moorhouse, G. 1973. *The Missionaries*. London: Eyre Methuen.

Mufwene, S. S. 1988. The small *pro* and inflectional morphology. *Linguistic Analysis* 18: 253–42.

   1996. The founder principle in Creole genesis. *Diachronica* 13: 83–134.

   1998. Native speaker, proficient speaker and norms. In Singh, R. (ed.), *The Native Speaker: Multilingual Perspectives*, 111–23. New Delhi: Sage.

   2001. *The Ecology of Language Evolution*. Cambridge: Cambridge University Press.

Myers-Scotton, C. 1976. Strategies of Neutrality: language choice in uncertain situations. *Language* 52: 919–41.

   1993a. *Duelling Languages: Grammatical Structure in Code-Switching*. Oxford: Clarendon Press.

   1993b. *Social Motivations for Code-Switching: Evidence from Africa*. Oxford: Clarendon.

Nelson, C. 1992. Bilingual writing for the monolingual reader: blowing up the canon. *World Englishes*, 11: 271–75.

Nesfield, J. C. 1895. *English Grammar Series, Book IV: Idiom, Grammar and Synthesis for High Schools*. Calcutta: Macmillan.

Nihalani, P., Tongue R. K., and Hosali, P. 1977. *Indian and British English: A Handbook of Usage and Pronunciation*. New Delhi: Oxford University Press.

Okara, G. 1964. *The Voice*. London: Heinemann.

Omoniyi, T. 2006. Hip-hop through the World Englishes lens: a response to globalization. *World Englishes* 25/2: 195–208.

Orsman, H. (ed.) 1997. *A Dictionary of New Zealand English on Historical Principles*. Auckland: Oxford University Press.

Paikeday, T. 1985. *The Native Speaker Is Dead*. Toronto: Paikeday Publishing Inc.

Pakir, A. 1992. Dictionary entries for discourse particles. In Pakir, A. (ed.), *Words in a Cultural Context*, 143–52. Singapore: Unipress.

   1994. English in Singapore: the codification of competing norms. In Gopinathan, S. A., Pakir, A., Ho, W. K., and Saravanan, V. (eds.), *Language, Society and Education in Singapore: Issues and Trends*, 92–118. Singapore: Times Academic Press (2nd edn 1998).

Palmer, H. E. 1917. *The Scientific Study and Teaching of Languages*. London: George G. Harrap.

Paradis, M. 1998. Neurolinguistic aspects of the native speaker. In Singh, R. (ed.), *The Native Speaker: Multilingual Perspectives*, 205–19. New Delhi: Sage.

Pemagbi, J. 1989. Still a deficient language? *English Today* 17: 20–4.

Penfield-Jasper, S. 1980. Selected grammatical characteristics of Mohave English. PhD dissertation, University of Arizona (Tucson).

Pennycook, A. D. 1994. *The Cultural Politics of English as an International Language*. London: Longman.

1998. *English and the Discourses of Colonialism*. London: Routledge.

2003. Global Englishes, rip slyme, and performativity. *Journal of Sociolinguistics* 7/4: 513–33.

Perullo, A., and Fenn, J. 2003. Language ideologies, choices, and practices in Eastern African hip-hop. In Berger, H. M., and Carrol, M. T. (eds.), *Global Popular Music: The Politics and Aesthetics of Language Choice*, 18–51. Jackson: University Press of Mississippi.

Petzold, R. 2002. Toward a pedagogical model for ELT. *World Englishes* 21/3: 422–26.

Phillipson, R. 1992. *Linguistic Imperialism*. Oxford: Oxford University Press.

Piggin, S. C. 1984. *Making Evangelical Missionaries 1789–1859*. Abingdon: Sutton Courtenay Press.

Platt, J. T. 1975. The Singapore English speech continuum and its basilect 'Singlish' as a creoloid. *Anthropological Linguistics* 17: 363–74.

1982. English in Singapore, Malaysia and Hong Kong. In Bailey, R. W., and Görlach, M. (eds.), *English as a World Language*, 384–414. Ann Arbor: University of Michigan Press.

1987. Communicative functions of particles in Singapore English. In Steele, R., and Threadgold, T. (eds.), *Language Topics: Essays in Honour of Michael Halliday*, Vol. I, 391–401. Amsterdam: John Benjamins.

Platt, J. T., and Ho, M. L. 1989. Discourse particles in Singaporean English: substratum influences and universals. *World Englishes* 8: 215–21.

Platt, J. T., and Weber, H. 1980. *English in Singapore and Malaysia*. Kuala Lumpur: Oxford University Press.

Platt, J., Weber, H., and Ho, M. L. 1983. *The New Englishes*. London: Routledge and Kegan Paul.

Plüddemann, P. (ms). Fear to fail: realising school language policy in South Africa. Cape Town: PRAESA, University of Cape Town.

Poplack, S. (ed.) 2000. *The English History of African American English*. Oxford: Blackwell.

Poplack, S., and Tagliamonte, S. 1991. African American English in the diaspora: evidence from old-line Nova Scotians. *Language Variation and Change* 3: 301–39.

Preston, D. 1989. *Sociolinguistics and Second Language Acquisition*. Oxford: Blackwell.

Pride, J. B. 1982. *New Englishes*. Rowley: Newbury House.

Prince, A., and Smolensky, P. 2004. *Optimality Theory: Constraint Interaction in Generative Grammar*. Malden, MA: Blackwell.

Prince E. 1981. Topicalisation, focus-movement and Yiddish-movement: a pragmatic differentiation. *Proceedings of the 7th meeting of the Berkeley Linguistics Society*, 249–64. Berkeley, CA: Berkeley Linguistics Society.

Pulcını, V. 1997. Attitudes toward the spread of English in Italy. *World Englishes* 16/1: 77–86.

Pullum, G. K. 1997. Language that dare not speak its name. *Nature* 328: 321–2.

Pyles, T. and Algeo, J. 1982. *The Origins and the Development of the English Language*. New York: Harcourt Brace Jovanovich.

Qiang, N., and Wolff, M. 2003. Chian and Chinese, or Chingland and Chinglish? *English Today* 19/2: 9–11.

Quirk, R. 1985. The English language in a global context. In Quirk, R., and Widdowson, H. (eds.), *English in the World: Teaching and Learning the Language and Literatures*, 1–6. Cambridge: Cambridge University Press.

(ed.) 1987. *Dictionary of Contemporary English: New Edition*. Harlow: Longman.

1990. Language varieties and standard language. *English Today* 21: 3–10.

1995. *Grammatical and Lexical Variance in English*. London and New York: Longman.

Quirk, R., Greenbaum, S., Leech, G., and Svartvik, J. 1985. *A Comprehensive Grammar of the English Language*. London: Longman.

Quirk, R., Greenbaum, S., and Svartvik, J. 1972. *A Communicative Grammar of English*. London: Longman.

Rampton, B. 2005. *Crossing: Language and Ethnicity among Adolescents*. 2nd edn. Manchester: St Jerome Publishing.

Rand, D., and Sankoff, D. 1990. Goldvarb: a variable rule application for Macintosch. *Centre de recherches mathématiques*, Université de Montreal.

Rao, R. 1938. *Kanthapura*. London: Allen and Unwin.

Ravem, R. 1974. Language acquisition in a second language environment. In Richards, J. C. (ed.), *Error Analysis: Perspectives on Second Language Acquisition*, 124–33. London: Longman.

Reinecke, J. 1937. Marginal languages: a sociological survey of the Creole languages and trade jargons. PhD thesis, Yale University.

Richards, J. C., and Tay, M. W. J. 1977. The *la* particle in Singapore English. In Crewe, W. (ed.), *The English Language in Singapore*, 141–56. Singapore: Eastern Universities Press.

Rickford, J. 1986. Social contact and linguistic diffusion: Hiberno English and New World Black English. *Language* 62: 245–89.

1997. Commentary: suite for ebony and phonics. *Discover* Dec: 82–7.

1999. The creole origin of African-American vernacular English: evidence from copula absence. In Mufwene, S., Rickford, J., Bailey, G., and Baugh, J. (eds.), *African American English: Structure, History and Use*, 155–200. London: Routledge.

Ritchie, W. C. 1986. Second-language acquisition research and the study of non-native varieties of English: some issues in common. *World Englishes* 5: 15–30.

Robertson, D. 2000. Variability in the use of the English article system by Chinese learners of English. *Second Language Research* 16: 135–72.

Robinson, J., Lawrence, H., and Tagliamonte, S. 2001. GOLDVARB 2001 for Windows. Department of Language and Linguistic Science, University of York, UK.

Romaine, S. 1982. English in Scotland. In Bailey, R. W., and Görlach, M. (eds.), *English as a World Language*, 56–83. Ann Arbor: University of Michigan Press.

1992. The evolution of linguistic complexity in pidgin and Creole languages. In Hawkins, J. A., and Gell-Mann, J. (eds.), *The Evolution of Human Languages*, Vol. X, 213–38. Reading, MA: Addison-Wesley.

1997. The British heresy in ESL revisited. In Eliasson, S., and Jahr, E. H. (eds.), *Language and its Ecology*, 417–32. Berlin: Mouton de Gruyter.

Romaine, S., and Nettle, D. 2000. *Vanishing Voices: The Extinction of the World's Languages*. Oxford: Oxford University Press.

Rosewarne, D. 1994. Estuary English – tomorrow's RP. *English Today* 10/1: 3–8.

Sahgal, A 1991. Patterns of language use in a bilingual setting in India. In Cheshire, J. (ed.), *English around the World*, 299–307. Cambridge: Cambridge University Press.

Sand, A. 2004. Shared morpho-syntactic features in contact varieties of English: Article use. *World Englishes* 23: 281–98.

Sankoff, G. 1994. An historical and evolutionary approach to variation in the Tok Pisin verb phrase. *Proceedings of the Chicago Linguistic Society* 30: 293–320.

Sankoff, G., and Laberge, S. 1973. On the acquisition of native speakers by a language. *Kivung* 6: 32–47.

Saville-Troike, M. 2003. *The Ethnography of Communication*. 3rd edn. Oxford: Basil Blackwell.

Savignon S., and Berns, M. 1984. *Initiatives in Communicative Language Teaching*. Reading, MA: Addison-Wesley.

Schiffrin, D. 1987. *Discourse Markers*. Cambridge: Cambridge University Press.

Schmidt, R. 1990. The role of consciousness in second language learning. *Applied Linguistics* 11: 129–58.

Schmied, J. 1991. *English in Africa: An Introduction*. London: Longman.

2004. East African English (Kenya, Uganda, Tanzania): phonology. In Kortmann, B., Schneider, E. W., Burridge, K., Mesthrie, R., and Upton, C. (eds.), *A Handbook of Varieties of English*, Vol. I, 918–30. Berlin: Mouton de Gruyter.

Schneider, E. W. 1990. The cline of creoleness in English-oriented Creoles and semi-creoles of the Caribbean. *English World-Wide* 11: 79–113.

2003. The dynamics of New Englishes: from identity construction to dialect birth. *Language* 79/2: 233–81.

2006. *Postcolonial Englishes*. Cambridge: Cambridge University Press.

2004. Schneider, E., Burridge, K., Kortmann, B., Mesthrie, R., and Upton, C. (eds) 2004. *A Handbook of Varieties of English*, Vol. I. Berlin: Mouton de Gruyter.

Schuchardt, H. 1882. Kreolische Studien I: Über das negerportugiesische von San Thome (Westafrika). *Sitzungsberichte der Kaiserlichen Akademie der Wissenschaften zu Wien* 101: 889–917.

1889. Beiträge zur Kenntnis des kreolischen Romanisch: Allgemeineres über das Indo-portugiesische (Asioportugiesische). *Zeitschrift fur Romanische Philologie* 13: 476–516.

1891. Beiträge zur Kenntnis des englische Creolisch III: Das Indo-Englische. *Englische Studien* 15: 286–305.

Schumann, J. H. 1974. Implications of pidginization and creolization for the study of adult second language acquisition. In Gingras, R. C. (ed.), *Second Language Acquisition and Foreign Language Teaching*: 137–51. Arlington: Center for Applied Linguistics.

1978. *The Pidginization Process: A Model for Second Language Acquisition.* Rowley, MA: Newbury House.

Schumann, J. H., and Stauble, A. 1983. A discussion of second language acquisition and decreolization. In Andersen, R. (ed.), 1983 *Pidginization and Creolization as Language Acquisition*, 260–74. Rowley, MA: Newbury House.

Scollon, R., and Scollon, S. W. 1991. Topic confusion in Asian-English discourse. *World Englishes* 10/2: 113–25.

2000. *Intercultural Communication: A Discourse Approach.* 2nd edn. Malden, MA: Blackwell.

Scotton, C. M. 1976. Strategies of neutrality: Language choice in uncertain situations. *Language* 52: 919–41.

1985. 'What the heck, Sir': style and lexical colouring as features of powerful language. In Street, R. L., and Cappella, J. N. (eds.), *Sequence and Pattern in Communicative Behaviour*, 103–19. London: Arnold.

Sebba, M. 1997. *Contact Languages: Pidgins and Creoles.* London: Macmillan.

Seidlhofer, B. 2005. English as a lingua franca. *ELT Journal* 59/4: 339–41.

Seidlhofer, B., and Widdowson, H. G. 1998. Applied linguistics, pragmatics, and language pedagogy. In de Beaugrande, R., Grosman, M., and Seidlhofer, B. (eds.), *Language Policy and Language Education in Emerging Nations: Focus on Slovenia and Croatia*, 3–14. London: Ablex.

Selinker, L. 1972. Interlanguage. *International Review of Applied Linguistics* 10: 209–30.

Selinker, L. 1993. Fossilization as simplification. In Tickoo, M. L. (ed.), *Simplification: Theory and Application.* Singapore: SEAMEO Regional Language Centre.

Sey, K. A. 1973. *Ghanaian English.* London: Macmillan.

Sharma, D. 2005a. Language transfer and discourse universals in Indian English article use. *Studies in Second Language Acquisition* 27/4: 535–66.

2005b. Dialect stabilisation and speaker awareness in non-native varieties of English. *Journal of Sociolinguistics* 9: 194–224.

Sharwood-Smith, M. 1986. Consciousness-raising and the second language learner. *Applied Linguistics* 2: 59–68.

Shivachi, C. 1999. A case study in language contact: English, Kiswahili and Luhyia amongst the Luhyia people of Kenya. Unpublished PhD dissertation, University of Cape Town.

Sidhu, C. D. 1976. *An Intensive Course in English.* New Delhi: Orient Longman.

Siegel, J. 1985. Koines and koineization. *Language in Society* 14: 357–78.

1987. *Language Contact in a Plantation Environment.* Cambridge: Cambridge University Press.

1994. Review of R. Mesthrie, English in language shift: the history, structure and sociolinguistics of South African Indian English. *Journal of African Languages and Linguistics* 15/1: 86–90.

1997a. Mixing, leveling, and Pidgin/Creole development. In Spears, A., and Winford, D. (eds.), *The structure and status of Pidgins and Creoles*: 111–49. Amsterdam: John Benjamins.

1997b. Pidgin and English in Melanesia: is there a continuum? *World Englishes* 16/2: 185–204.

2003. Substrate influence in Creoles and the role of transfer in second language acquisition. *Studies in Second Language Acquisition* 25: 185–209.

Simo Bobda, A. 1994. *Aspects of Cameroon English Phonology.* Bern: Peter Lang.

2004. Cameroon English: phonology. In Kortmann, B., Schneider, E. W., Burridge, K., Mesthrie, R., and Upton, C. (eds.), *A Handbook of Varieties of English*, Vol. I, 885–901. Berlin: Mouton de Gruyter.

Singh, F. B. 1987. Power and politics in the content of grammar books: the example of India. *World Englishes* 6/3: 253–61.

Singh, K. 1959. *I Shall Not Hear the Nightingale.* London: John Calder.

Singh, R. (ed.) 1998. *The Native Speaker: Multilingual Perspectives.* New Delhi: Sage.

Singler, J. V. 1990. On the use of sociohistorical criteria in the comparison of Creoles. In Seuren, P., and Mufwene, S. (eds.), *Issues in Creole Linguistics*, 645–59 (Special Issue of Linguistics: 28/4).

2004. Liberian Settler English: phonology. In Kortmann, B., Schneider, E. W., Burridge, K., Mesthrie, R., and Upton, C. (eds.), *A Handbook of Varieties of English*, Vol. I, 874–84. Berlin: Mouton de Gruyter.

Singler, J., and Kouwenberg, S. (in press). *A Handbook of Pidgins and Creoles.* Oxford: Blackwell.

Slobin, D. I. 1973. Cognitive prerequisites for the development of grammar. In Ferguson, C. A., and Slobin, D. I. (eds.), *Studies in Child Language Development*, 175–208. New York: Holt, Rinehart and Wilson.

1977. Language change in childhood and in history. In Macnamara, J. (ed.), *Language Learning and Thought*, 185–214. New York: Academic Press.

1983. What the natives have in mind. In Andersen, R. (ed.), *Pidginization and Creolization as Language Acquisition*, 246–53. Rowley, MA: Newbury House.

1985. Cross-linguistic evidence for the language-making capacity. In Slobin, D. I. (ed.), *The Cross-Linguistic Study of Language Acquisition*, Vol. II, 1157–256. Hillsdale, NJ: Lawrence Erlbaum.

Smalley, R. L., and Hank, M. R. 1982. *Refining Composition Skills*. New York: Macmillan.

Smith, A. M. 1978. The Papua New Guinea Dialect of English. Educational Research Unit report No. 25, University of Papua New Guinea.

Smith, L. E. 1987. Introduction: discourse strategies and cross-cultural communication. In Smith, L. (ed.), *Discourse across Cultures: Strategies in World Englishes*, 1–6. New York: Prentice-Hall.

(ed.) 1987. *Discourse Across Cultures: Strategies in World Englishes*. London: Prentice-Hall.

1992. Spread of English and issues of intelligibility. In Kachru, B. B. (ed.), *The Other Tongue: English across Cultures*, 75–90. Urbana: University of Illinois Press.

Smith, L. E., and Nelson, C. L. 1985. International intelligibility of English: directions and resources. *World Englishes* 4/3: 333–42.

Smith, L. E., and Rafiqzad, K. 1979. English for cross-cultural communication: the question of intelligibility. *TESOL Quarterly* 13/3: 371–80.

Sood, K. S., and Bright, P. S. n.d. *Bright's Handbook of Common Errors in English and How to Avoid Them*. New Delhi: Bright Careers Institute.

Spencer, J. 1971. West Africa and the English language. In Spencer J. (ed.), *The English Language in West Africa*, 1–34. London: Longman.

Sridhar, K. K. 1991. Speech acts in an indigenized variety: sociocultural values and language variation. In Cheshire, J. (ed.), *English around the World: Sociolinguistic Perspectives*, 308–18. Cambridge: Cambridge University Press.

1982. English in a South Indian Urban context. In Kachru, B. B (ed.), *The Other Tongue: English across Cultures*, 141–53. Urbana: University of Illinois Press.

1992. The ecology of bilingual competence: language interaction in indigenized varieties of English. *World Englishes* 11: 141–50.

1996. The pragmatics of South Asian English. In R. Baumgardner (ed.), *South Asian Englishes: Structure, Use and Users*, 141–57. Urbana and Chicago: University of Illinois Press.

Sridhar, K. K., and Sridhar, S. N. 1986. Bridging the paradigm gap: second language acquisition research and indigenized varieties of English. *World Englishes* 5/1: 3–14.

Sridhar, S. N. 1992. The ecology of bilingual competence: Language interaction in indigenized varieties of English. *World Englishes* 11/2–3:141–50.

Stauble, A. M. E. 1978. The process of decreolisation: a model for second language development. *Language and Learning* 28: 29–54.

Stern, H. H. 1983. *Fundamental Concepts of Language Teaching*. Oxford: Oxford University Press.

Strang, B. 1970. *A History of English*. London: Methuen.

Swann, M., and Smith, B. 1987. *Learner English: A Teacher's Guide to Interference and Other Problems*. Cambridge: Cambridge University Press.

Tajima, A. 2004. Fatal miscommunication: English in aviation safety. *World Englishes* 23/3: 451–70.

Tarone, E. 1983. On the variability of interlanguage systems. *Applied Linguistics* 4: 143–63.

Tayao, Ma. L. G. 2004. Philippine English: phonology. In Kortmann, B., Schneider, E. W., Burridge, K., Mesthrie, R., and Upton, C. (eds.), *A Handbook of Varieties of English*, Vol. I, 1047–59. Berlin: Mouton de Gruyter.

Taylor, D. 1971. Grammatical and lexical affinities of Creoles. In Hymes, D. (ed.), *Pidginisation and Creolisation of Languages*, 293–6. Cambridge: Cambridge University Press.

Taylor, J. 2002. China's English language push. In *ABC News Online*, 3 November. See www.abc.net.au/correspondents/s717371.htm.

Taylor, P. and Bain, P. 2005. 'India calling to the faraway towns': the call center labour process and globalization. *Work, Employment, Society* 19: 261–82.

Tent, J., and Mugler, F. 1996. Why a Fiji corpus? In Greenbaum, S. (ed.), *Comparing English Worldwide: The International Corpus of English*, 249–61. Oxford: Clarendon.

Teo, A. 1995. Analysis of editorials: a study of argumentative text structure. PhD dissertation, University of Illinois (Urbana).

Thomas, M. 1989. The acquisition of English articles by first-and second-language learners. *Applied Psycholinguistics* 10: 335–55.

Thomason, S. G. 2001a. *Language Contact: An Introduction*. Edinburgh: Edinburgh University Press.

2001b. Contact languages. In Mesthrie, R. (ed.), *Concise Encyclopaedia of Sociolinguistics*, 461–4. Oxford: Pergamon.

Thomason, S. G., and Kaufman T. 1988. *Language Contact, Creolization and Genetic Linguistics*. Berkeley: University of California Press.

Thomson, G. 1972. *The Greek Language*. Cambridge: Heffer.

Times of London, 10/27/86: 17.

Times of India news-brief, www.timesofindia.com, 12 October 2001.

Times of India, 12 May 2002: 10.

8 March 2006, p. 1.

Tingley, C. 1981. Deviance in English in Ghanaian newspapers. *English World-Wide* 2: 39–62.

Tipping, L. 1933. *Matriculation English Grammar for Modern English Usage*. London: Macmillan.

Tirkkonen-Condit, S. 1985. *Argumentative Text Structure and Translation*. Jyvaskyla: University of Jyvaskyla.

Todd, L. 1982. The English language in West Africa. In Bailey, R. W., and Görlach, M. (eds.), *English as a World Language*, 281–305. Ann Arbor: University of Michigan Press.

1984. *Modern Englishes: Pidgins and Creoles*. London: Routledge.

1985. Review of Platt, Weber and Ho, The New Englishes. *English World-Wide* 6/1: 155–63.

Tollefson, J. W. 1991. *Planning Language, Planning Inequality*. London: Longman.

Tristram, H. 2006. *The Celtic Englishes* IV. Potsdam: University of Potsdam Press.

Troike, M. 1977. The future of English. Editorial. *Linguistics Reporter* 19/8: 2.

Truchot, C. 1997. The spread of English: from France to a more general perspective. *World Englishes* 16/1: 65–76.

Trudgill, P. 1975. *Accent, Dialect and the School*. London: Edward Arnold.

1986. *Dialects in Contact*. Oxford: Basil Blackwell.

1998. Review of John Honey, *Language is Power: The Story of Standard English and its Enemies. Journal of Sociolinguistics*, 2/3: 457–473.

Trudgill, P., and Hannah, J. 1985. *International English: A Guide to Varieties of Standard English*. London: Edward Arnold.

Trudgill, P., and Watts, R. 2002. *The History of English: Alternative Perspectives*. London: Routledge.

Valdman, A. 1977. Creolisation: elaboration in the development of Creole French dialects. In Valdman, A. (ed.), *Pidgin and Creole Linguistics*, 155–89. Bloomington: Indiana University Press.

van Essen, A. 1997. English in Mainland Europe: A Dutch Perspective. *World Englishes* 16/1: 95–103.

van Name, A. (1869-70). Contributions to Creole grammar. *Transactions of the American Philological Association* 1: 123–67.

van Rooy, B. 2004. Black South African English: phonology. In Kortmann, B., Schneider, E. W., Burridge, K., Mesthrie, R., and Upton, C. (eds.), *A Handbook of Varieties of English*, Vol. I, 943–52. Berlin: Mouton de Gruyter.

Vandergriff, J. 1982. Kotzebue English: some Notes on Inupiaq English. In Bartelt, H. G., Penfield-Jasper, S., and Hoffer, B. (eds.), *Essays in Native American English*, 121–56. San Antonio: Trinity University Press.

Varonis, E., and Gass, S. 1982. The comprehensibility of non-native speech. *Studies in Second Language Acquisition* 4: 114–36.

Vavrus, F. 1991. When paradigms clash: the role of institutionalized varieties in language teacher education. *World Englishes* 10: 181–95.

Verma, S. 1982. Swadeshi English: form and function. In Pride, J. (ed.), *New Englishes*, 174–87. Rowley, MA: Newbury House.

Visser, F. Th. 1963. *An Historical Syntax of the English Language*. Leiden: Brill.

von Stutterheim, C., and Klein, W. 1987. A concept-orientated approach to second language studies. In Pfaff, C. (ed.), *First and Second Language Acquisition Processes*, 191–205. Rowley, MA: Newbury House.

Warren, M. 1967. *Social History and Christian Mission*. London: SCM Press.

Watts, R. J. 1989. Taking the pitcher to the 'well': native speakers' perception of their use of discourse markers in conversation. *Journal of Pragmatics* 18: 203–37.

Wee, L. 2004. Singapore English: phonology. In Kortmann, B., Schneider, E. W., Burridge, K., Mesthrie, R., and Upton, C. (eds.), *A Handbook of Varieties of English*, Vol. I, 1017–33. Berlin: Mouton de Gruyter.

Weinreich, U. 1953. *Languages in Contact*. New York: Publications of the Linguistics Circle of New York, No 1.

Wells, J. C. 1982. *Accents of English* (3 vols.). Cambridge: Cambridge University Press.

White, L., and Genessee, F. 1996. How native is near native? The issue of ultimate attainment in adult second language acquisition. *Second Language Research* 12: 233–65.

Williams, J. 1987. Non-native varieties of English: a special case of language acquisition. *English World-Wide* 8: 161–99.

1992. Planning, discourse marking and the comprehensibility of international teaching assistants. *TESOL Quarterly* 26/4 (Winter): 693–711.

Winefield, H. R., Chandler, M. A., and Bassett, D. L. 1989. Tag questions and powerfulness: quantitative and qualitative analyses of a course of psychotherapy. *Language in Society* 18: 77–86.

Winford, D. 2000. Introduction: on the structure and status of pidgins and Creoles. In Spears, A., and Winford, D. (eds.), *The Structure and Status of Pidgins and Creoles*, 1–31. Amsterdam: John Benjamins.

Wingstedt, M., and Schulman, R. 1984. Comprehension of foreign accents. In Dressler, W. (ed.), *Phonologica 1984: Proceedings of the 5th international phonology meeting*, 339–44. Cambridge: Cambridge University Press.

Wong, J. 1994. A Wierzbickan approach to Singlish particles. MA dissertation, National University of Singapore.

2004. The particles of Singapore English: a semantic and cultural interpretation. *Journal of Pragmatics* 36: 739–93.

Wren. P. C., and Martin, H. 1954. *High School English Grammar and Composition*. New Delhi: S. Chand.

Yajun, J. 2003. English as a Chinese language. *English Today* 19/2: 3–8.

Zobl, H. 1980. The formal and developmental selectivity of L1 influence on L2 acquisition. *Language Learning* 30/1: 43–57.

Author index

Subject index